OXFORD

P

Atlas

Editorial Adviser
Dr Patrick Wiegand

OXFORD
UNIVERSITY PRESS

Great Clarendon Street, Oxford OX2 6DP

Oxford University Press is a department of the University of Oxford.
It furthers the University's objective of excellence in research, scholarship,
and education by publishing worldwide in

Oxford   New York

Auckland   Cape Town   Dar es Salaam   Hong Kong   Karachi
Kuala Lumpur   Madrid   Melbourne   Mexico City   Nairobi
New Delhi   Shanghai   Taipei   Toronto

With offices in

Argentina   Austria   Brazil   Chile   Czech Republic   France   Greece
Guatemala   Hungary   Italy   Japan   Poland   Portugal   Singapore
South Korea   Switzerland   Thailand   Turkey   Ukraine   Vietnam

Oxford is a registered trade mark of Oxford University Press
in the UK and in certain other countries

© Oxford University Press 2006

First published 2006

© Maps copyright Oxford University Press

ISBN-13: 978 0 19 832198 9 (hardback)
ISBN-10: 0 19 832198 8 (hardback)

ISBN-13: 978 0 19 832199 6 (paperback)
ISBN-10: 0 19 832199 6 (paperback)

1 3 5 7 9 10 8 6 4 2

Printed in Singapore

2 Contents

Understanding topographic maps 4–5

Europe

Physical 6–7
Political 8–9
British Isles 10–11
Ireland 12
Scotland 13
England and Wales 14–15
Scandinavia and Iceland 16–17
Belgium and Netherlands 18–19
Central Europe 20–21
France and Switzerland 22–23
Spain and Portugal 24–25
Italy 26–27
South East Europe 28–29
East Europe and Turkey 30–31

Asia

Physical 32–33
Political 34–35
Northern Eurasia 36–37
Middle East 38–39
South Asia 40–41
China 42–43
Japan 44–45
South East Asia 46–47
Mainland South East Asia 48–49

Africa

Physical 50–51
Political 52–53
Northwest Africa 54–55
Northeast Africa 56–57
East Africa 58–59
Southern Africa 60–61

North America

Physical 62–63
Political 64–65
Canada 66–67
United States of America 68–69

Contents 3

Northeast USA _____ 70–71
California _____ 72–73
Mexico _____ 74–75
Central America and the Caribbean ____ 76–77

South America

Physical _____ 78–79
Political _____ 80–81
Northern South America _____ 82–83
Southern South America _____ 84–85

Oceania

Physical _____ 86–87
Political _____ 88–89
Australia _____ 90–91
New Zealand _____ 92–93

Oceans and Poles

Atlantic Ocean _____ 94
Indian Ocean _____ 95
Pacific Ocean _____ 96–97
Arctic Ocean _____ 98
Antarctica _____ 99

World

Physical _____ 100–101
Political _____ 102–103
Plate tectonics _____ 104–105
Temperature and ocean currents _____ 106–107
Precipitation _____ 108
Climate hazards _____ 109
Climate regions _____ 110–111
Environments _____ 112–113
Population _____ 114–115
Time zones _____ 116
Travel _____ 117
Flags and statistics _____ 118–134

Index

How to use the index _____ 135
Abbreviations _____ 135
Index _____ 136–160

© Oxford University Press

4 Understanding topographic maps

Topographic maps show the main features of the physical landscape as well as settlements, communications, and boundaries. Background colours show the height of the land.

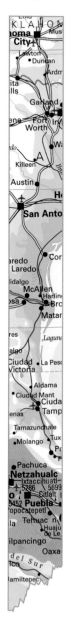

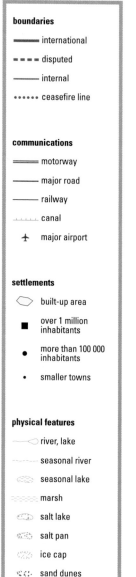

boundaries

━━━━━ international

▬ ▬ ▬ disputed

───── internal

•••••• ceasefire line

communications

═══ motorway

──── major road

──── railway

⊥⊥⊥⊥ canal

✈ major airport

settlements

⬡ built-up area

■ over 1 million inhabitants

● more than 100 000 inhabitants

• smaller towns

physical features

◦⁓ river, lake

----- seasonal river

⬭ seasonal lake

⬱⬱⬱ marsh

⬭ salt lake

⬭ salt pan

⬭ ice cap

⬭ sand dunes

Place names

This atlas has been designed for English speaking readers and so all places have be named using the Roman alphabet and anglicised spellings are often used.

Brackets are used to show former place names, alternative names and spellings of the country to which a territory belongs.

Type style

Contrasting type styles are used to show the difference between physical features, settlements, and administrative areas.

Physical features are separated into two categories: land and water. Land features are shown in roman type:

e.g. Ural Mountains   ANDES

Water features are shown in italics:

e.g. *Mozambique Channel*

Mississippi

Peaks are shown in condensed type:

e.g. Mt. Logan 5951

Settlement names are shown in upper and lower case:

e.g. Shanghai

Country names are shown in bold capital letters:

e.g. **AUSTRALIA**

Administrative areas are shown in light capital letters:

e.g. ONTARIO

The size of settlements is shown by the size of the type and whether the type face is bold or medium:

e.g. **Madrid**   Florence   Cherbourg

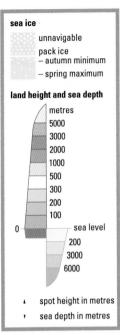

sea ice

- unnavigable
- pack ice
  – autumn minimum
  – spring maximum

land height and sea depth

metres
5000
3000
2000
1000
500
300
200
100
0 — sea level
200
3000
6000

▲ spot height in metres

▼ sea depth in metres

Sea ice

White stipple patterns over the sea colour show the seasonal extent of sea ice.

Land height and sea depth

Colours on topographic maps refer only to the height of the land or the depth of the sea. They do not give information about land use or other aspects of the environment.

Scale

The relationship between a map and the real world it represents is defined by the map's *scale*.

Scale is shown on the maps in this atlas by a representative fraction.

Scale 1: 5 000 000

In this example, 1 centimetre on the map represents 5 million centimetres, or 50 kilometres, on the Earth's surface.

Abbreviations used on the maps

ACT	Australian Capital Territory	Peg.	Pegunungan *(mountain range)*
Admin.	administrative area	Pen; Penin.	Peninsula
Arch.	Archipelago	Pk.	Peak
Aust.	Australia	Port.	Portugal
B.	Bay	Pt.	Point
C.	Cape; Cabo; Cap	Pta.	Punta *(cape; point)*
Cord.	Cordillera *(mountain range)*	Pte.	Pointe
Den.	Denmark	Pto.	Porto; Puerto *(bay; harbour)*
Eq. Guinea	Equatorial Guniea	Ra.	Range
Fr.	France	Rep.	Republic
Ft.	Fort	Res.	Reservoir
FYROM	Former Yugoslav Republic of Macedonia	RSA	Republic of South Africa
		S.	South
G.	Gulf; Gunung; Gebel	Sa.	Serra *(hills; mountains)*
I.	Island; Île; Isla; Ilha	Sd.	Sound
Is.	Islands; Îles; Islas; Ilhas	Sp.	Spain
Jct.	Junction	St.	Saint
Kep.	Kepulauan *(islands)*	Sta.	Santa
L.	Lake; Lac; Lago; Lough	Ste.	Sainte
M.	Mys *(cape; point)*	Str.	Strait
Mt.	Mount; Mountain; Mont	Terr.	Territory
Mts.	Mountains; Monts	UK	United Kingdom
N.	North	USA	United States of America
Neths.	Netherlands	Vdkhr.	Vodokhranilishche *(reservoir)*
NZ	New Zealand	Vdskh.	Vodoskhovyshche *(reservoir)*
P.	Pulau *(island)*	W.	Wadi *(watercourse)*

Scale 1: 25 00

20°W

0°

GREENLAND SEA

Iceland
Vatnajökull
•1491
Hekla

Norwegian Basin

•-3970

Arctic

60°N

Faroe Islands

Shetland Islands

Prime Meridian

Skerriegard

Josted

Rockall Bank

Outer Hebrides

C. Wrath

Orkney Islands

Hardanger vidda

ATLANTIC

OCEAN

Malin Head

Ben Nevis
•1344
Grampians

NORTH SEA

Skage

Ireland

Central Plain

Southern Uplands

Great Britain

Pennines

Iylland

Shannon

St. George's Channel

Cambrian Mts.

The Wash

•-36

Frisian Islands

Scilly Is.

English Channel

Thames

Str. of Dover

Ijsselmeer
Waal
Maas

Weser

Harz

West

European

Basin

Channel Islands

Cotentin

Seine

Meuse

Ardennes

Rhine

Brittany Pen.

Paris Basin

Marne

Vosges

Schwäbische

40°N

Bay of Biscay

Loire

Saône

L. Geneva

Jura

Bodense

C. Finisterre

Cantabrian Mts.

Dordogne

Massif
Central

Mont Blanc
4807

ALPS

Iberian Basin

Doure

Duero

Ebro

Garonne

Pyrénées

Rhône

Alpes
Maritimes

Po

Central Cordilleras

Tagus

3404

Gulf of Lyons

LIGURIAN SEA

A

Guadiana

La Manche

Corsica

Sierra Morena

Balearic Islands

Ves

C. de São Vicente

Guadalquivir

Betican Cordilleras

Ibiza

Mallorca

Menorca

Sardinia

TYRRHENI
SEA

Str. of Gibraltar

MEDITERR

ATLAS MOUNTAINS

Grand Erg Occidental

0°

Conical Orthomorphic Projection

8 **Europe** Political

Scale 1: 25 000

international boundary
- - - disputed boundary
■ capital city
• other important city

ICELAND
■ Reykjavik

Arctic Ci

Prime Meridian

20°W

0°

ATLANTIC
OCEAN

•Edinburgh   NORTH SEA

REPUBLIC
OF IRELAND   •Manchester
■ Dublin

UNITED

•Birmingham   KINGDOM

NETHERLANDS

•Rotterdam   **Amsterdam**

■ London

BELGIUM   **Brussels**

■ **Paris**   LUXEMBOURG   •Düsseldorf
Luxembourg   Frank
am Ma

GERM

Göt

DENM
Copenh

Ha

FRANCE   Bern   •Munich

•Bordeaux   ■   LIECHTENS

•Lyons   SWITZERLAND

•Milan

•Oporto

PORTUGAL   SPAIN   ANDORRA   •Marseilles   MONACO

■ **Lisbon**   ■ **Madrid**   •Barcelona

■ Rome

Nap

•Valencia

•Seville

Gibraltar
(UK)

Ceuta
(Sp.)

Melilla
(Sp.)

MEDITERRANEAN

ITA

Lju

40°N

MOROCCO   ALGERIA   TUNISIA   Valle

10°W   0°   10°E

© Oxford University Press   Conical Orthomorphic Projection

20°E 40°E 60°E

60°N

N O R W A Y

S W E D E N

FINLAND

RUSSIAN FEDERATION (RUSSIA)

Perm

■ Helsinki · St. Petersburg

■ Stockholm ■ Tallinn
ESTONIA

Nizhniy-Novgorod

BALTIC SEA

L A T V I A
■ Riga

Moscow ■

LITHUANIA
■ Vilnius
KALININGRAD (Russia)

■ Minsk

B E L A R U S

P O L A N D

■ Warsaw
· Łódź

· Kiev

· Kharkov

Volgograd

ue
· Kraków

U K R A I N E

· Donets'k

· Rostov-on-Don

REP.
SLOVAKIA
a ■ Bratislava

MOLDOVA
■ Chişinău · Odessa

■ Budapest
HUNGARY

R O M A N I A

agreb

BLACK SEA

GEORGIA
■ T'bilisi

40°N

BOSNIA–
RZEGOVINA
■ Belgrade ■ Bucharest

rajevo
SERBIA AND
MONTENEGRO

B U L G A R I A

■ Skopje
Tiranë FYRO
MACEDONIA
ALBANIA

■ Sofia

· İstanbul

■ Ankara

T U R K E Y

GREECE

· İzmir

· Adana

SYRIA IRAQ

■ Athens

Nicosia ■
CYPRUS

LEBANON

EA

20°E 40°E

© Oxford University Press

Scale 1: 5 00

NORTH SEA

ATLANTIC OCEAN

Shetland Islands

Lerwick

Foula

Fair Isle

Orkney Islands

Kirkwall

Duncansby Head

Wick

Thurso

Cape Wrath

The Minch

Loch Shin

Ullapool

Stornoway

Lewis

Harris

North Uist

South Uist

St. Kilda

Outer Hebrides

Skye

Kyle of Lochalsh

Mallaig

Rhum

Coll

Tree

Jura

Islay

Campbeltown

Malin Head

Inner Hebrides

Mull

Firth of Lorn

Oban

Loch Lomond

Arran

Clyde

Greenock

Paisley

Glasgow

Kilmarnock

Ayr

Motherwell

Edinburgh

Firth of Forth

Dunfermline

Stirling

Perth

Loch Forth

Dundee

Dee

Don

Aberdeen

Peterhead

Berwick-upon-Tweed

Tweed

Cairngorms

Ben Macdhui 1310

Spey

Tay

Moray Firth

Inverness

Loch Ness

Fort William

Ben Nevis 1344

Loch Lomond

Grampian Mountains

Northwest Highlands

SCOTLAND

UNITED

Uplands

Southern

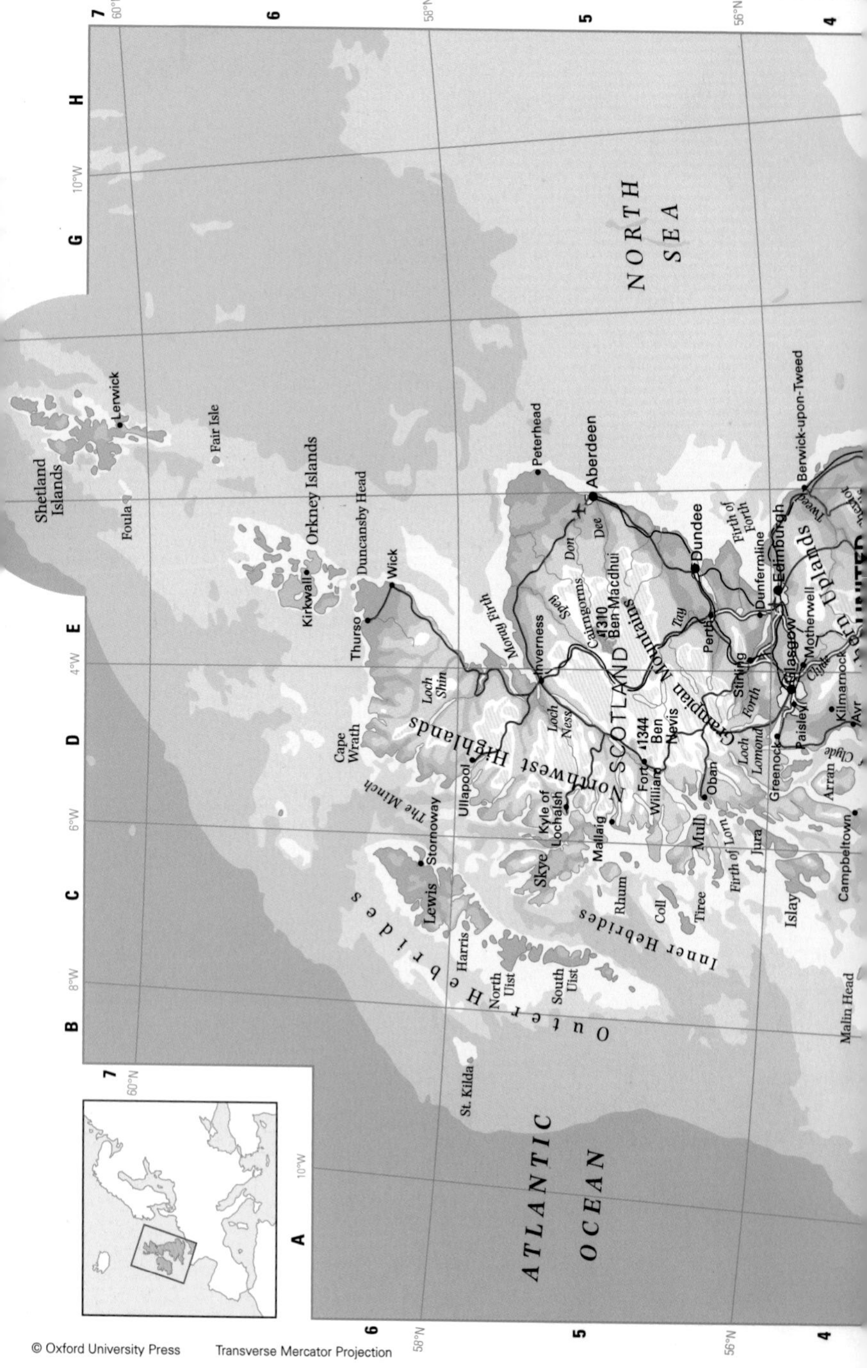

© Oxford University Press   Transverse Mercator Projection

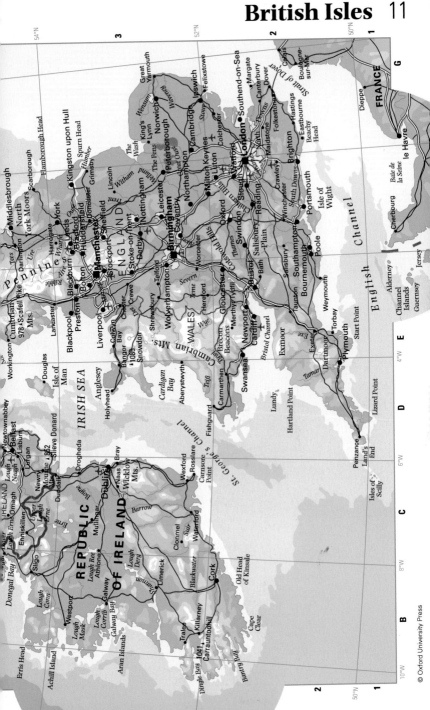

© Oxford University Press

Scale 1: 3 000 000 (both r

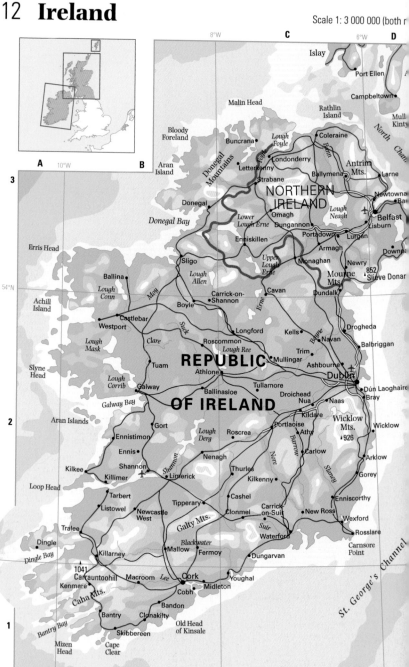

Transverse Mercator Projection

Shetland Islands
Unst
Yell
Fetlar
Mainland
Lerwick
Foula
Sumburgh Head

Westray
Sanday
Stronsay
Mainland
Kirkwall
Orkney Islands
Hoy
Pentland Firth
Thurso
John o'Groats
Duncansby Head
Thurso
Wick

Cape Wrath
Butt of Lewis
The Minch
Lewis
Stornoway
Helmsdale
Loch Shin
Dornoch Firth
Ullapool
Ben Wyvis
1046
Dingwall
Tain
Moray Firth
Banff
Fraserburgh
Elgin
Outer Hebrides
North Uist
Lochmaddy
Uig
Portree
Skye
Kyle of Lochalsh
1009
1183
Loch Ness
Inverness
Huntly
Peterhead
Inverurie
Aberdeen
Benbecula
Little Minch
Spey
Deveron
Don
Lochboisdale
Aviemore
Cairngorms
Dee
Barra
Rhum
Eigg
Mallaig
Monadhliath Mountains
1310
Ben Macdhui
Stonehaven

SCOTLAND
Inner Hebrides
Coll
Tiree
Iona
Mull
Oban
Crianlarich
Inveraray
Colonsay
Jura
Port Askaig
Rothesay
Islay
Bute
Port Ellen
Arran
Brodick
Campbeltown
Mull of Kintyre

Fort William
1344
Ben Nevis
Loch Linnhe
Grampian Mountains
Pitlochry
Blairgowrie
Forfar
N. Esk
S. Esk
Montrose
Arbroath
Carnoustie
Tay
Sidlaw Hills
Dundee
St. Andrews
Loch Tay
Perth
Glenrothes
NORTH SEA
Loch Lomond
Forth
Stirling
Alloa
Kirkcaldy
Firth of Forth
Falkirk
Dunfermline
Grangemouth
Cumbernauld
Greenock
Dumbarton
Clydebank
Glasgow
Coatbridge
Livingston
Edinburgh
Haddington
St. Abb's Head
Paisley
Motherwell
Lammermuir Hills
East Kilbride
Hamilton
Clyde
Galashiels
Ardrossan
Kilmarnock
Jedburgh
Berwick-upon-Tweed
Irvine
Tweed
Southern Uplands
Cheviot Hills
Firth of Clyde
Ayr
840
Hawick
Girvan
UNITED KINGDOM
Mull of Galloway
Rathlin Island
North Channel
Newton Stewart
Dumfries
Lockerbie
Coleraine
Bann
Stranraer
Castle Douglas
Carlisle
Antrim Mts.
NORTHERN IRELAND
Ballymena
Larne
Kirkcudbright
Solway Firth
Dee
Eden
Lough Foyle
Londonderry

© Oxford University Press

Scale 1: 3 000

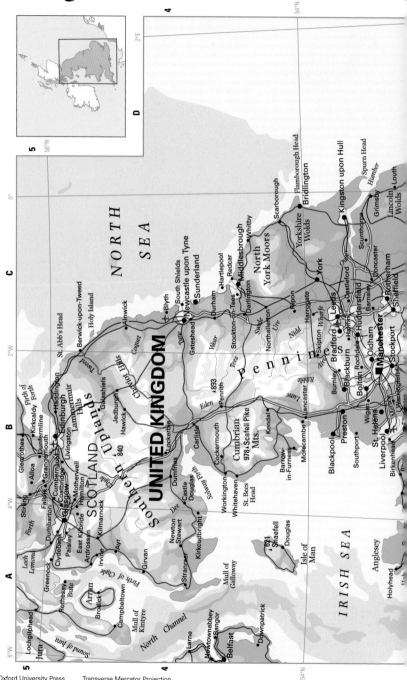

Transverse Mercator Projection

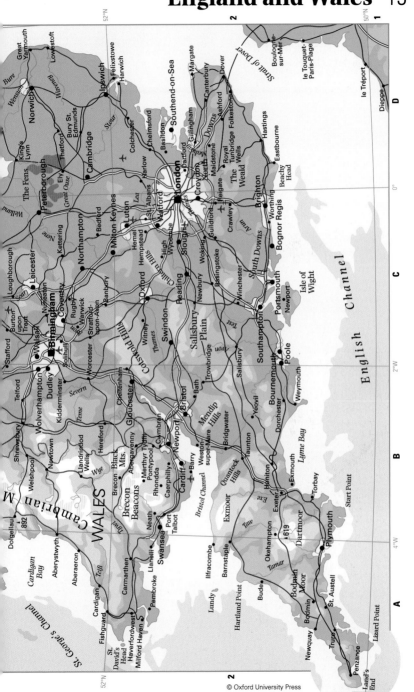

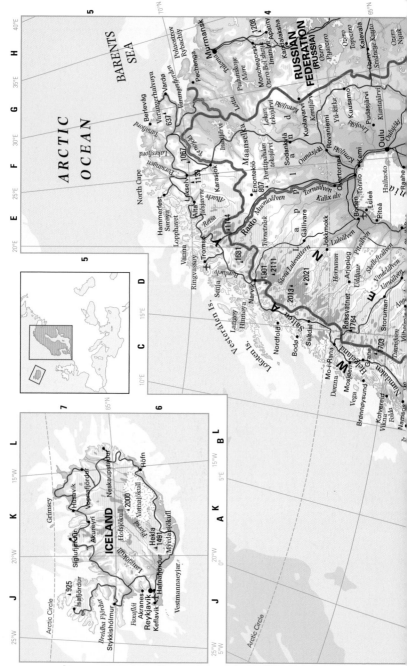

Conical Orthomorphic Projection

Scale 1: 2 500

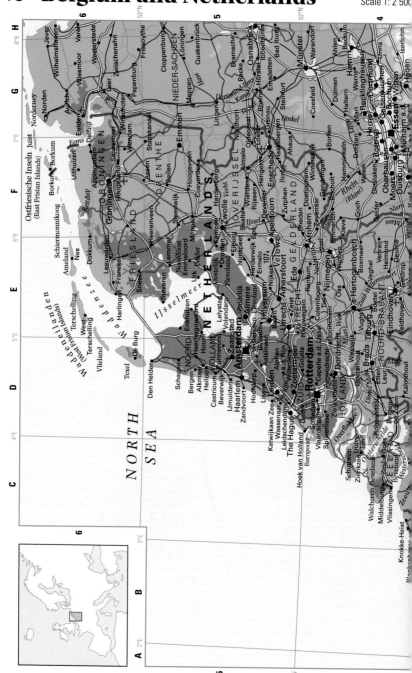

Conical Orthomorphic Projection

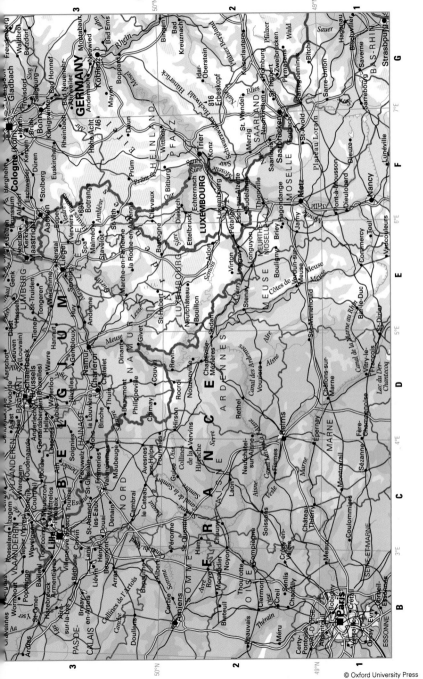

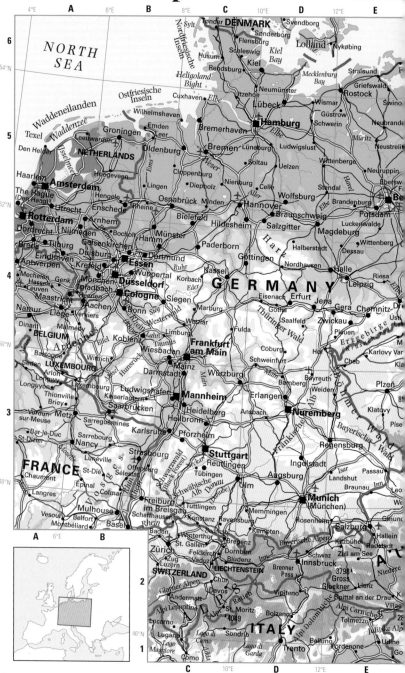

Conical Orthomorphic Projection

Scale 1: 6 00

Conical Orthomorphic Projection

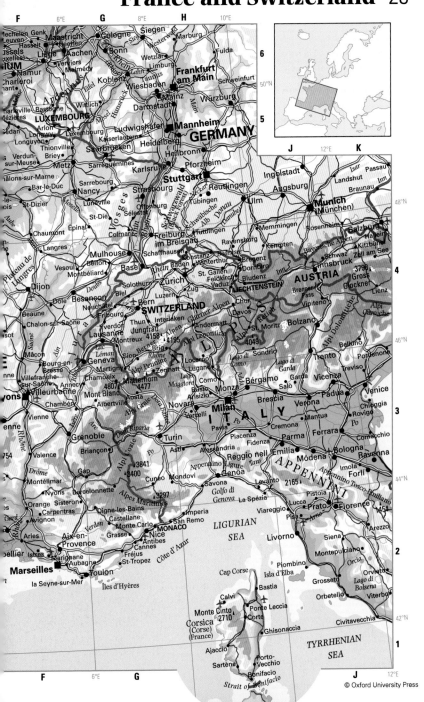

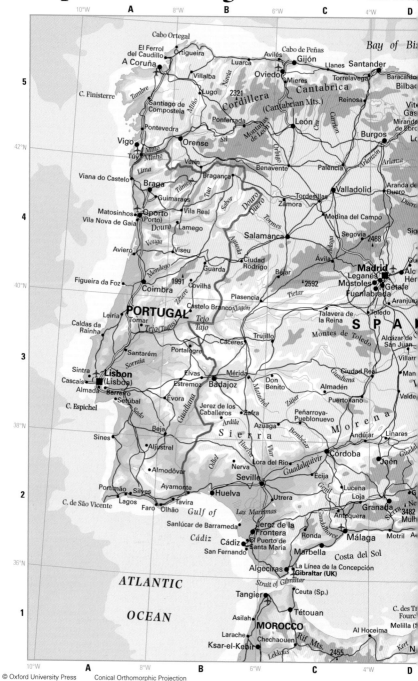

Conical Orthomorphic Projection

Scale 1: 6 0

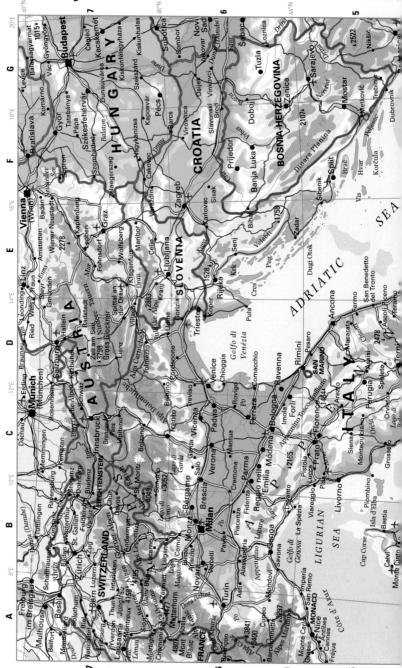

© Oxford University Press   Conical Orthomorphic Projection

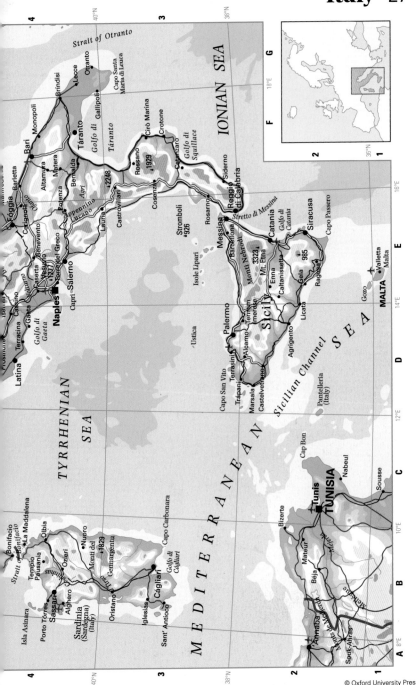

Strait of Otranto

IONIAN SEA

TYRRHENIAN SEA

MEDITERRANEAN SEA

Sicilian Channel SEA

Brindisi
Lecce
Otranto
Capo Santa Maria di Leuca
Bari
Monopoli
Altamura
Matera
Gioia del Colle
Barletta
Foggia
Taranto
Golfo di Táranto
Cirò Marina
Crotone
Rossano
•1929
Catanzaro
Golfo di Squillace
Siderno
Reggio di Calabria
Stretto di Messina
Messina
Barcellona
Monti Nebrodi
3323
Mt. Etna
Catania
Golfo di Catania
Siracusa
Capo Passero
Stromboli •926
Isole Lipari
Palermo
Termini Imerese
Enna
Caltanissetta
Gela 985
Ragusa
Ustica
Alcamo
Trapani
Terrasini
Marsala
Castelvetrano
Agrigento
Licata
Capo San Vito
Sicilia
Pantelleria (Italy)
Cap Bon
Nabeul
Sousse
Bizerte
Tunis
TUNISIA
Meteur
Béja
Medjerda
Ahmadu
Mteur
Mts Medjerda
Souk-Ahras
Gozo
MALTA
Valletta
Malta
Naples
Capri
Salerno
Castrovillari
Laurìa
Cosenza
•2248
Potenza
Appennino Lucano
Bernalda
Benevento
Caserta
Cassino
Gaeta
Golfo di Gaeta
Terracina
Latina
Rosarno
Castelvetrano

Isla Asinara
Porto Torres
Sassari
Alghero
Ozieri
Tempio Pausania
Olbia
La Maddalena
Bonifacio
Strait of Bonifacio
Nuoro
Monti del Gennargentu
•1829
Oristano
Tirso
Iglesias
Sant'Antioco
Cagliari
Golfo di Cagliari
Capo Carbonara
Sardinia (Sardegna) (Italy)

Strait of Otranto

© Oxford University Press

40°N 4
38°N 3
38°N 2
G F E D C B A
40°N 4
38°N 3
18°E 16°E 14°E 12°E 10°E 8°E
36°N 1

Scale 1: 6 00

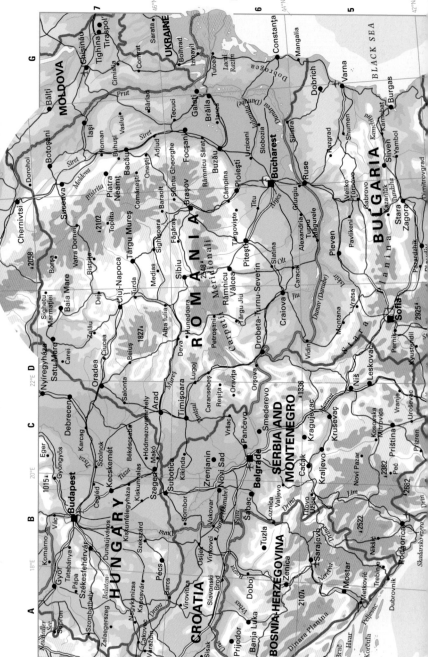

© Oxford University Press

Scale 1: 12 50

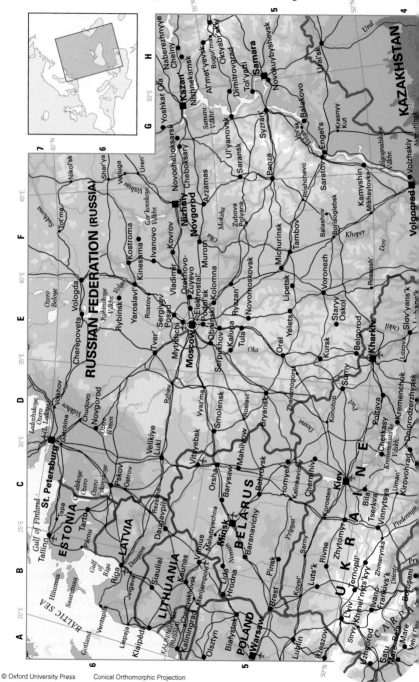

Conical Orthomorphic Projection

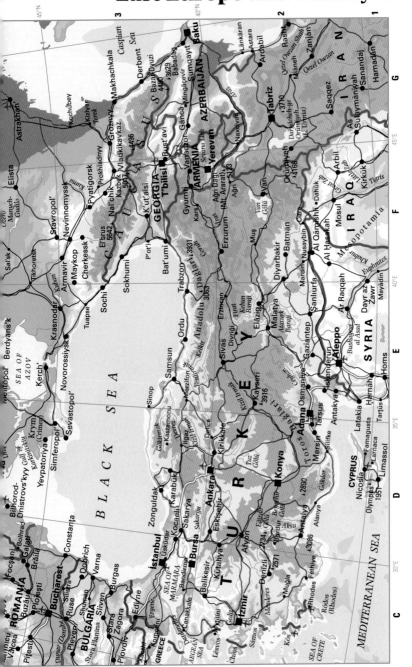

60°N   20°E   40°E   80°N   80°E   100°

Scandinavia

Pyrenees
Massif
Central
Loire
ALPS
Corsica
Sardinia
APPENNINI
Rhine
Danube
North European Plain
Jura
BALTIC SEA
G. of Bothnia
WHITE SEA
Kola Peninsula
BARENTS SEA
Novaya Zemlya
KARA SEA
Taymyr Pe

Carpathians
Dniester
Danube
Lake Peipus
Lake Ladoga
Lake Onega
Central Russian Uplands
Pechora
Ob'
Arctic Circle
Vaygach Peninsula
G. of Ob'

Pindus
Dnieper
Dniester
Don
Volga
Siberian Lowland
Yenisey
Nizhnyay
Ang

Peloponnese
Crete
Cyprus
MEDITERRANEAN SEA
Anatolian Plateau
Toros Daglari
BLACK SEA
Caucasus
Mt. Elbrus 5642
Sea of Azov
Ural Mountains
Kazakh Upland
Tobol
Irtysh
Western Sayan
Tannu-
Altai Mount
Easte

Nile
Nile Delta
Dead Sea
Syrian Desert
Euphrates
Tigris
Mt. Ararat 5122
Lake Urmia
Mesopotamia
Caspian Sea
Aral Sea
Syr Dar'ya
Lake Balkhash
Dzungarian Basin
Turfan Depression 154
Qilc

Tropic of Cancer
RED SEA
An Nafud
Arabian Peninsula
Zagros Mts.
Elburz Mts.
Dasht-e-Kavir
Dasht-e-Lut
The Gulf
Kara Bogaz Gol
Ust Urt Plateau
Kara Kum
Kyzyl Kum
Amu Dar'ya
Qullai Garmo 7495
Pamirs
Hindu Kush
Tien Shan
Tarim Basin
Kunlun Shan
Altun Shan
Nan S
Qaidam Basin
Am

Asir Mountains
Rub' al Khali
Gulf of Oman
Str. of Hormuz
Helmand
Sulaiman Range
Indus
K2 8611
Karakoram
Ladakh Ra.
Gandisê Shan
Plateau of Tibet
Mt. Nyainqêntanglha
Tsangpo

Hadhramaut
Gulf of Aden
Socotra
Thar Desert
Rann of Kachchh
Yamun
Ganga
Himalaya
Mt. Everest 8848
Brahmaputra

ARABIAN SEA
Satpura Ra.
Mahanadi
Mouths of the Ganga
Irrawad

Shebeli
Somali Basin
Equator
Godavari
Deccan
Western Ghats
Eastern Ghats
Malabar Coast
Coromandel Coast
Laccadive Islands
Bay of Bengal
Andaman Islands
ANDAM SEA

-5340
Seychelles Ridge
Chagos-Laccadive Ridge
Maldive Archipelago
Cape Comorin
2518 Pidurutalagala
Nicobar Islands
Menta

INDIAN OCEAN

60°E   80°E

Wrangel
New Siberian Islands
Chukotsk Range
Koryak Range
Arctic Circle
BERING SEA
Kolyma Lowland
Kolyma
Kolyma (Gydan) Range
Cherskiy Range
3147
Aleutian Trench
Emperor Seamounts
Verkhoyansk Range
Lena
Vilyuy
Aldan
Kamchatka
SEA OF OKHOTSK
Sakhalin
Kuril Islands
Kuril Trench
Stanovoy Range
180°
Lake Baykal
Yablonovy Range
Amur (Heilong Jiang)
Sikhote Alin
Hokkaido
Northwest Pacific Basin
Greater Khingan Range
Liao
SEA OF JAPAN
Honshu
Mt. Fuji 3776
Japan Trench
PACIFIC
20°N
Tropic of Cancer
Bo Hai
Shandong Peninsula
YELLOW SEA
Shikoku
Kyushu
OCEAN
Huang He
ng Shan
EAST CHINA SEA
Ryukyu Islands
Ryukyu Trench
g Jiang (Yangtze)
Dongting Hu
Poyang Hu
Wuyi Shan
Nan Ling
Xi Jiang
Taiwan Strait
Taiwan
Mariana Trench
160°E
Gulf of Tongking
Leizhou Peninsula
Hainan
Luzon
PHILIPPINE SEA
-11022 Challenger Deep
Equator
-Koi
Annam Range
Mekong
Tonle Sap
SOUTH CHINA SEA
Mindoro
Panay
Negros
Palawan
SULU SEA
Mindanao
Samar
-10497
Philippine Trench
East Caroline Basin
0°
4094 Kinabalu
Borneo
CELEBES SEA
Halmahera
West Caroline Basin
New Guinea
sula
Sulawesi
Seram
BANDA SEA
ARAFURA SEA
Arnhem Land
ra
JAVA SEA
Java
Bali
Lesser Sunda Islands
Flores
Timor

© Oxford University Press

Scale 1: 55 00

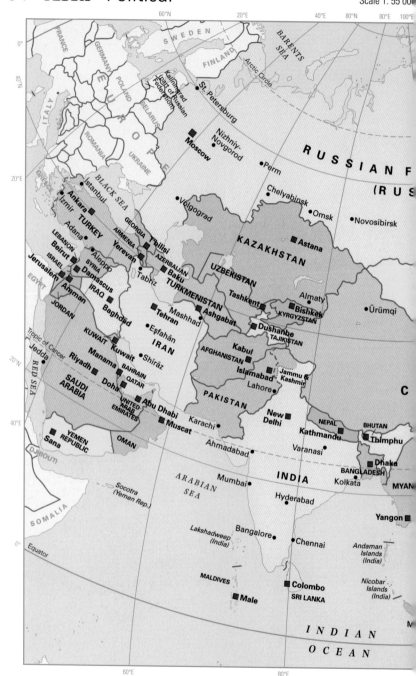

international boundary
disputed boundary
capital city
other important city

Arctic Circle

SEA OF
OKHOTSK

Kuril
Islands
(Russia)
Administered by Russia.
Claimed by Japan

180°

· Sapporo

ATION

·lan Bator
GOLIA

· Harbin

20°N

Tropic of Cancer

PACIFIC

Shenyang ·

NORTH
KOREA
■ Pyongyang
■ Seoul
SOUTH
KOREA

■ Tokyo

JAPAN

Beijing ·
· Tianjin

· Pusan
Osaka

OCEAN

· Fukuoka

nzhou
· Xi'an

· Shanghai

Ryukyu
Islands
(Japan)

· Wuhan

160°E

ngqing

■ **Taipei**

· Guangzhou

TAIWAN

· Hong Kong

■ **Hanoi**
entiane

■ Manila · Quezon City

THE
PHILIPPINES

0°

Equator

AND
gkok
VIETNAM

AMBODIA
■ **Phnom Penh**
· Hô Chi Minh

BRUNEI

■ Bandar
Seri Begawan

M A L A Y S I A

·uala Lumpur
■ SINGAPORE

PAPUA
NEW GUINEA

I N D O N E S I A

· Palembang

· Ujung
Pandang

■ Dili

EAST
TIMOR

AUSTRALIA

■ **Jakarta**
· Semarang
· Surabaya

Scale 1: 32 000

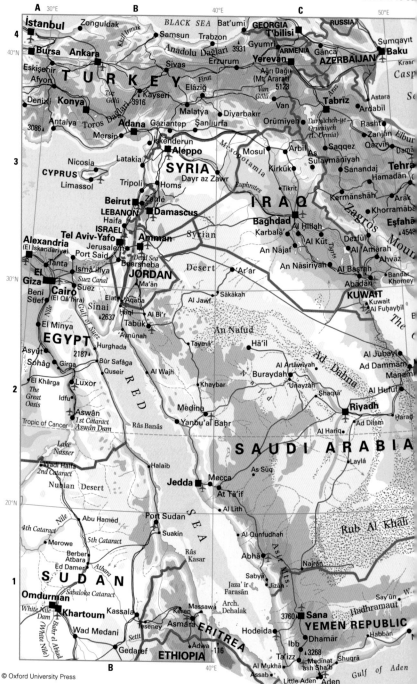

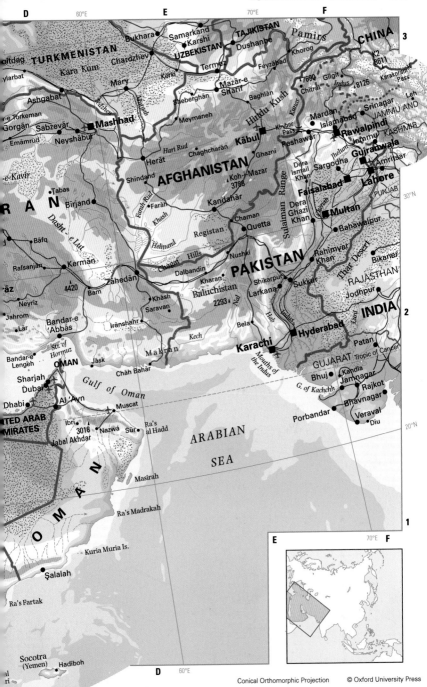

Conical Orthomorphic Projection   © Oxford University Press

Scale 1: 15 000

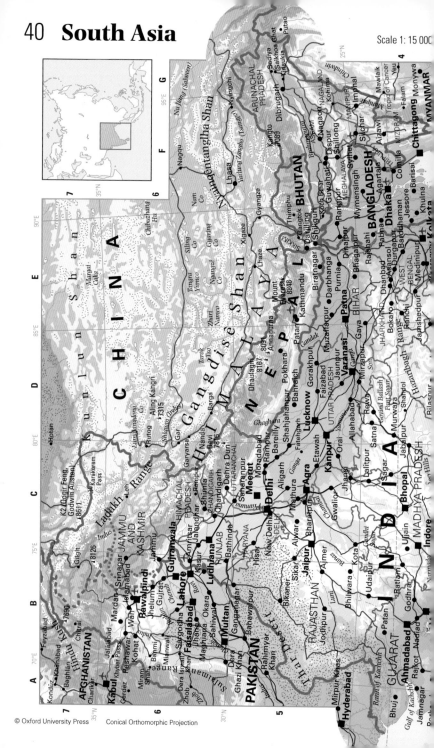

Conical Orthomorphic Projection

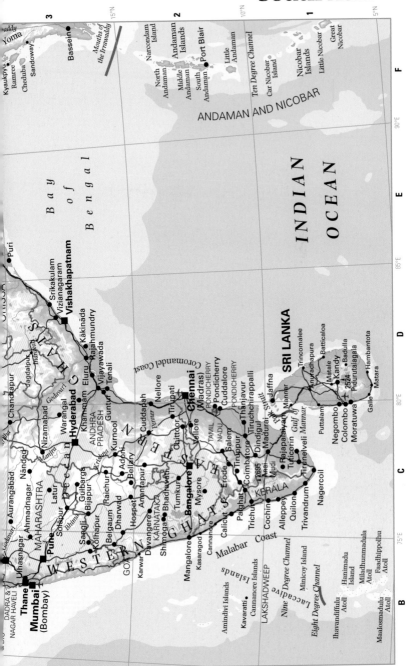

© Oxford University Press

Scale 1: 22 000

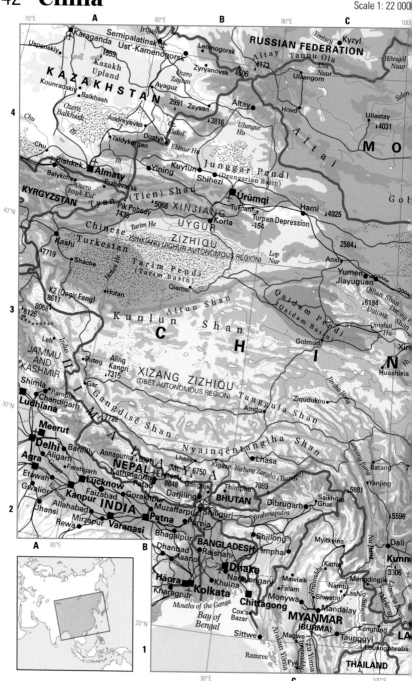

© Oxford University Press   Conical Orthomorphic Projection

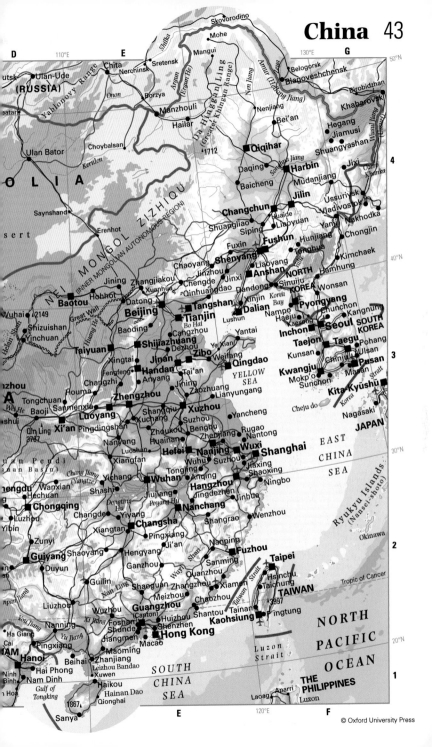

© Oxford University Press

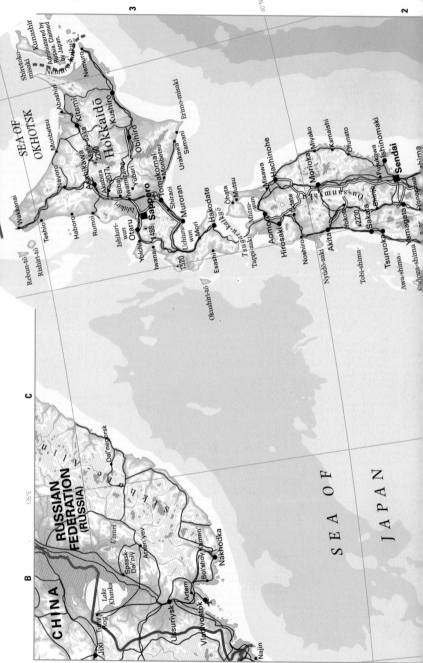

SEA OF OKHOTSK

SEA OF JAPAN

JAPAN

RUSSIAN FEDERATION (RUSSIA)

CHINA

Kunashir
Shiretoko-misaki
Nemuro
Zemlya Kuril'Ju
Administered by Russia. Claimed by Japan.
Abashiri
Kitami
Kushiro
Erimo-misaki
Monbetsu
Nayoro
Asahikawa
Asahi-dake 2290
Hokkaidō
Obihiro
Urakawa
Samani
Wakkanai
Teshio
Haboro
Rumoi
Bibai
Iwamizawa
Yūbari
Tomakomai
Monbetsu
Sapporo
Ishikari-wan
Otaru
Yoichi
Iwanai
1488
Chitose
Shiraoi
Muroran
Uchiura-wan
Mori
Hakodate
Kōyayū
1520
Esashi
Okushiri-tō
Rebun-tō
Rishiri-tō
Tsugaru
Tappi-zaki
Mutsu
Ōhata
Misawa
Hachinohe
Morioka
Miyako
Kamaishi
Ōfunato
Ishinomaki
Sendai
Fukushima
Mutsu-wan
Aomori
Noshiro
Nyūdō-zaki
Akita
Yokote
2230
Sakata
Tobi-shima
Tsuruoka
Yamagata
Awa-shima
Sadoga-shima
Konoze-wan
Ōu-sanmyaku

© Oxford University Press   Zenithal Equidistant Projection

135°E
40°N
40°N

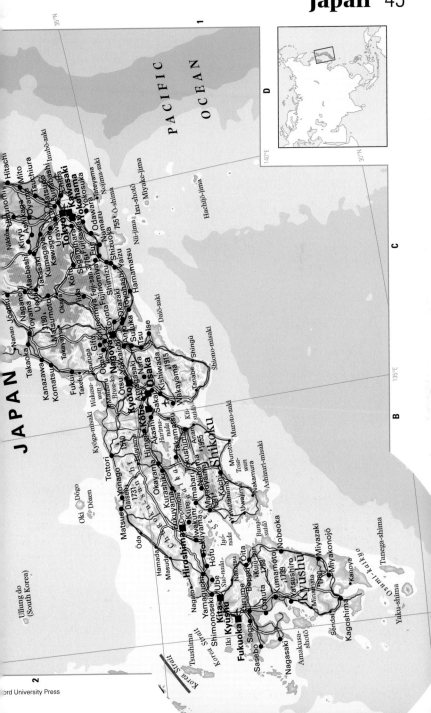

PACIFIC

OCEAN

JAPAN

Scale 1: 23 0

© Oxford University Press   Conical Orthomorphic Projection

shsiung
ngtung
AIWAN

on
it

Aparri
on
Ilagan
gupan
Cabanatuan
Quezon City
Manila
San Pablo
ngas •Naga
2488
Masbate
Roxas
Panay
Iloilo
Bacolod
San Carlos
Negros
Cadiz Tacloban
Cebu
Bohol Leyte
Samar

PACIFIC

OCEAN

-11022
**Challenger
Deep**
10°N

Yap

**FEDERATED STATES
OF MICRONESIA**

PALAU •Koror

Butuan
2560 Cagayan
Dipolog de Oro
Pagadian Iligan
anga •Datu Piang **Mindanao** **Davao**
2954
*Moro
Gulf*
hipelago

THE PHILIPPINES

Kep.
Talaud

**LEBES
SEA**

Kep. Sangir

Morotai

Manado
Ternate ‡1508 Halmahera
Minahassa Peninsula Sao-Siu
Gorontalo

Waigeo

Manokwari P. Biak
•Sorong
‡3000 •Sarmi **Jayapura**
P. Yapen
Pegunungan Van Rees
IRIAN
Nabire Pegunungan Moake New
Puntjak Jaya **JAYA**
5030 4700

Maluku
Kep.
Obi
Misoöl
SERAM
SEA
•Fakfak
Seran •Bula
Kaimana
Amamapare **Guinea**

Ampana
est
Kep. Sula

2799
Kendari
ampone
Muna
S

Buru
Ambon
I **A**

•Baubau
BANDA SEA

Buton

Kep.
Kai

Mapi

Kep.
Aru

Pulau
Dolak
•Merauke

Wetar
Kep.
Babar
Kep.
Tanimbar

Lomblen
ndeh Alor Dili
Maumere Pantar 2960 **EAST TIMOR**
SAWU SEA Timor
Kupang

ARAFURA SEA
10°S

ES SEA

**TIMOR
SEA**
Melville I.
Bathurst I. **AUSTRALIA**

Scale 1: 11 00

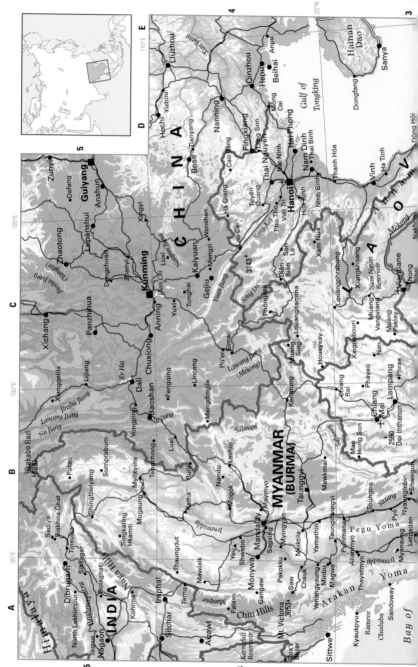

Conical Orthomorphic Projection

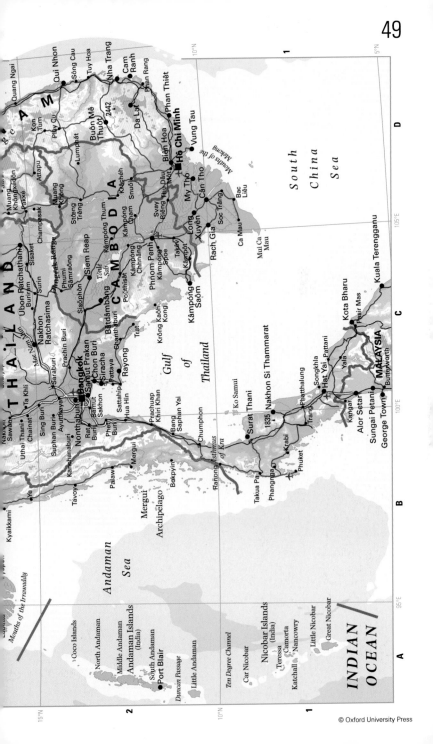

Scale 1: 42 0

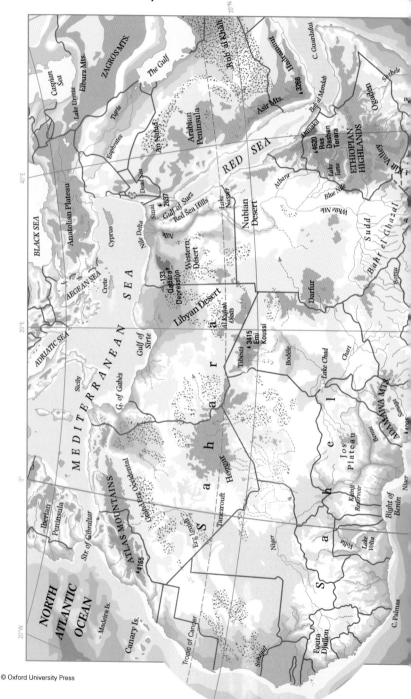

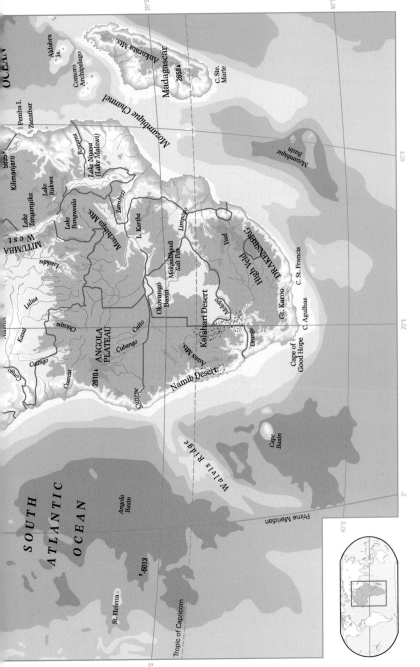

Aldabra Is.

Comoro Archipelago

Ankaratra Mts.

Madagascar

2658

C. Ste. Marie

Pemba I.

Zanzibar

OCEAN

Mozambique Channel

Mozambique Basin

Rovuma

Lake Nyasa (Lake Malawi)

Kilimanjaro

Lake Rukwa

Lake Tanganyika

Zambezi

L. Kariba

Lake Bangweulu

Muchinga Mts.

Luapula

MITUMBA West

Makgadikgadi Salt Pan

Limpopo

Vaal

High Veld

DRAKENSBERG

C. St. Francis

Gt. Karoo

Okovango Basin

Molopo

Kasai

Lulua

Okapa

Chicapa

ANGOLA PLATEAU

Cubango

Cuito

Kalahari Desert

Orange

Cape of Good Hope

C. Agulhas

Cuango

Cuanza

2610

Auas Mts.

Chicamba

Namib Desert

Cunene

SOUTH

ATLANTIC

OCEAN

Angola Basin

Walvis Ridge

Cape Basin

St. Helena

-6013

Prime Meridian

Tropic of Capricorn

20°S

20°S

20°S

0°

20°E

40°E

40°S

Zenithal Equal Area Projection   © Oxford University Press

Scale 1: 42 0(

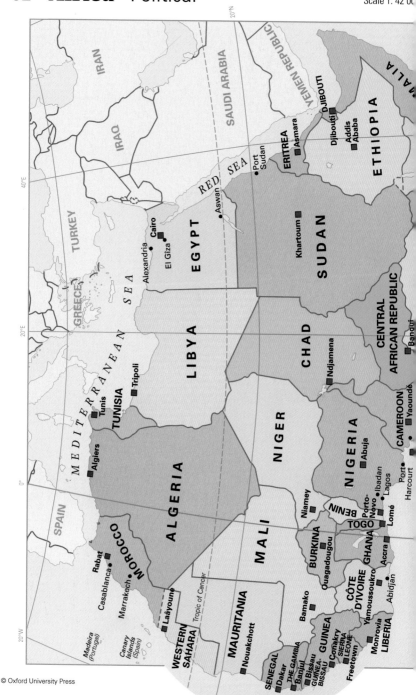

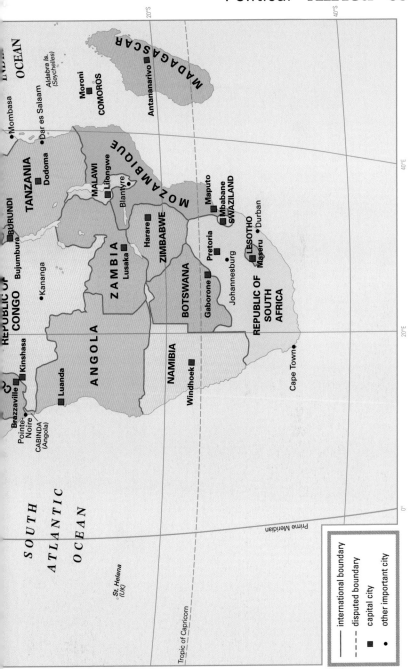

INDIAN OCEAN

MADAGASCAR

Aldabra Is.
(Seychelles)

Moroni
COMOROS

Antananarivo

Mombasa

Dar es Salaam

TANZANIA

Dodoma

BURUNDI

Bujumbura

REPUBLIC OF CONGO

Kananga

Kinshasa

Brazzaville

Pointe-Noire

CABINDA
(Angola)

Luanda

ANGOLA

MALAWI

Lilongwe

Blantyre

MOZAMBIQUE

ZAMBIA

Lusaka

ZIMBABWE

Harare

NAMIBIA

Windhoek

BOTSWANA

Gaborone

Maputo

SWAZILAND

Mbabane

Pretoria

Johannesburg

LESOTHO

Maseru

Durban

REPUBLIC OF SOUTH AFRICA

Cape Town

SOUTH ATLANTIC OCEAN

St. Helena
(UK)

Tropic of Capricorn

Prime Meridian

20°S

40°S

40°E

20°E

0°

20°S

international boundary
disputed boundary
■ capital city
• other important city

Zenithal Equal Area Projection

© Oxford University Press

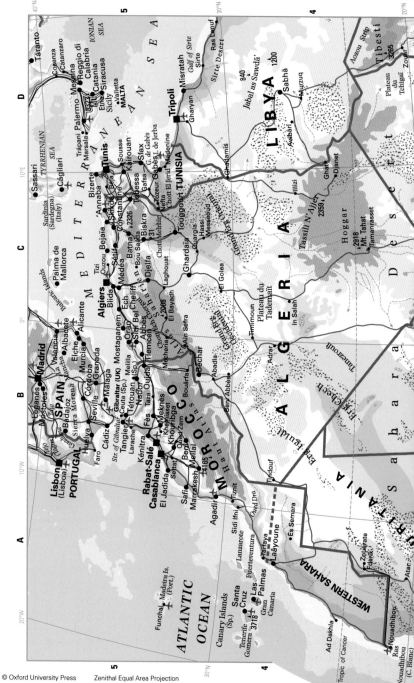

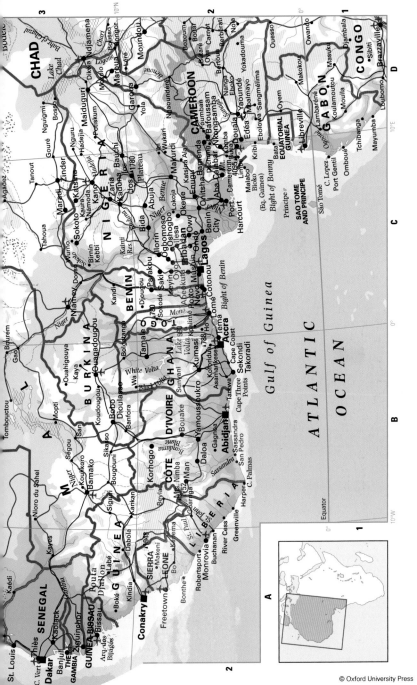

Scale 1: 21 00

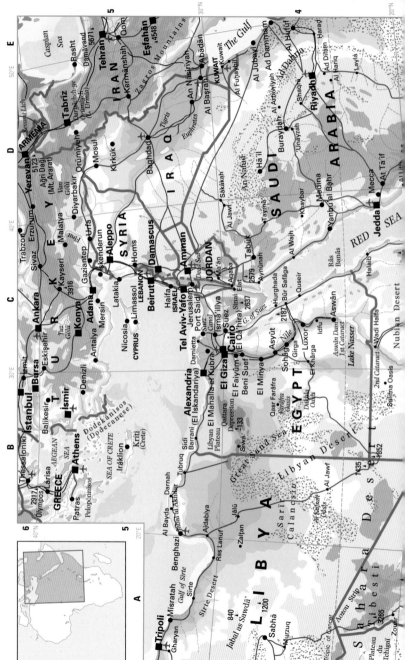

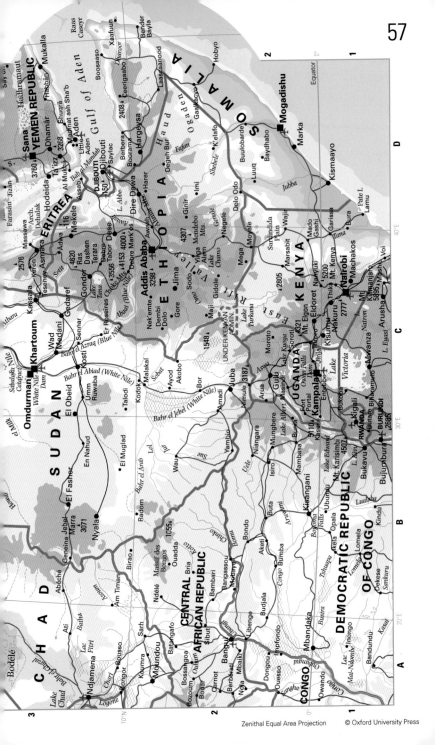

Raas Caseyr
Raas Xaafuun
Bandar Beyla
Bender Cassim
Boosaaso
Dhuudo
Mukalla
Say'un
Hadhramaut
Ambûn
Shuqrâ
Jawf
Maqnat ash Sha'b
Aden
Little Aden
Bab al Mandab
Saylac
Djibouti
Assab
L. Abbe
Dire Dawa
Harer
2408
Gaakaayo
Hobyo
Gulf of Aden
Mukalla
Hadhrenaut
SOMALIA

Farasān Jizān
Archi.
Dehalak
Massawa
Hodeida
Ta'izz
3268
3760
Sana'
YEMEN REPUBLIC
Dhamār

ERITREA
Mekele
Adwa
Asmara
Keren
Gonder
2576

Beseney
Gedaref
4620
Ras Dashen
Terara
Chercs Mts.
3556
4153
4001
Dese
Tabor
Debre Markos
Desë
Gidabo

Awash
Addis Ababa
3298

Hargeysa
Berbera
Booraama

Djibouti
150

L. Tana
Abal (Blue Nile)
Er Roseires
Sennar
Blue Nile

Kassala
Atbara
Gedaref

Khartoum
Omdurman
Cataract
White Nile
Dam
Wad Medani
Bahr el Azraq (Blue Nile)
Kosti
Bahr El Abiad (White Nile)
El Obeid
Umm Ruwaba
Sennar

SUDAN

El Fasher
Geneina Jebel Marra
3071
Nyala

CHAD
Abéché
Ati
Bodélé
Lake Chad
Bahr el Ghazal
Ndjamena
Logone
10°N

el Milk
Sabaloka
Kaduqli
Talodi
Kadugli
Malakal
Sobat
Kodok
Ayod
Akobo
Bor
3187
Nmule

Bahr el Arab
El Muglad
En Nahud
Lol
Radom
Wau
Juba
Amadi
Yei
Yambio
Niangara
Uele
Bondo
Buta

UNDER KENYA
ADMIN.
1548
Nek'emte
Dembi Dolo
Gore
Maji
Omo
Jima
Soda
Soto
4307
Viga
Alem Mts.
Mega
Negele
Moyale
Marsabit

ETHIOPIA

East Rift Valley
Lake Chamo
Lake Chew Bahir
Gidole
Lake Turkana
Moroto
Lodwar
Kitale
Mt. Elgon
4321
Soroti
Lake Kyoga
Lira
5110
Mt. Elgon
Kasese
Lake Edward
4507
2685

KENYA
Nairobi
Machakos
2777
Mt. Kenya
5200
Nyeri
Nanyuki
Eldoret
Nakuru
Kisumu
Thika
Mombasa
Voi
5895
Mt. Kilimanjaro
L. Natron
L. Eyasi
Arusha
Mwanza

Sarh
Dolo Odo
Ginir
Imi
Shebele
Degeh Bur
Fafan
Kelafo
Luuq
Baydhabo
Buulobarde
Ceerigaabo
Laascaanood
Haud
Ogaden
Mandebo Mts.
Garadse
Mado Gashi
Wajir
Garissa
Tana
Sarhdinida Plain
2805
Garsen
Lamu
Pate I.
Kismaayo
Jubba
Marka
Mogadishu

Shibut
Bangassou
Bambari
Bria
Ndélé
Massif des Bongos
1055
Birao
Am Timan
Ouaddaï

CENTRAL AFRICAN REPUBLIC
Bangui
Berbérati
Bossangoa
Bozoum
Bouar
Carnot
Mbaïki
Nola
Ouham
Bamingui

Kaga Bandoro
Batangafo
Moundou
Kélo
Bongor
Kaumra
Rousso

Libenge
Budjala
Bumba
Aketi
Akula
Bondo
Gemena
Lisala
Mbandaka
Inongo
Lac Mai-Ndombe

Ubangi
Uele
Isiro
Kisangani
Boyoma Falls
Opala

DEMOCRATIC REPUBLIC OF CONGO

Lomela
Oshwe
Dekese
Lodja
Lomami
Sankuru
Lubefu
Lubao
Kasai
Kindu
Lualaba
Bukavu
Goma
L. Kivu
Uvira
Bujumbura

RWANDA
Kigali
Butare
Bijharamulo
BURUNDI

UGANDA
Kampala
Entebbe
Fort Portal
Masindi
Gulu
Arua
Juba
Bukoba
Jinja
Lake Victoria
Lake Albert
Mubende
Lake Kyoga

CONGO
Ouesso
Owando
Mbandaka
Impfondo
Dongou
Sangha
Likouala
Mossaka

Bangassou
Obo

Zenithal Equal Area Projection © Oxford University Press

Scale 1: 7 00

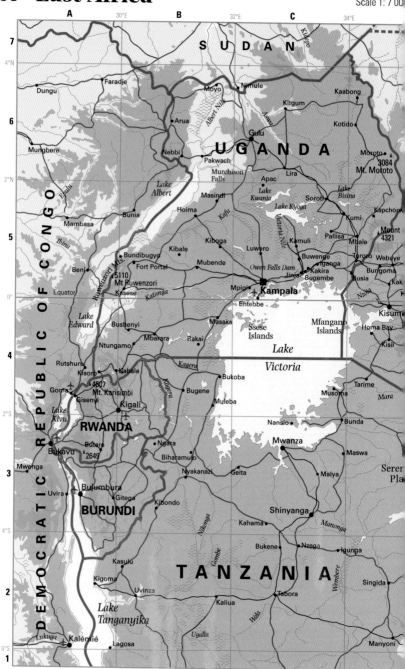

© Oxford University Press   Zenithal Equal Area Projection

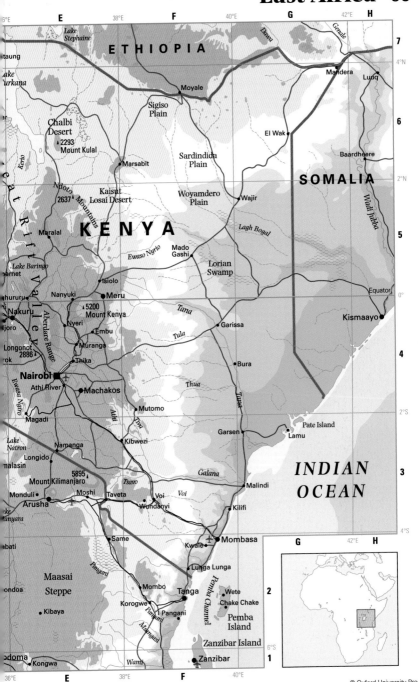

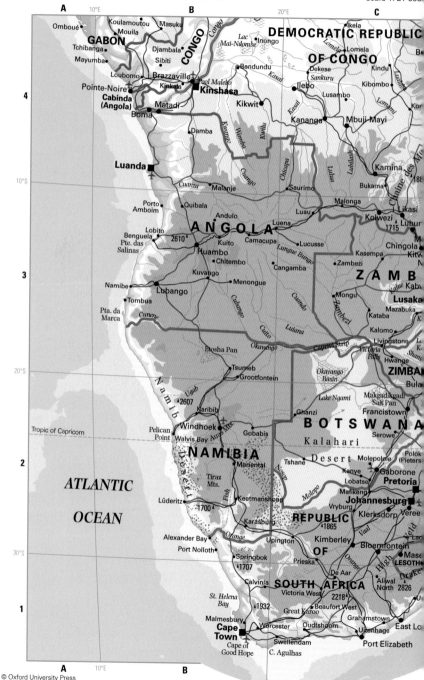

A 10°E · B · 20°E · C

Omboué
Koulamoutou
Mouila
Masuku
GABON
Tchibanga
Djambala
Mayumba
Sibiti
Loubomo
CONGO
Congo
Lac Mai-Ndombe
Inongo
Ikela
DEMOCRATIC REPUBLIC
Lomela
Lomela
OF CONGO
Kindu
Dekese
Sankuru
Kibombo
Bandundu
Ilebo
Lusambo
Kor
Pointe-Noire
Brazzaville
Kinkala
Pool Malebo
Kinshasa
Kikwit
Kasai
Kananga
Mbuji-Mayi
Kamina
Cabinda (Angola)
Matadi
Boma
Damba
Kwango
Wamba
Kwilu
Bukama
Likasi
Luanda
Cuanza
Malanje
Chicapa
Saurimo
Malonga
Kolwezi
Likasi
Lubur
1715
Porto Amboim
Quibala
Andulo
A N G O L A
Luau
Luena
Lucusse
Kasempa
Chingola
Kitw
Lobito
2610
Kuito
Camacupa
Lungue Bungo
Zambezi
Z A M B
Benguela
Pte. das Salinas
Huambo
Chitembo
Cangamba
Kasai
Mongu
Lusaka
Namibe
Kuvango
Menongue
Cubango
Cuando
Zambezi
Mazabuka
Kataba
Tombua
Lubango
Cuito
Luiana
Kalomo
Pta. da Marca
Cunene
Livingstone
L. K
Etosha Pan
Okavango
Capivi Strip
Victoria Falls
Hwange
ZIMBA
Tsumeb
Grootfontein
Okavango Basin
Bula
2607
Ugab
Ghanzi
Lake Ngami
Makgadikgadi Salt Pan
Francistown
Karibib
Windhoek
Gobabis
B O T S W A N A
Serowe
Pelican Point
Walvis Bay
Auas Mts.
Kalahari
Desert
Molepolole
Polok (Pieters
N A M I B I A
Mariental
Tshane
Kanye
Gaborone
Tiraz Mts.
Nossob
Lobatse
Pretoria
Lüderitz
Keetmanshoop
Molopo
Mafikeng
Johannesburg
1700
Karasburg
Vryburg
Klerksdorp
Veree
ATLANTIC
REPUBLIC
1865
Alexander Bay
Orange
Upington
Kimberley
Bloemfontein
OCEAN
Port Nolloth
Springbok
Prieska
OF
Orange
Mase
LESOTH
1707
De Aar
Aliwal North
2826
Calvinia
SOUTH AFRICA
Victoria West
2218
St. Helena Bay
1932
Great Karoo
Beaufort West
Grahamstown
East Lo
Malmesbury
Worcester
Oudtshoorn
Uitenhage
Cape Town
Swellendam
Port Elizabeth
Cape of Good Hope
C. Agulhas

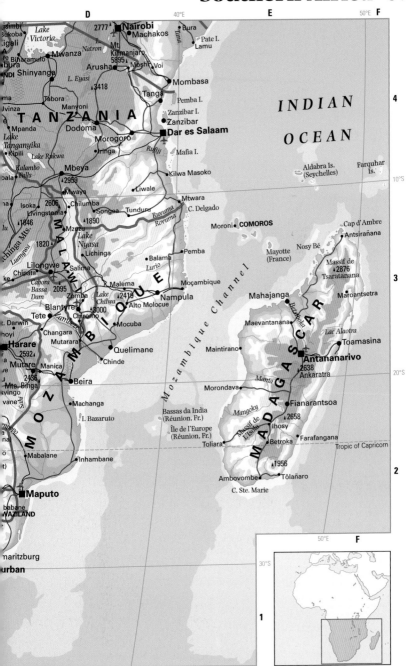

Zenithal Equal Area Projection   © Oxford University Press

Scale 1: 40 00

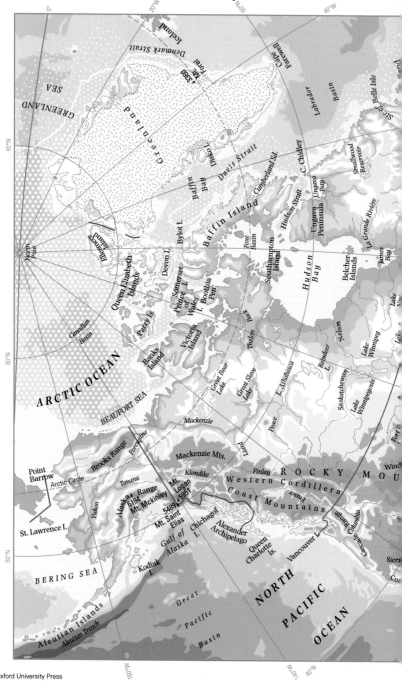

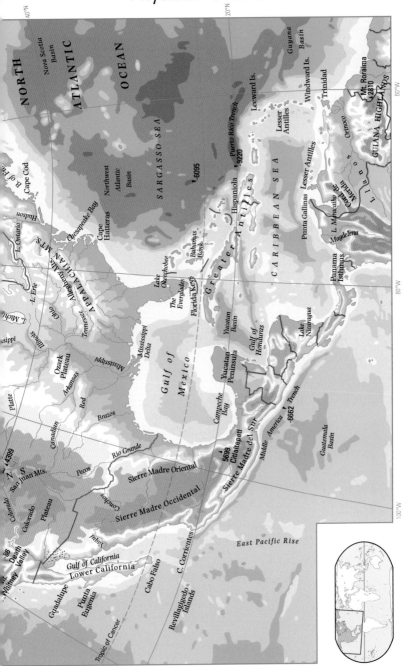

NORTH

ATLANTIC

OCEAN

Nova Scotia Basin

Cape Cod

B. of Fundy

Hudson

Chesapeake Bay

Cape Hatteras

Northwest Atlantic Basin

SARGASSO SEA

•-6095

Puerto Rico Trench
•-9220

Leeward Is.

Windward Is.

Trinidad

Guiana Basin

Mt. Roraima
2810

GUIANA HIGHLANDS

Orinoco

Cordillera de Mérida

Sierra Nevada de Santa Marta

L. Ontario

L. Erie

L. Michigan

Mississippi

Ohio

Illinois

Tennessee

ALLEGHENY MTS.

APPALACHIAN MTS.

Bahamas Bank

Hispaniola

Greater Antilles

Lesser Antilles

Lesser Antilles

CARIBBEAN SEA

Punta Gallinas

L. Maracaibo

Magdalena

Lake Okeechobee

The Everglades

Florida Keys

Yucatan Basin

Gulf of Honduras

Lake Nicaragua

Panama Isthmus

Ozark Plateau

Arkansas

Mississippi Delta

Mississippi

Red

Canadian

Brazos

Rio Grande

Pecos

Conchos

Gulf of Mexico

Campeche Bay

Yucatan Peninsula

Sierra Madre del Sur

Middle America Trench •-6662

Guatemala Basin

Platte

San Juan Mts.

•4399

N S

Colorado

Plateau

Death Valley

Mt. Whitney •-86

Guadalupe

Punta Eugenia

Gulf of California

Lower California

Cabo Falso

Balsas

C. Corrientes

Revillagigedo Islands

Sierra Madre Oriental

Citlaltepetl
5699 •

Sierra Madre Occidental

Sierra Madre del Sur

East Pacific Rise

Tropic of Cancer

40°N

20°N

60°W

80°W

100°W

20°N

Scale 1: 40 00

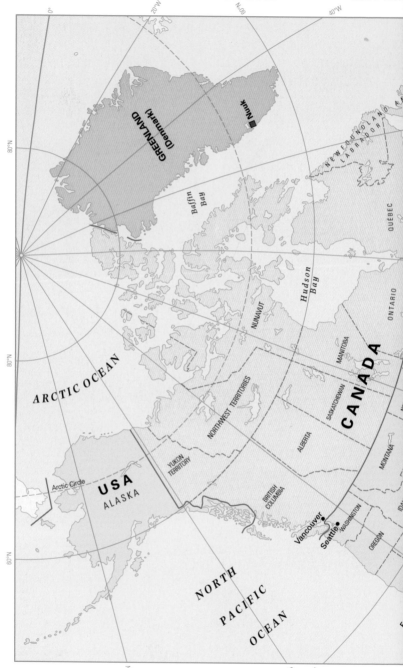

GREENLAND
(Denmark)

Nuuk

Baffin
Bay

NEWFOUNDLAND
AND
LABRADOR

QUÉBEC

Hudson
Bay

ONTARIO

NUNAVUT

MANITOBA

ARCTIC OCEAN

SASKATCHEWAN

C A N A D A

NORTHWEST TERRITORIES

MONTANA

ALBERTA

YUKON
TERRITORY

Arctic Circle

USA
ALASKA

BRITISH
COLUMBIA

Vancouver
Seattle
WASHINGTON

IDAHO

OREGON

N O R T H

P A C I F I C

O C E A N

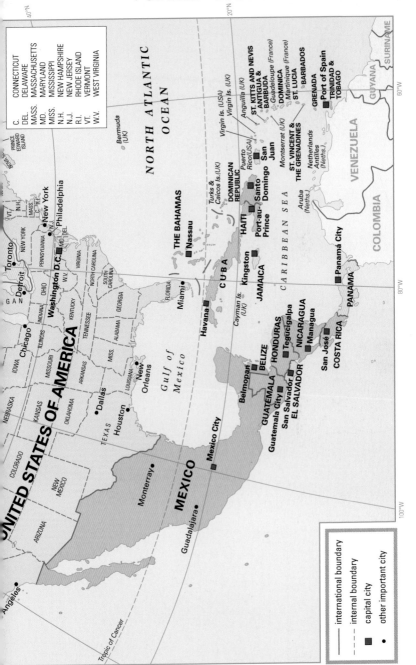

C.	CONNECTICUT
DEL.	DELAWARE
MASS.	MASSACHUSETTS
MD.	MARYLAND
MISS.	MISSISSIPPI
N.H.	NEW HAMPSHIRE
N.J.	NEW JERSEY
R.I.	RHODE ISLAND
VT.	VERMONT
W.V.	WEST VIRGINIA

NORTH ATLANTIC OCEAN

Bermuda (UK)

THE BAHAMAS
Nassau

CUBA
Havana

Turks & Caicos Is.(UK)

DOMINICAN REPUBLIC
HAITI
Santo Domingo
Port-au-Prince

Puerto Rico(USA)
San Juan
Virgin Is. (USA)
Virgin Is. (UK)
Anguilla (UK)
ST. KITTS AND NEVIS
ANTIGUA & BARBUDA
Guadeloupe (France)
DOMINICA
Martinique (France)
ST. LUCIA
Montserrat (UK)
ST. VINCENT & THE GRENADINES
BARBADOS
Netherlands Antilles (Neths.)
GRENADA
Port of Spain
TRINIDAD & TOBAGO

Aruba (Neths.)

VENEZUELA

COLOMBIA

GUYANA

SURINAME

Cayman Is. (UK)

Kingston
JAMAICA

CARIBBEAN SEA

Miami
FLORIDA

Panamá City
PANAMA

San José
COSTA RICA

Managua
NICARAGUA

Tegucigalpa
HONDURAS

Belmopan
BELIZE

GUATEMALA
Guatemala City
San Salvador
EL SALVADOR

New Orleans

Gulf of Mexico

MEXICO
Mexico City
Monterray
Guadalajara

UNITED STATES OF AMERICA

Washington D.C.
New York
Philadelphia
Toronto
Detroit
Chicago
Dallas
Houston
Los Angeles

NEW YORK
PENNSYLVANIA
OHIO
INDIANA
ILLINOIS
IOWA
MISSOURI
KANSAS
NEBRASKA
OKLAHOMA
ARKANSAS
LOUISIANA
TEXAS
NEW MEXICO
ARIZONA
COLORADO
KENTUCKY
TENNESSEE
VIRGINIA
NORTH CAROLINA
SOUTH CAROLINA
GEORGIA
ALABAMA
MISS.
W.V.
VT.
N.H.
MASS.
C.
R.I.
N.J.
DEL.
MD.
PRINCE EDWARD ISLAND

Tropic of Cancer

40°N
20°N
100°W
80°W
60°W

international boundary
internal boundary
capital city
other important city

Oblique Mercator Projection   © Oxford University Press

Scale 1: 28 000

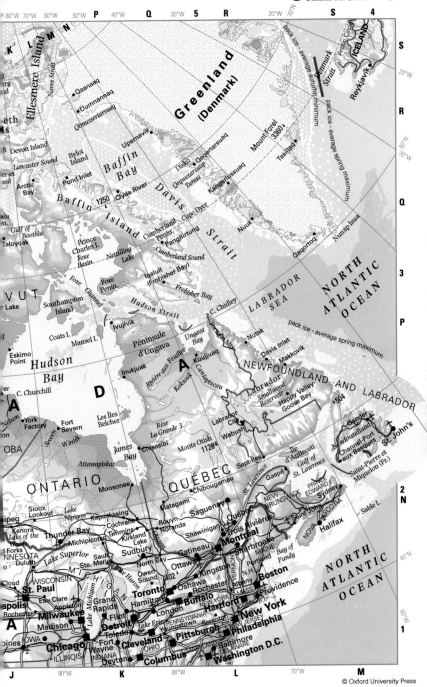

© Oxford University Press

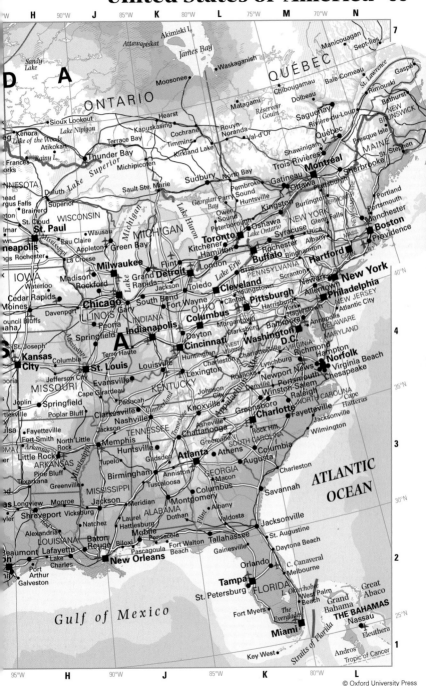

Scale 1: 6 250

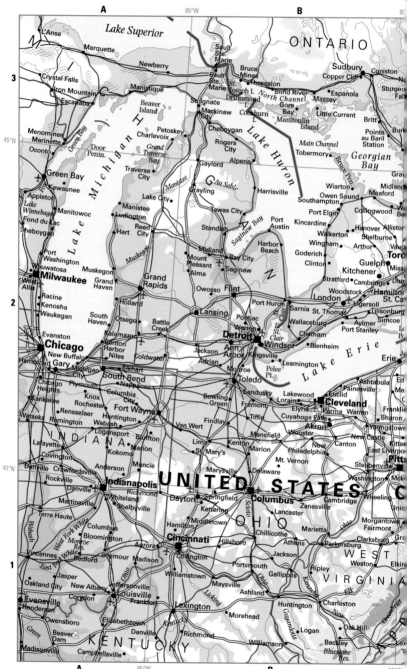

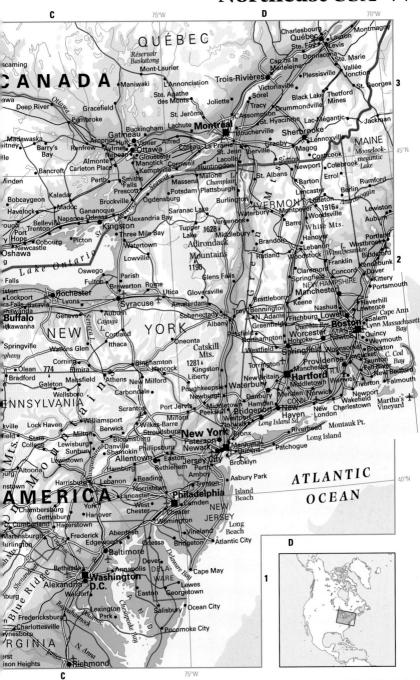

C   75°W   D   70°W

QUÉBEC

Réservoir Baskatong

scaming
Mont-Laurier
Maniwaki   L'Annonciation
Charlesbourg Québec
Lauzon Montmagny
Cap de la Madeleine   Ste. Foy   Lévis
Ste. Marie
Ste. Agathe des Monts   Donnacona   Vallée Jonction
CANADA   Trois-Rivières   Plessisville   St. Georges   3
awa   Deep River   Ottawa   Victoriaville
Gracefield   St. Jérôme   Sorel   Black Lake   Thetford Mines
Pembroke   Joliette   Tracy   Drummondville   Jackman
Madawaska   Barry's Bay   Buckingham   Lachute   **Montréal**   St. Hyacinthe   Lac-Mégantic   **MAINE**
itney   Renfrew   Arnprior   Hull   Gatineau   Vanier   Alfred   Boucherville   Granby   Lennoxville
le   Almonte   Aylmer   Nepean   Coteau   La Prairie   Sutton   **Sherbrooke**   Mooselookmeguntic Lake   45°N
Bancroft   Carleton Place   Manotick   Gloucester   St. Jean   Iberville   Magog   Coaticook
linden   Perth   Kemptville   Cornwall   Huntingdon   Lacolle   Newport   Colebrook   Rumford
Bobcaygeon   Kaladar   Smiths Falls   Seaway   Massena   Malone   St. Albans   Barton   Berlin   Androscoggin
Havelock   Madoc   Brockville   Prescott   Potsdam   Plattsburgh   Lancaster   Errol   Lewiston
ough   Belleville   Gananoque   Ogdensburg   Champlain   L.   **VERMONT**   Littleton   1916   Auburn
Port   Napanee   Odessa   **Kingston**   Alexandria Bay   Saranac Lake   Burlington   Waterbury   Montpelier   White Mts.
Hope   Trenton   Kaladar   Three Mile Bay   Tupper   1628   Vergennes   Barre   Woodsville   Portland
Cobourg   Picton   Lake   Middlebury   Hanover   Winnipesaukee   Biddeford
Oshawa   St.   Watertown   **Adirondack**   Brandon   L. Westbrook   Kennebunk
g   Lowville   **Mountains**   Rutland   Woodstock   Franklin   Concord   Dover
Falls   Oswego   Parish   Glens Falls   1190   Claremont   Portsmouth   2
iston   Fulton   Rome   Gloversville   Springfield   **NEW HAMPSHIRE**   Kittery
Lockport   **Rochester**   Brewerton   Utica   Brattleboro   Keene   **Manchester**
ra Falls Batavia   Lyons   Syracuse   Amsterdam   Troy   Bennington   Nashua   Haverhill
hawanda   **Buffalo**   Geneva   Cayuga   Schenectady   N. Adams   Fitchburg   Lowell   Lawrence   Cape Ann
ckawanda   **NEW**   Auburn   L.   **Albany**   Greenfield   Quabbin Res.   **Boston**   Lynn   Massachusetts Bay
Springville   Watkins Glen   Cortland   Pittsfield   Northampton   Worcester   **MASS.**   Newton   Quincy
gheny   Corning   Ithaca   **YORK**   Oneonta   Westfield   Holyoke   Weymouth
Olean   774   Elmira   Binghamton   **Catskill Mts.**   Torrington   **Springfield**   Woonsocket   Brockton
Bradford   Galeton   Mansfield   Athens   New Milford   1281   Kingston   Middletown   Providence   Taunton   C. Cod Bay
Wellsboro   Carbondale   Liberty   Hancock   New Britain   Menden   **Hartford**   Warwick   New Bedford   Falmouth
NNSYLVANIA   Scranton   Port Jervis   Poughkeepsie   Newburgh   Danbury   Hamden   **CONN.**   Norwich   Newport   Martha's
kville   Lock Haven   Williamsport   Wilkes-Barre   Milford   Middletown   New   Charlestown   Vineyard
field   State College   Milton   Berwick   Stroudsburg   Peekskill   Bridgeport   Haven   New London
Lewisburg   Bloomsburg   Danville   Westport   Long Island Sd.   Riverhead   Montauk Pt.
urg   Altoona   Lewistown   Sunbury   Shamokin   Phillipsburg   **New York**   Bronx   Long Island
nstown   Harrisburg   Allentown   Easton   Paterson   Newark   Manhattan   Queens   Patchogue
AMERICA   Hamburg   Bethlehem   Perth Amboy   Jersey City   Brooklyn   Asbury Park   **ATLANTIC**   40°N
Chambersburg   Lebanon   Reading   Norristown   Island   **OCEAN**
Gettysburg   Hanover   Lancaster   West   **Philadelphia**   Beach   **NEW**
Cumberland   York   Chester   Camden   Long   **JERSEY**
Martinsburg   Hagerstown   Frederick   Aberdeen   Wilmington   Beach
urlington   Edgewood   Odessa   Vineland   Atlantic City   D
Baltimore   Bridgeton
Bethesda   Annapolis   Dover   **DELA-**   Cape May   1
Alexandria   **Washington**   Waldorf   **D.C.**   Easton   **WARE**   Lewes
Lexington Park   Georgetown   Ocean City
urg   Fredericksburg   Potomac   Salisbury
Charlottesville   Pocomoke City
ynesboro   Chesapeake Bay
RGINIA   N. Anna
son Heights   **Richmond**

C   75°W

Scale 1 : 5 50

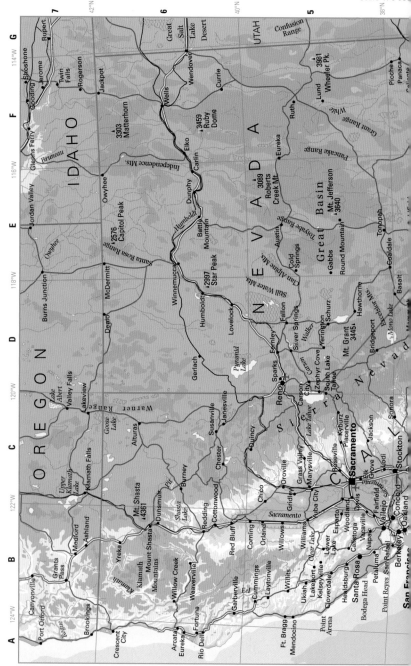

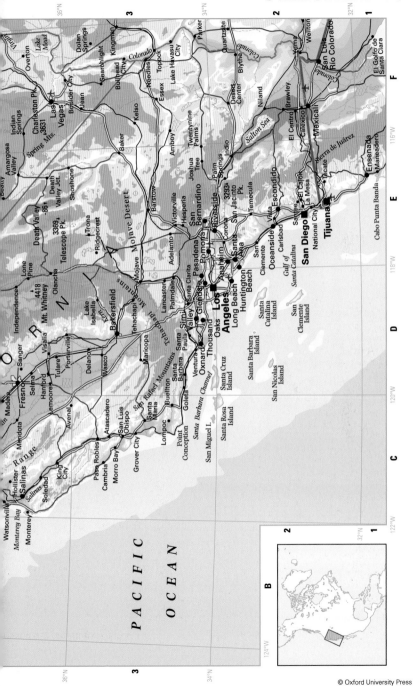

Scale 1: 15 0

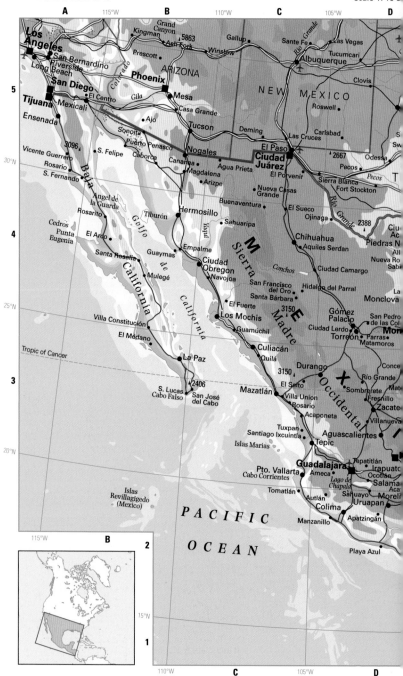

© Oxford University Press   Zenithal Equidistant Projection

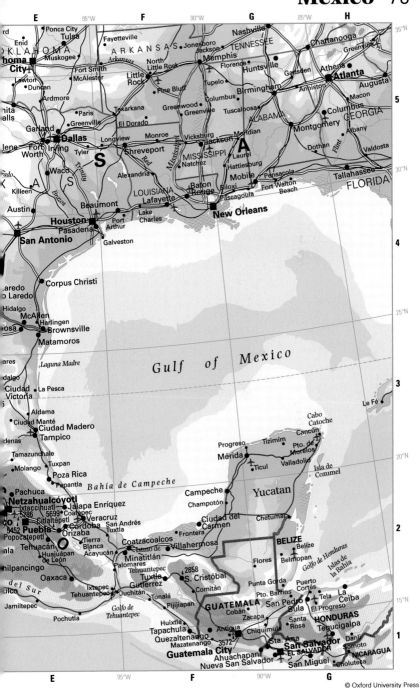

Gulf of Mexico

Bahía de Campeche

Yucatan

ARKANSAS

TENNESSEE

OKLAHOMA

ALABAMA

GEORGIA

MISSISSIPPI

LOUISIANA

FLORIDA

TEXAS

Laguna Madre

Golfo de
Tehuantepec

GUATEMALA

HONDURAS

BELIZE

EL SALVADOR

NICARAGUA

Golfo de Honduras

Islas de
la Bahía

Isla de
Cozumel

del Sur

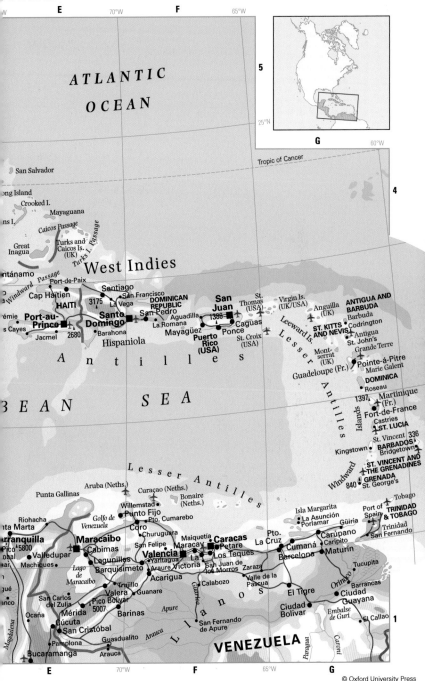

E 70°W F 65°W

G 60°W

ATLANTIC

OCEAN

5

25°N

G

Tropic of Cancer

San Salvador

ong Island

Crooked I.

ans I.   Mayaguana

Caicos Passage

Great   Turks and

Inagua   Caicos Is.

(UK)   *Turks I. Passage*

ntánamo   **West Indies**

Windward Passage   Port-de-Paix   Santiago

Cap Haïtien   San Francisco

émie   **HAITI**   3175   La Vega   **DOMINICAN**   **San**

Port-au-   Santo   San Pedro   **REPUBLIC**   **Juan**

s Cayes   **Prince**   **Domingo**   Aguadilla   1388   St.

Jacmel   2680   Barahona   La Romana   **Mayagüez**   Caguas   Thomas   Virgin Is.

   Hispaniola   Ponce   **Puerto**   St. Croix   (UK/USA)

   A n t i l l e s   **Rico**   (USA)

   (USA)

4

Anguilla   **ANTIGUA AND**

(UK)   **BARBUDA**

   Barbuda

ST. KITTS   Codrington

AND NEVIS   Antigua

   St. John's

Mont-   Grande Terre

serrat   **Pointe-á-Pitre**

(UK)   Marie Galent

Guadeloupe (Fr.)   **DOMINICA**

   Roseau

B E A N   S E A   1397   Martinique

   (Fr.)

   Fort-de-France

   Castries

   ST. LUCIA

L e s s e r   A n t i l l e s   St. Vincent   336

Kingstown   **BARBADOS**

   Bridgetown

   ST. VINCENT AND

   THE GRENADINES

   GRENADA

   840   St. George's

Aruba (Neths.)   Curaçao (Neths.)

Punta Gallinas   Bonaire   Isla Margarita   Port of   Tobago

   (Neths.)   La Asunción   Spain   **TRINIDAD**

Riohacha   Willemstad   Pto. Cumarebo   Porlamar   Güiria   **& TOBAGO**

ta Marta   *Golfo de*   **Punto Fijo**   Carúpano   Trinidad

   Venezuela   Coro   Maiquetía   **Caracas**   Pto.   Cumaná   San Fernando

rranquilla   **Maracaibo**   San Felipe   Maracay   Petare   La Cruz

   Cabimas   **Valencia**   La   Los Teques   Barcelona   Maturín

bal   Valledupar   Lagunillas   Yaritagua   Victoria   San Juan de

Machiques   *Lago*   Barquisimeto   Araure   los Morros   Zaraza   Caripito

   de   Acarigua   Calabozo   Valle de la   El Tigre   Tucupita

jué   San Carlos   Trujillo   Guanare   Pascua   Barrancas

nco   del Zulia   **Pico Bolívar**   *Apure*   **Ciudad**   Ciudad   *Orinoco*

Ocaña   Mérida   5007   Barinas   **Bolívar**   Guayana

Cúcuta   San Fernando   *Embalse*   El Callao

San Cristóbal   Guasdualito   de Apure   *de Gurí*

Pamplona   *Arauca*   **VENEZUELA**   *Caroní*

Bucaramanga   Arauca   *Paraguá*

E 70°W F 65°W G

© Oxford University Press

Scale 1: 35 000

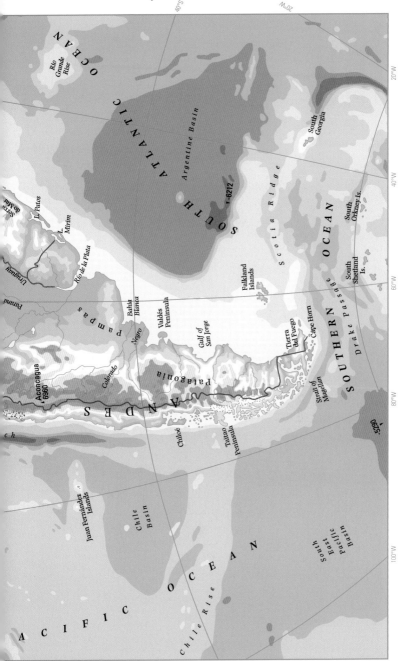

Rio Grande Rise

SOUTH ATLANTIC OCEAN

OCEAN

Argentine Basin

South Georgia

-6212

Scotia Ridge

Serra do Mar

L. Patos

L. Mirim

Uruguay

Rio de la Plata

Paraná

Falkland Islands

SCOTIA

South Orkney Is.

Pampas

Bahía Blanca

Negro

Valdés Peninsula

Gulf of San Jorge

Patagonia

Tierra del Fuego

Cape Horn

Drake Passage

South Shetland Is.

SOUTHERN OCEAN

Aconcagua 6960

Colorado

ANDES

Strait of Magellan

...ch

Chiloé

Taitao Peninsula

-5290

Juan Fernández Islands

Chile Basin

PACIFIC OCEAN

Chile Rise

South East Pacific Basin

Scale 1: 35 00

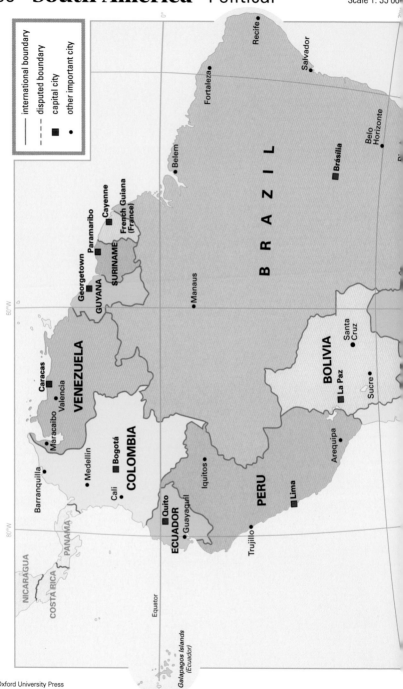

international boundary
disputed boundary
capital city
other important city

Recife

Salvador

Fortaleza

Belo
Horizonte

Belem

Brásilia

B R A Z I L

Cayenne

French Guiana
(France)

Paramaribo

SURINAME

Georgetown

GUYANA

Manaus

Santa
Cruz

Caracas

VENEZUELA

BOLIVIA

Valencia

La Paz

Sucre

Maracaibo

Medellin

Bogotá

COLOMBIA

Iquitos

Arequipa

Cali

Quito

Guayaquil

PERU

Lima

Barranquilla

ECUADOR

Trujillo

PANAMA

NICARAGUA

COSTA RICA

Equator

Galapagos Islands
(Ecuador)

60°W

80°W

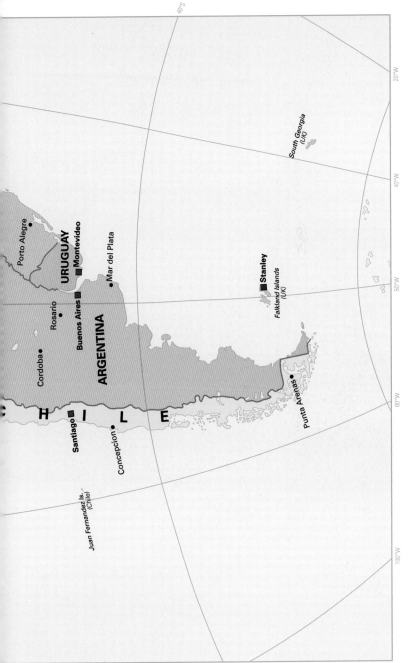

Oblique Mercator Projection   © Oxford University Press

Scale 1: 21 50

Transverse Mercator Projection

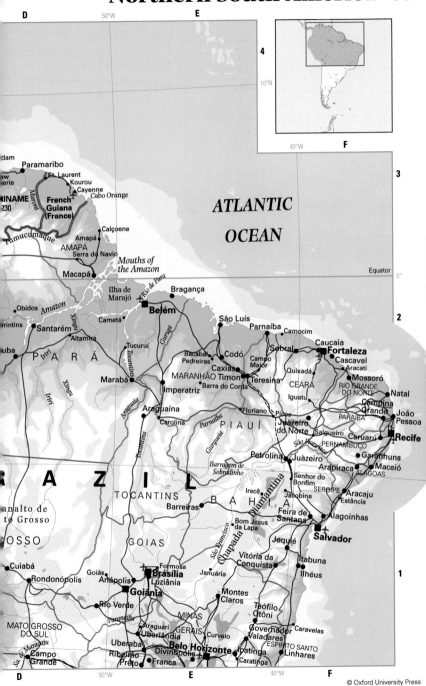

D   50°W   E   10°N   40°W   F

4

ATLANTIC

OCEAN

Equator   0°

3

dam
Paramaribo
•St. Laurent
w   Kourou
erie   Cayenne
RINAME   Cabo Orange
230   French
Guiana
(France)
Tumucumaque
Calçoene
Amapá
AMAPÁ
Serra do Navio
Macapá

Mouths of
the Amazon

Ilha de   Bragança
Marajó   Rio de Pará
•Obidos   Belém   São Luís
rintins   Amazon   Cametá   Parnaíba   Camocim
•Santarém   Xingu   Caucaia
uba   Altamira   Tucuruí   Bacabal   Codó   Sobral   Fortaleza
P A R Á   Pedreiras   Campo   Cascavel
Xingu   Maranhão Timon   Maior   Quixadá   Aracati
Iriri   Marabá   Caxias   Teresina   CEARÁ   Mossoró
Imperatriz   Barra do Corda   RIO GRANDE
Araguaia   Iguatú   DO NORTE   Natal
Araguaína   Floriano   Picos   Campina   João
Carolina   P I A U Í   Juàzeiro   Grande   Pessoa
Parnaíba   do Norte   Salgueiro   PARAÍBA   Recife
R   Gurguéia   São Francisco   Caruaru
Petrolina   PERNAMBUCO   Garanhuns
A   Juàzeiro   Arapiraca   Maceió
Barragem de   ALAGOAS
Z   Sobradinho   Senhor do   SERGIPE
Bonfim   Aracaju
analto de   I   Irecê   Jacobina   Estância
to Grosso   T O C A N T I N S   B A H I A   Feira de   Alagoinhas
OSSO   Barreiras   Bom Jesus   Santana   Salvador
da Lapa   Chapada
G O I A S   Vitória da   Itabuna
•Cuiabá   Conquista   Ilhéus
Rondonópolis   Goiás   Formosa   Januária
Anápolis   Brasília   Montes
Luziânia   Claros
MATO GROSSO   Goiânia   Teófilo
DO SUL   Rio Verde   Otôni
MINAS   Araguari   Governador   Caravelas
Campo   Uberlândia   Curvelo   Valadares   Linhares
Grande   Uberaba   GERAIS   Ipatinga   ESPÍRITO SANTO
Ribeirão   Divinópolis   Belo Horizonte   Caratinga
Preto   Franca

1

B R   R A   Z   I   L

D   50°W   E   40°W   F

© Oxford University Press

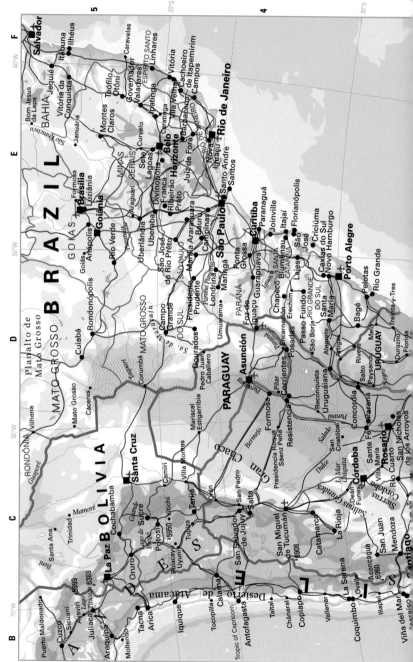

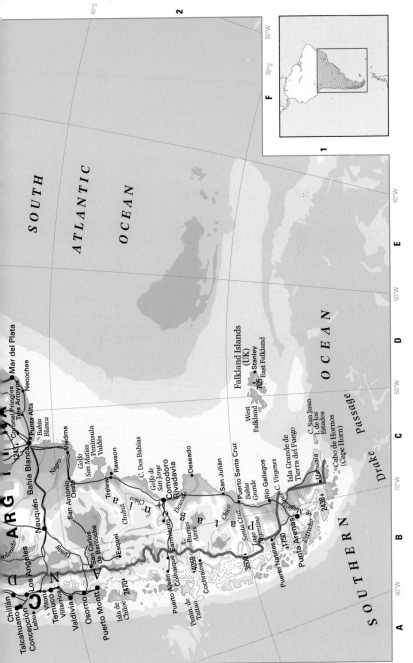

SOUTH ATLANTIC OCEAN

SOUTH

ATLANTIC

OCEAN

F

30°W

50°S

1

Mar del Plata
Neocochea
Coronel Pringles
Tres Arroyos
1243 Punta Alta
Bahía Blanca
Bahía Blanca

Viedma

Golfo
San Matías
Península
Valdés

Rawson

C. Dos Bahías

Golfo de
San Jorge
Comodoro
Rivadavia

Deseado

San Julián

Puerto Santa Cruz

Bahía
Grande

Río Gallegos

C. Vírgenes

C. San Juan
I. de los
Estados

Isla Grande de
Tierra del Fuego

Ushuaia
Cabo de Hornos
(Cape Horn)

Falkland Islands
(UK)
Stanley
East Falkland

West
Falkland

Drake Passage

OCEAN

ARGENTINA

Chillán
Talcahuano
Concepción
Leubú
Temuco
Villarrica
Valdivia
Osorno
Puerto Montt
Isla de
Chiloé
Penín. de
Taitao
Cochrane
Victoria
Los Angeles
Neuquén
San Carlos
de Bariloche
Esquel
Puerto Aisén
Coihaique
Balmaceda
4058
2470
Colorado
Limay
Negro
San Antonio
Oeste
Chubut
Trelew
Chico
Deseado
Santa Cruz
Lago
Argentino
360
Puerto Natales
1750
Punta Arenas
C. Magallanes
2438
Estrecho

SOUTHERN

80°W   70°W   60°W   50°W   40°W

2

40°S

© Oxford University Press

Scale 1: 30 00

120°E   140°E

0° Equator

Borneo

Sulawesi   Seram

Buru

BANDA SEA   Jaya Peak 5030▲

Aru Is.   New

FLORES SEA   Guinea

Tanimbar
Is.

ARAFURA   SEA

Lombok   Torres S
Flores   Timor   Melville   C
Bali   Sumbawa   I.
Sumba   TIMOR   Cape
SEA   York
Penins.
Bathurst I.   Arnhem Land
Joseph   Gulf of
Bonaparte   Carpentaria
Gulf   Daly   Mitch

INDIAN   Kimberley   Barkly Tableland   Flinders
Plateau

OCEAN   Fitzroy   Georgina

Eighty   Great   Macdonnell Ranges
Mile   Sandy Desert   Lake   Simpson
Beach   Mackay   Desert   Th
North West   Lake   867▲
Cape   Hamersley   Disappointment   Ayers
Range ▲1235   Rock   Cooper Creek
Ashburton   Mt. Tom   Gibson Desert
Price   Lake
L. Carnegie   Eyre
Gascoyne   Great   Victoria   Desert   L.
Murchison   Torrens   Ra.
L. Barlee   Flinders
Nullarbor Plain   L.
L. Moore   Gairdner   Murray
Eyre
Penin.
Great Australian Bight   Spencer Gulf
Kangaroo I.
C. Leeuwin

SOUTHERN

40°S   OCEAN

© Oxford University Press   Zenithal Equidistant Projection

120°E   140°E

20°S

Tropic of Capricorn

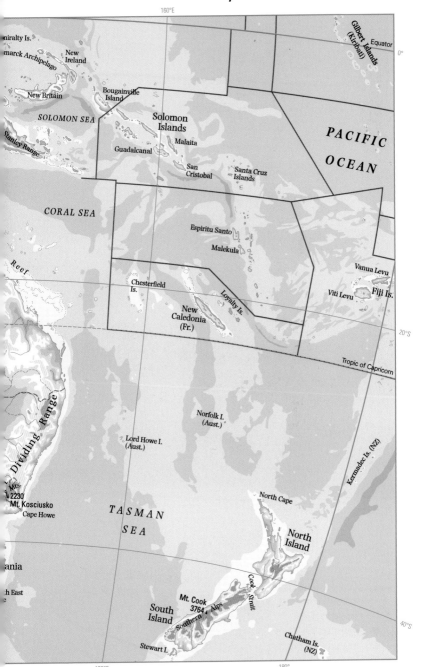

miralty Is.

Bismarck Archipelago

New Ireland

New Britain

Bougainville Island

SOLOMON SEA

Stanley Range

Solomon Islands

Malaita

Guadalcanal

San Cristobal

Santa Cruz Islands

Gilbert Islands (Kiribati)

Equator

0°

PACIFIC

OCEAN

CORAL SEA

Reef

Espiritu Santo

Malekula

Chesterfield Is.

Loyalty Is.

New Caledonia (Fr.)

Vanua Levu

Viti Levu

Fiji Is.

20°S

Tropic of Capricorn

Great Dividing Range

Norfolk I. (Aust.)

Lord Howe I. (Aust.)

Kermadec Is. (NZ)

Mts.

2230

Mt. Kosciusko

Cape Howe

TASMAN SEA

North Cape

North Island

ania

h East

Mt. Cook 3764 Southern Alps

South Island

Cook Strait

Stewart I.

Chatham Is. (NZ)

40°S

160°E

180°

160°E

Zenithal Equidistant Projection

© Oxford University Press

Scale 1: 30 00(

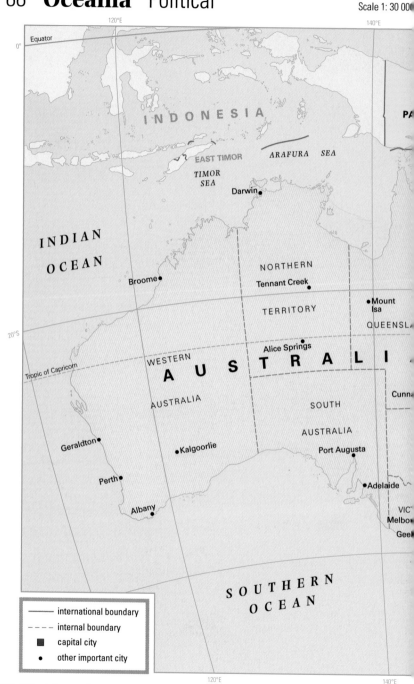

120°E

Equator

0°

INDONESIA

PA

EAST TIMOR

ARAFURA SEA

TIMOR
SEA

Darwin

INDIAN

OCEAN

NORTHERN

Broome

Tennant Creek

•Mount
Isa

TERRITORY

QUEENSL

20°S

Alice Springs

WESTERN

Tropic of Capricorn

A U S T R A L I

AUSTRALIA

SOUTH

Cunn

AUSTRALIA

Geraldton

•Kalgoorlie

Port Augusta

Perth

•Adelaide

Albany

VIC

Melbo

Gee

SOUTHERN

OCEAN

—— international boundary

--- internal boundary

■ capital city

• other important city

Zenithal Equidistant Projection

120°E   140°E

NAURU

Gilbert Islands (Kiribati)

Equator 0°

160°E

GUINEA

SOLOMON SEA

rt esby

SOLOMON ISLANDS

Honiara

PACIFIC

OCEAN

TUVALU

CORAL SEA

VANUATU

Port Vila

FIJI

Suva

vnsville

New Caledonia (Fr.)

Nouméa

20°S

Rockhampton

Tropic of Capricorn

Brisbane
Gold Coast

Norfolk I. (Aust.)

EW
UTH
LES

Lord Howe I. (Aust.)

Newcastle
Sydney
Wollongong
Canberra

Kermadec Is. (NZ)

TASMAN

SEA

Auckland
Hamilton

ANIA
bart

Wellington

NEW ZEALAND

Christchurch

Chatham Is. (NZ)

Dunedin

160°E

180°

40°S

Scale 1: 20 000

INDIAN
OCEAN

TIMOR
SEA

*TIMOR
SEA*

Bathurst I.

Melv

C. Talbot

Bonaparte
Archipelago

*Joseph
Bonaparte
Gulf*

Ka

Wyndham

Kununurra

C. Lévêque

Argyle

786

Derby

Kimberley
Plateau

Broome

Halls Creek

Fitzroy

Eighty
Mile
Beach

Sturt Creek

Goldsworthy

*Great
Sandy Desert*

20°S

NORTH

Barrow I.

Dampier

Port Hedland

Marble Bar

North West.
Cape

Onslow

Fortescue

*Lake
Mackay*

Exmouth

Hamersley
Range

Ashburton

1235

Lake
Disappointment

Mac
Ra

Mt. Tom
Price

Newman

Paraburdoo

WESTERN

Tropic of Capricorn

L. Macleod

Gascoyne

Gibson Desert

867

Ayers'
Rock

1722

A   U   S   T

Carnarvon

Murchison

Meekatharra

Wiluna

L. Carnegie

AUSTRALIA

Great Victoria Dese

Mt. Magnet

Laverton

Northampton

Leonora

L. Raeside

Geraldton

L. Barlee

L. Moore

Kalgoorlie

Forrest

Moora

Coolgardie

Zanthus

Nullarbor Plain

30°S

Perth

Northam

Eucla

Fremantle

Norseman

Great Australian B

Narrogin
Wagin

Ravensthorpe

Bunbury

Collie

Esperance

C. Naturaliste

Augusta

1042

Arch. of the
Recherche

C. Leeuwin

Albany

SOUTHERN

OCEAN

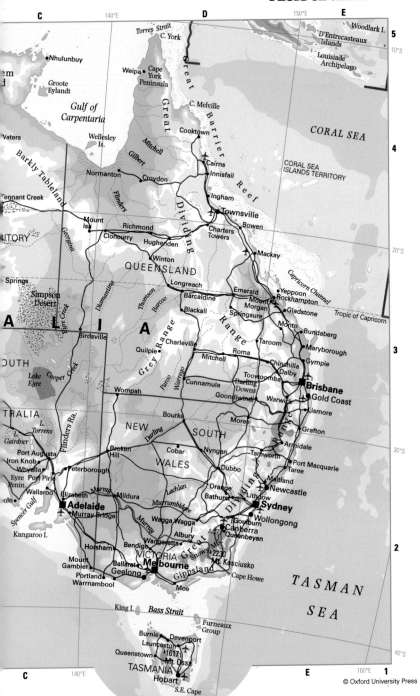

C 140°E **D** 150°E **E**

Woodlark I.
D'Entrecasteaux Islands
Louisiade Archipelago

Torres Strait
C. York

Nhulunbuy

Weipa Cape York Peninsula

Groote Eylandt

Gulf of Carpentaria

C. Melville

CORAL SEA

Wellesley Is.

Barkly Tableland

Mitchell
Gilbert

Normanton Croydon

Cooktown

Cairns

Innisfail

Ingham

Great Barrier Reef

CORAL SEA ISLANDS TERRITORY

Tennant Creek

Flinders

Mount Isa

Richmond

Townsville

Bowen

Cl

Springs

Simpson Desert

Georgina

Cloncurry Hughenden

Winton

Charters Towers

Mackay

QUEENSLAND

Longreach

Capricorn Channel

Tropic of Capricorn

Diamantina

Thomson

Barcoo

Barcaldine

Blackall

Emerald

Mount Morgan

Yeppoon

Rockhampton

Gladstone

Springsure

Monto

Bundaberg

Birdsville

Grey Range

Charleville

Range

Taroom

Maryborough

Quilpie

Mitchell

Roma

Chinchilla
Dalby

Gympie

Cooper Creek

Lake Eyre

Warrego

Paroo

Cunnamula

Toowoomba

Darling Downs

Brisbane
Gold Coast

Wompah

Goondiwindi

Warwick

Lismore

Bourke

NEW

Darling

Moree

Grafton

Broken Hill

Cobar

SOUTH

Nyngan

Tamworth

Armidale

Port Macquarie

Port Augusta
Iron Knob
Whyalla
Port Pirie
Renin.
Wallaroo

Peterborough

WALES

Dubbo

Orange

Taree

Maitland

Newcastle

L. Torrens
L. Gairdner

Flinders Ra.

Murray

Mildura

Lachlan

Bathurst

Lithgow

Sydney

Wollongong

Elizabeth

Adelaide

Murray Bridge

Murrumbidgee

Wagga Wagga

Goulburn

Canberra
Queanbeyan

Spencer Gulf

Kangaroo I.

Murray

Albury

Wangaratta

ACT

•2230

Snowy Mts.

Horsham

Bendigo

VICTORIA

Gippsland

Mt. Kosciusko

Cape Howe

Mount Gambier

Ballarat

Geelong

Melbourne

Portland

Warrnambool

Moe

TASMAN

SEA

King I.

Bass Strait

Furneaux Group

Burnie

Devonport

Launceston

•1617

Mt. Ossa

Queenstown

TASMANIA

Hobart

S.E. Cape

C 140°E **E** 160°E **1**

© Oxford University Press

5
10°S
4
20°S
3
30°S
2
40°S

Scale 1: 6 000

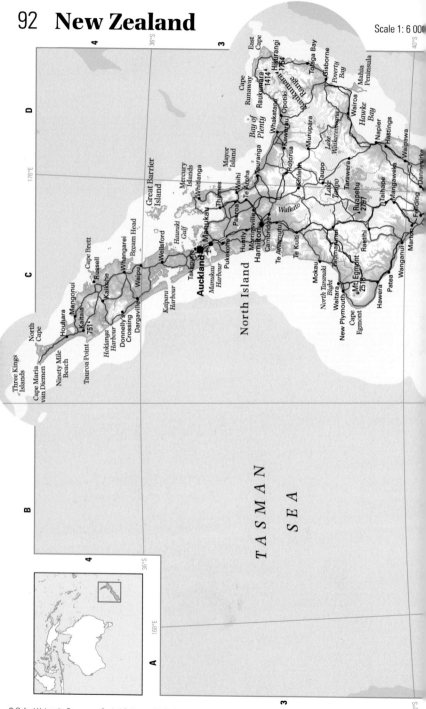

T A S M A N

S E A

North Island

Auckland

TASMAN

168°E

36°S

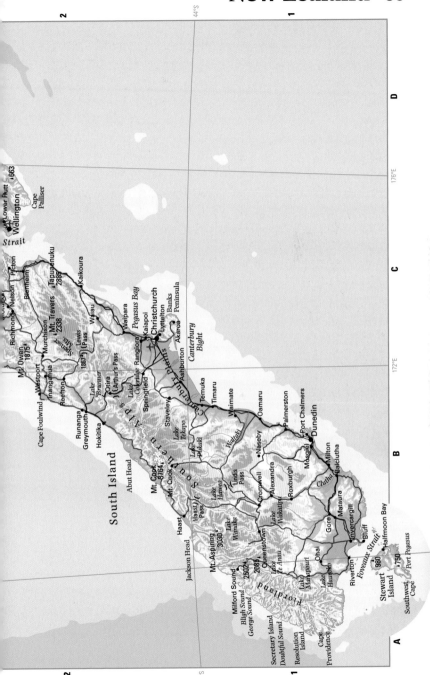

Scale 1: 90 000 000 (both

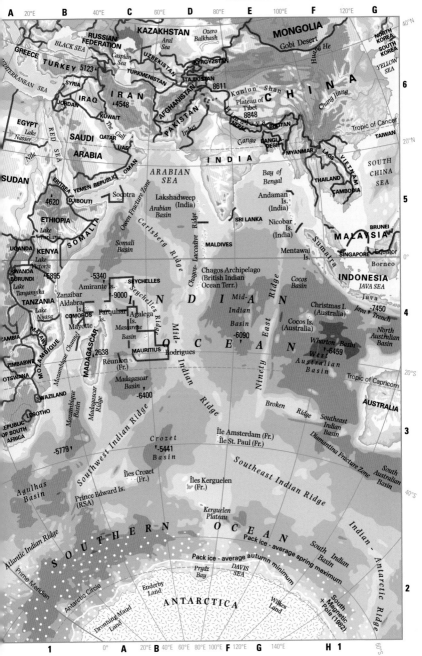

A 20°E B 40°E C 60°E D 80°E E 100°E F 120°E G

40°N

GREECE
MEDITERRANEAN SEA
TURKEY 5123
SYRIA
JORDAN
IRAQ
EGYPT
Lake Nasser
RED SEA
SUDAN
SAUDI ARABIA
KUWAIT
QATAR
UAE
The Gulf
OMAN
IRAN 4548
AFGHANISTAN
KAZAKHSTAN
Aral Sea
Ozero Balkhash
Caspian Sea
UZBEKISTAN
TURKMENISTAN
KYRGYZSTAN
TAJIKISTAN
8611
PAKISTAN
Indus
Kunlun Shan
Plateau of Tibet
8848
Himalaya
NEPAL
BHUTAN
MONGOLIA
Gobi Desert
Huang He
CHINA
Chang Jiang
NORTH KOREA
SOUTH KOREA
YELLOW SEA
TAIWAN
Tropic of Cancer

6

20°N

ETHIOPIA
ERITREA
YEMEN REPUBLIC
DJIBOUTI
4620
Socotra
Lake Turkana
UGANDA
KENYA
Lake Victoria
RWANDA
BURUNDI
5895
Lake Tanganyika
Lake Nyasa
TANZANIA
ZAMBIA
ZIMBABWE
MOZAMBIQUE
BOTSWANA
Mozambique Basin
SWAZILAND
LESOTHO
REPUBLIC OF SOUTH AFRICA
Agulhas Basin
Atlantic Indian Ridge
Prime Meridian
SOMALI
Somali Basin
Zanzibar
COMOROS
Mayotte
Aldabra Is.
-9000
Amirante Is.
-5340
SEYCHELLES
Farquhar Is.
Agalega Is.
Mascarene Basin
MADAGASCAR
2638
Madagascar Ridge
Madagascar Basin
-6400
-5779
Mozambique Channel
MAURITIUS
Réunion (Fr.)
Rodrigues
Seychelles Ridge
Carlsberg Ridge
Owen Fracture Zone
ARABIAN SEA
Arabian Basin
Lakshadweep (India)
Chagos - Laccadive Ridge
MALDIVES
SRI LANKA
INDIA
Ganga
BANGLADESH
MYANMAR
Bay of Bengal
Andaman Is. (India)
Nicobar Is. (India)
LAOS
THAILAND
CAMBODIA
VIETNAM
SOUTH CHINA SEA
Chagos Archipelago (British Indian Ocean Terr.)
Mentawai Is.
Mid-Indian Basin
-6090
Ninety East Ridge
Sumatra
SINGAPORE
MALAYSIA
BRUNEI
INDONESIA
Borneo
Equator
JAVA SEA
Java
Cocos Basin
Christmas I. (Australia)
Cocos Is. (Australia)
Wharton Basin
-6459
West Australian Basin
North Australian Basin
Java Trench
-7450
Tropic of Capricorn
AUSTRALIA

5

4

0°

20°S

INDIAN OCEAN
Mid-Indian Ridge
Southwest Indian Ridge
Crozet Basin
-5441
Îles Crozet (Fr.)
Prince Edward Is. (RSA)
Île Amsterdam (Fr.)
Île St. Paul (Fr.)
Îles Kerguelen (Fr.)
Kerguelen Plateau
Broken Ridge
Southeast Indian Ridge
Southeast Indian Basin
Diamantina Fracture Zone
South Australian Basin
Indian - Antarctic Ridge

40°S

SOUTHERN OCEAN
Pack ice - average spring maximum
Pack ice - average autumn minimum
South Indian Basin
South Magnetic Pole (1982)
ANTARCTICA
Antarctic Circle
Dronning Maud Land
Enderby Land
Prydz Bay
DAVIS SEA
Wilkes Land

3

2

1   0° A 20°E B 40°E C 60°E D 80°E E 100°E F 120°E G 140°E H 1

60°S

Modified Zenithal Equidistant Projection   © Oxford University Press

Scale 1: 90 00

Modified Zenithal Equidistant Projection

MONGOLIA
Yablonovy Range
RUSSIAN FEDERATION (RUSSIA)
Gobi Desert
Arctic Circle
SEA OF OKHOTSK
Kamchatka
BERING SEA
Mt. M
Bering Strait
Huang He
Amur
Sakhalin
Aleutian Islands
Aleutian Trench
-7822
CHINA
Chang Jiang
Hokkaido
Kuril Islands
Kuril Trench
-10542
NORTH KOREA
SOUTH KOREA
Honshū
JAPAN
Northwest Pacific Basin
Emperor Seamounts
-7168
Kyūshū
Shikoku
Japan Trench
-10374
Shatsky Rise
NORTH PACIFIC OC
Tropic of Cancer
Ryukyu Is.
TAIWAN
Midway Is.
Hawaiian Islands (U
-6987
Hawaiian R
SOUTH CHINA SEA
PHILIPPINE SEA
Southern Honshū Ridge
Kyushu–Palau Ridge
Mid-Pacific
International Date Line
West Marianas Basin
-8724
Mountains
N.W. Christmas Island Ridge
THE PHILIPPINES
Northern Marianas (USA)
Guam (USA)
East Marianas Basin
MARSHALL ISLANDS
Central Pacific Basin
Philippine Trench
-10497
Yap Trench
-11022
MICRONESIA
PALAU
Caroline Islands
FEDERATED STATES OF MICRONESIA
West Caroline Basin
New Guinea Rise
Gilbert Is.
Equator
Halmahera
MELANESIA
Phoenix Islands
KIRIBATI
Borneo
Sulawesi
Seram
Admiralty Is.
NAURU
INDONESIA
BANDA SEA
-7440
New Guinea
PAPUA NEW GUINEA
New Britain
SOLOMON ISLANDS
Vityaz Trench
TUVALU
SAMOA
American Samoa (USA)
Flores
EAST TIMOR
ARAFURA SEA
-9140
Wallis & Futuna (France)
Timor
CORAL SEA
VANUATU
New Hebrides Trench
FIJI
TONGA
Niue (NZ)
Co Islan
North Australian Basin
Great Barrier Reef
New Caledonia (Fr.)
-7570
Hunter Trench
-10024
Tonga Trench
Macdonnell Ranges
Great Dividing Range
South Fiji Basin
Tropic of Capricorn
AUSTRALIA
Lord Howe Rise
Norfolk Island Trough
Kermadec Is. (NZ)
Kermadec Trench
-10047
-1088
Sou P
Norfolk I. (Australia)
Southeast Indian Basin
Great Australian Bight
South Australian Basin
TASMAN SEA
NEW ZEALAND
Chatham I. (NZ)
Tasmania
Tasman Plateau
Auckland Is. (NZ)
Indian–Antarctic Ridge
Macquarie Ridge
SOUTHERN
Indian Antarctic Basin
Balleny Islands
pack ice – spring maxim
pack ice – autumn

H 120°W J 100°W K 80°W L 60°W M 40°W N

CANADA

Great Slave Lake

Hudson Bay

Canadian Shield

St. Lawrence

of ka

Queen Charlotte Islands

Vancouver Island

Rocky Mountains

Saskatchewan

Great Lakes

NORTH ATLANTIC OCEAN

6

UNITED STATES OF AMERICA

Mendocino Seascarp

Murray Seascarp

Northwest Atlantic Basin

Tropic of Cancer

20°N

Guadalupe (Mexico)

Rio Grande

Gulf of Mexico

MEXICO

THE BAHAMAS

CUBA

DOMINICAN REPUBLIC

Puerto Rico (USA)

HAITI

Islas Revillagigedo (Mexico)

Clarion Fracture Zone

Middle America Trench

East Pacific Rise

GUATEMALA **BELIZE**

Cayman Trench

JAMAICA

CARIBBEAN SEA

Windward Is.

5

st fic sin

Clipperton Fracture Zone

Clipperton I. (Fr.)

HONDURAS

EL SALVADOR

Guatemala Basin

NICARAGUA

COSTA RICA

PANAMA

Cocos Ridge

Orinoco

VENEZUELA

– –5298

S

COLOMBIA

Islas Galápagos (Ecuador)

Carnegie Ridge

ECUADOR

Equator

0°

•6310

Amazonas

E

Marquesas Islands (France)

Galápagos Rise

P E R U

B R A Z I L

ch Polynesia (France)

ety Is. nce)

Tuamotu Ridge

Tuamotu Archipelago (France)

Pacific Ridge

–5469

Peru Basin

Peru–Chile Trench

•6768 –6601

4

al Ridge

Pitcairn Islands (United Kingdom)

Easter Island Fracture Zone

Nasca Ridge

L. Titicaca

BOLIVIA

Easter Island (Chile)

–8066

OUTH PACIFIC OCEAN

East

Challenger Fracture Zone

Chile Basin

Tropic of Capricorn

20°S

PARAGUAY

Eltanin Fracture Zone

Pacific Ridge

Chile Rise

•6960

C H I L E

ARGENTINA

URUGUAY

3

cific–

Antarctic Zone

South East Pacific Basin

Patagonia

Argentine Basin

O C E A N

Antarctic Circle

Cabo de Hornos

Falkland Islands (UK)

H 120°W J 100°W K 80°W L 60°W M 40°W N

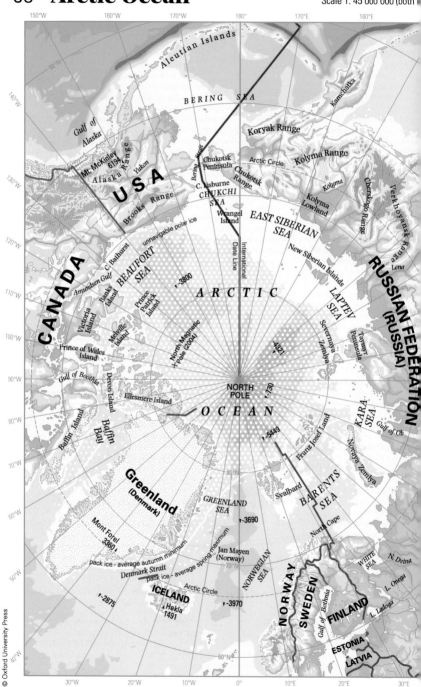

Aleutian Islands

BERING SEA

Gulf of Alaska

Koryak Range

Kamchatka

Arctic Circle

Kolyma Range

Mt. McKinley 6194

Alaska Range

Yukon

Chukotsk Peninsula

Bering Strait

Chukotsk Range

Kolyma

Kolyma Lowland

Verkhoyansk Range

USA

Brooks Range

C. Lisburne

CHUKCHI SEA

Wrangel Island

EAST SIBERIAN SEA

Cherskogo Range

Lena

unnavigable polar ice

C. Bathurst

BEAUFORT SEA

•3800

A R C T I C

New Siberian Islands

International Date Line

CANADA

Amundsen Gulf

Banks Island

Prince Patrick Island

Victoria Island

Melville Island

Prince of Wales Island

North Magnetic Pole (2004)

LAPTEV SEA

Severnaya Zemlya

Taymyr Peninsula

RUSSIAN FEDERATION (RUSSIA)

•4321

Gulf of Boothia

Devon Island

Ellesmere Island

NORTH POLE

•730

O C E A N

KARA SEA

Gulf of Ob

Baffin Island

Baffin Bay

Franz Josef Land

•5449

Novaya Zemlya

80°N

Svalbard

BARENTS SEA

Greenland (Denmark)

GREENLAND SEA

North Cape

WHITE SEA

N. Dvina

Mont Forel 3360

•3690

L. Onega

pack ice - average autumn minimum

Jan Mayen (Norway)

Denmark Strait

pack ice - average spring maximum

70°N

NORWEGIAN SEA

NORWAY

Gulf of Bothnia

SWEDEN

L. Ladoga

ICELAND

Arctic Circle

Hekla 1491

•-3970

60°N

FINLAND

ESTONIA

•-2875

LATVIA

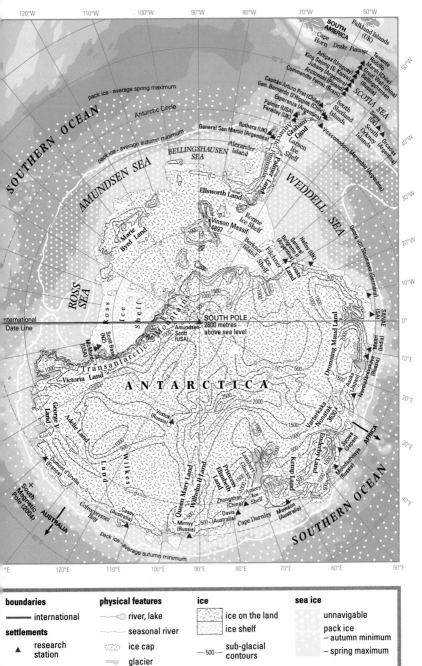

Zenithal Equidistant Projection   © Oxford University Press

Equatorial scale 1: 162 00

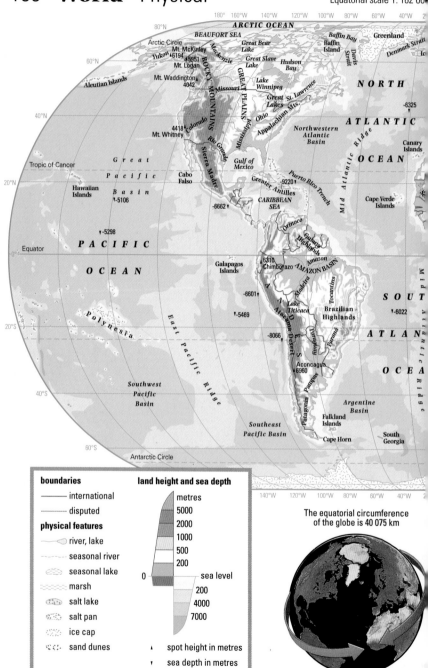

boundaries

— international

·········· disputed

physical features

~⬭ river, lake

- - - seasonal river

⬭ seasonal lake

marsh

salt lake

salt pan

ice cap

sand dunes

land height and sea depth

metres
5000
2000
1000
500
200
0 — sea level
200
4000
7000

▲ spot height in metres

▾ sea depth in metres

The equatorial circumference of the globe is 40 075 km

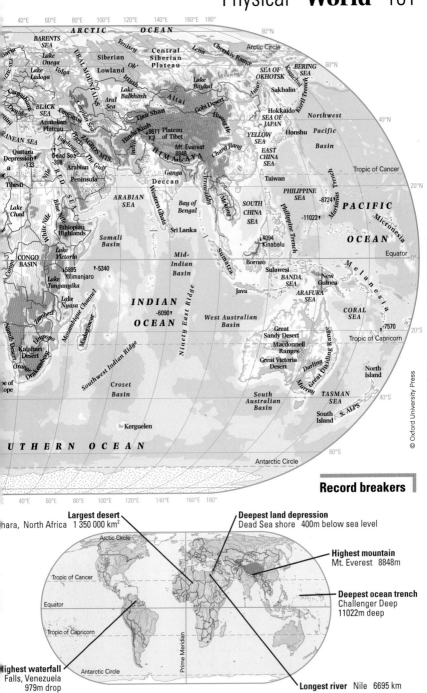

ARCTIC OCEAN

BARENTS SEA
Lake Onega
Volga
URAL MOUNTAINS
Lake Ladoga
Siberian Lowland
Ob'
Irtysh
Yenisey
Central Siberian Plateau
Lena
Cherskiy Range
Arctic Circle
80°N
60°N
BERING SEA
Kamchatka
Kuril Trench
SEA OF OKHOTSK
Sakhalin
Northwest Pacific Basin
40°N
Lake Baykal
Altai
Gobi Desert
Huang He
Amur
Hokkaido
SEA OF JAPAN
Honshu
BLACK SEA
Anatolian Plateau
Caspian Sea
Aral Sea
Lake Balkhash
Tien Shan
Hindu Kush
K2
8611
Plateau of Tibet
Chang Jiang
YELLOW SEA
EAST CHINA SEA
Taiwan
Tropic of Cancer
ZAGROS MTS.
Tigris
Euphrates
The Gulf
Dead Sea -398
Mt. Everest 8848
HIMALAYA
20°N
MEDITERRANEAN SEA
Qattara Depression -133
Nile
RED SEA
Arabian Peninsula
Ganga
Deccan
Irrawaddy
Mekong
PHILIPPINE SEA
-8724
Mariana Trench
PACIFIC OCEAN
Micronesia
Tibesti
Lake Chad
Blue Nile
White Nile
Ethiopian Highlands
ARABIAN SEA
Western Ghats
Bay of Bengal
Sri Lanka
SOUTH CHINA SEA
Philippine Trench -11022
4094 Kinabalu
Equator 0°
CONGO BASIN
Lake Victoria
Somali Basin
5895
-5340
Mid-Indian Basin
Sumatra
Borneo
Sulawesi
BANDA SEA
New Guinea
Melanesia
Congo
Kilimanjaro
Lake Tanganyika
Lake Nyasa
INDIAN OCEAN
-6090
Java
ARAFURA SEA
CORAL SEA
-7570
Zambezi
Mozambique Channel
Madagascar
Ninety East Ridge
West Australian Basin
Great Sandy Desert
Macdonnell Ranges
Great Victoria Desert
Tropic of Capricorn 20°S
Namib Desert
Limpopo
Orange
Kalahari Desert
Drakensberg
Southwest Indian Ridge
Crozet Basin
South Australian Basin
Darling
Murray
Great Dividing Range
North Island
e of ope
Kerguelen
TASMAN SEA
South Island
S. ALPS
40°S
SOUTHERN OCEAN
Antarctic Circle
60°S

© Oxford University Press

40°E 60°E 80°E 100°E 120°E 140°E 160°E 180°

Record breakers

Largest desert
hara, North Africa 1 350 000 km²

Deepest land depression
Dead Sea shore 400m below sea level

Highest mountain
Mt. Everest 8848m

Deepest ocean trench
Challenger Deep 11022m deep

ighest waterfall
Falls, Venezuela 979m drop

Longest river Nile 6695 km

Arctic Circle
Tropic of Cancer
Equator
Tropic of Capricorn
Antarctic Circle
Prime Meridian

Equatorial scale 1: 162 00

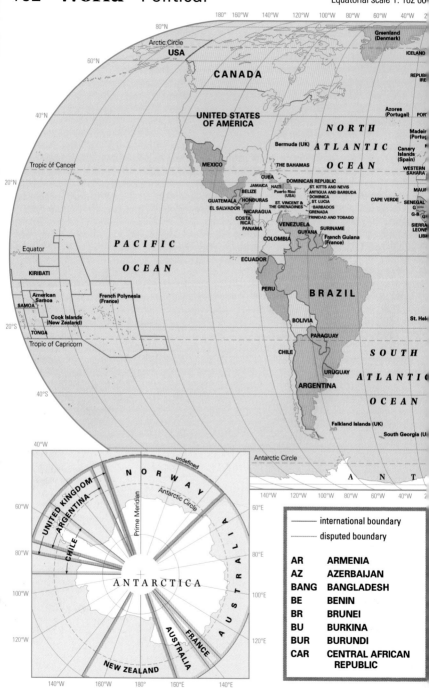

180° 160°W 140°W 120°W 100°W 80°W 60°W 40°W 2

80°N

Arctic Circle

USA

Greenland
(Denmark)

ICELAND

60°N

CANADA

REPUBI
IRE

40°N

**UNITED STATES
OF AMERICA**

Azores
(Portugal) POR

NORTH

Madeir
(Portu

Bermuda (UK)

ATLANTIC

Canary
Islands
(Spain)

Tropic of Cancer

WESTERN
SAHARA

MEXICO

20°N

OCEAN

CUBA

THE BAHAMAS

DOMINICAN REPUBLIC

MAUF

JAMAICA

HAITI ST. KITTS AND NEVIS
ANTIGUA AND BARBUDA

BELIZE

Puerto Rico
(USA) DOMINICA

GUATEMALA

HONDURAS ST. LUCIA
BARBADOS

CAPE VERDE

SENEGAL

EL SALVADOR

ST. VINCENT &
THE GRENADINES GRENADA

G

NICARAGUA

G-B

COSTA
RICA

TRINIDAD AND TOBAGO

SIERRA
LEONE

VENEZUELA

LIB

PANAMA

SURINAME

Equator

COLOMBIA

GUYANA

French Guiana
(France)

0°

PACIFIC

ECUADOR

KIRIBATI

OCEAN

PERU

BRAZIL

American
Samoa

French Polynesia
(France)

SAMOA

St. Hel

Cook Islands
(New Zealand)

BOLIVIA

20°S

TONGA

PARAGUAY

Tropic of Capricorn

CHILE

SOUTH

URUGUAY

ARGENTINA

ATLANTIC

40°S

OCEAN

Falkland Islands (UK)

South Georgia (U

Antarctic Circle

A   N   T

40°W

N O R W A Y

undefined

60°W

Antarctic Circle

UNITED KINGDOM

Prime Meridian

140°W 120°W 100°W 80°W 60°W 40°W 2

ARGENTINA

60°E

—— international boundary

------- disputed boundary

80°W

CHILE

80°E

AR   **ARMENIA**

AZ   **AZERBAIJAN**

BANG **BANGLADESH**

100°W

ANTARCTICA

100°E

BE   **BENIN**

BR   **BRUNEI**

AUSTRALIA

BU   **BURKINA**

FRANCE

120°W

AUSTRALIA

120°E

BUR   **BURUNDI**

CAR   **CENTRAL AFRICAN
REPUBLIC**

NEW ZEALAND

140°W 160°W 180° 160°E 140°E

Eckert IV Projection   © Oxford University

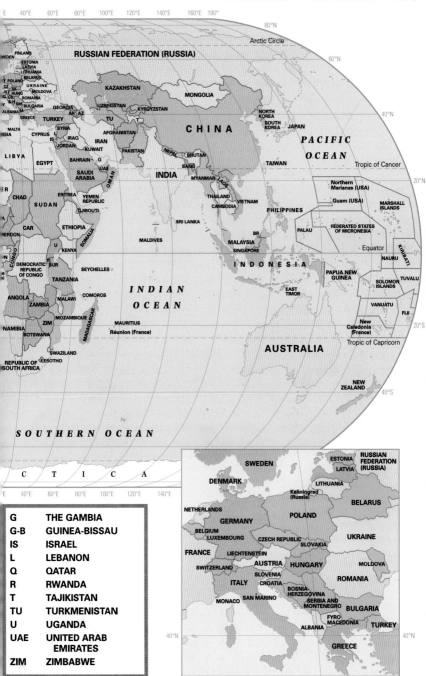

Equatorial scale 1: 180 00[C]

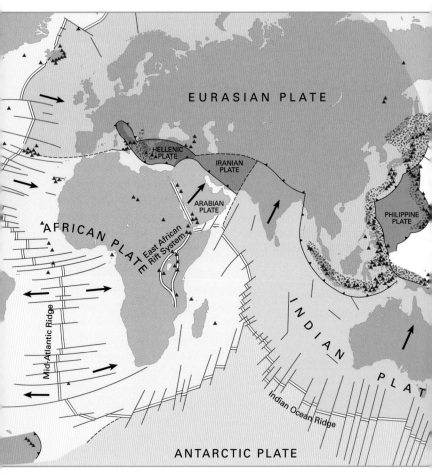

EURASIAN PLATE

HELLENIC PLATE

IRANIAN PLATE

ARABIAN PLATE

PHILIPPINE PLATE

AFRICAN PLATE

East African Rift System

Mid-Atlantic Ridge

INDIAN

PLAT

Indian Ocean Ridge

ANTARCTIC PLATE

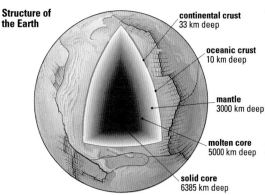

plate boundaries

— constructive (moving apart)

▲— destructive (colliding)

--- passive

— transform faults

→ direction of plate movement

▲ active volcanoes

🝈 areas of deep focus earthquakes

Structure of the Earth

continental crust 33 km deep

oceanic crust 10 km deep

mantle 3000 km deep

molten core 5000 km deep

solid core 6385 km deep

Gall Projection

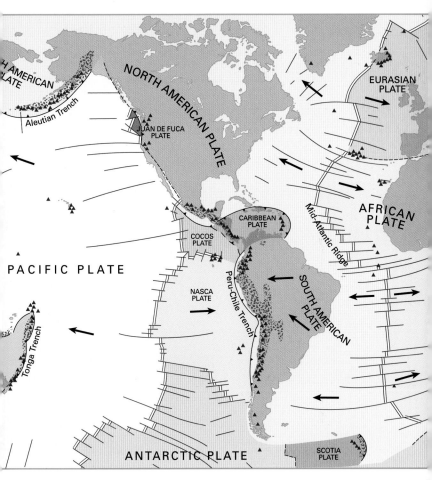

NORTH AMERICAN PLATE

Aleutian Trench

EURASIAN PLATE

JUAN DE FUCA PLATE

AFRICAN PLATE

Mid-Atlantic Ridge

CARIBBEAN PLATE

COCOS PLATE

PACIFIC PLATE

NASCA PLATE

Peru-Chile Trench

SOUTH AMERICAN PLATE

Tonga Trench

ANTARCTIC PLATE

SCOTIA PLATE

s section of the crust and upper mantle

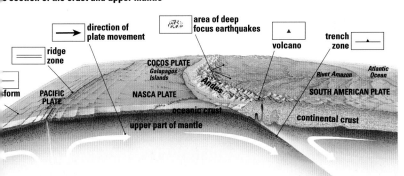

direction of plate movement

area of deep focus earthquakes

volcano

trench zone

ridge zone

form

COCOS PLATE
Galapagos Islands

Andes

River Amazon

Atlantic Ocean

PACIFIC PLATE

NASCA PLATE

oceanic crust

SOUTH AMERICAN PLATE

continental crust

upper part of mantle

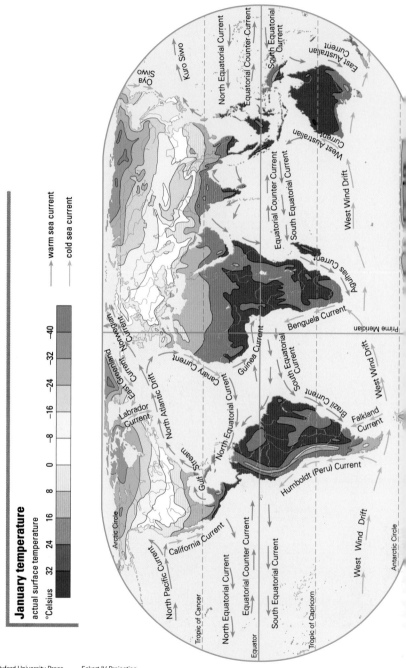

January temperature

actual surface temperature

°Celsius 32 24 16 8 0 -8 -16 -24 -32 -40

→ warm sea current
→ cold sea current

Eckert IV Projection

e 1: 230 000 000 (both maps)

July temperature
actual surface temperature

°Celsius 32 24 16 8 0 -8 -16 -24 -32 -40

→ warm sea current
→ cold sea current

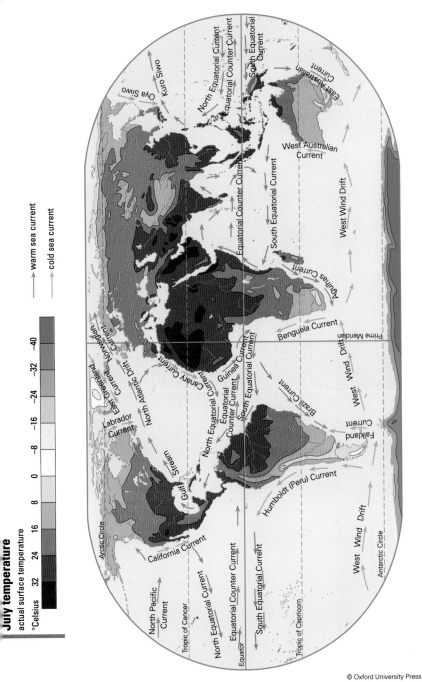

© Oxford University Press

Equatorial scale 1: 230 000 000 (both r

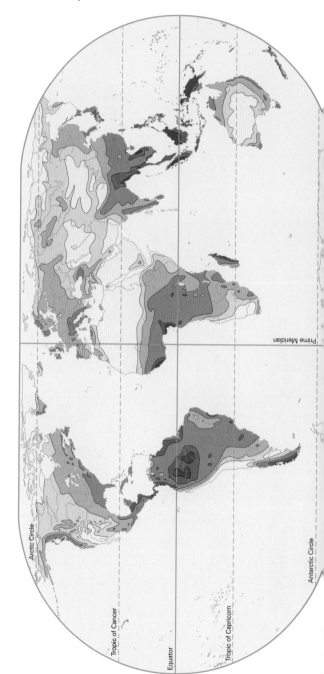

Precipitation

average annual precipitation

| mm | 3000 | 2000 | 1000 | 500 | 250 |

© Oxford University Press   Eckert IV Projection

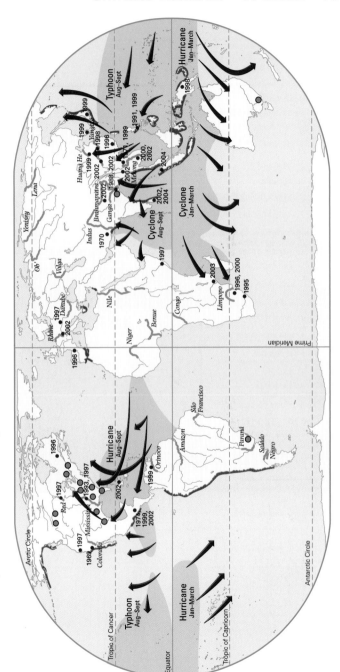

Storms

- paths of revolving tropical storms
- areas affected by tropical storms
- areas affected by tornadoes

— coasts vulnerable to tsunamis (seismic sea waves)
— major river flood plains susceptible to flooding
- major floods

Equatorial scale 1: 162 0C

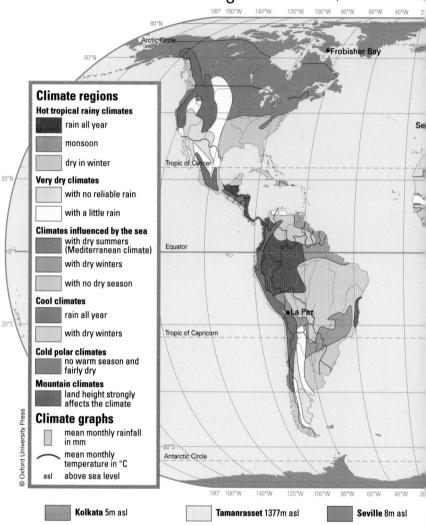

Climate regions

Hot tropical rainy climates

rain all year

monsoon

dry in winter

Very dry climates

with no reliable rain

with a little rain

Climates influenced by the sea

with dry summers (Mediterranean climate)

with dry winters

with no dry season

Cool climates

rain all year

with dry winters

Cold polar climates

no warm season and fairly dry

Mountain climates

land height strongly affects the climate

Climate graphs

mean monthly rainfall in mm

mean monthly temperature in °C

asl   above sea level

© Oxford University Press

80°N

Arctic Circle

60°N

●Frobisher Bay

Tropic of Cancer

20°N

Equator

●La Paz

20°S

Tropic of Capricorn

60°S

Antarctic Circle

180° 160°W 140°W 120°W 100°W 80°W 60°W 40°W

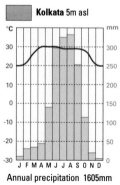

Kolkata 5m asl

Annual precipitation 1605mm

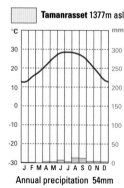

Tamanrasset 1377m asl

Annual precipitation 54mm

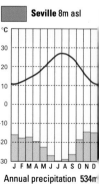

Seville 8m asl

Annual precipitation 534m

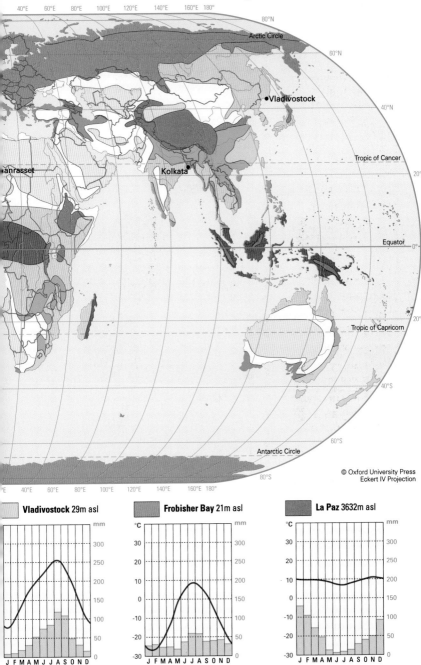

Vladivostock 29m asl

Annual precipitation 600mm

Frobisher Bay 21m asl

Annual precipitation 427mm

La Paz 3632m asl

Annual precipitation 610mm

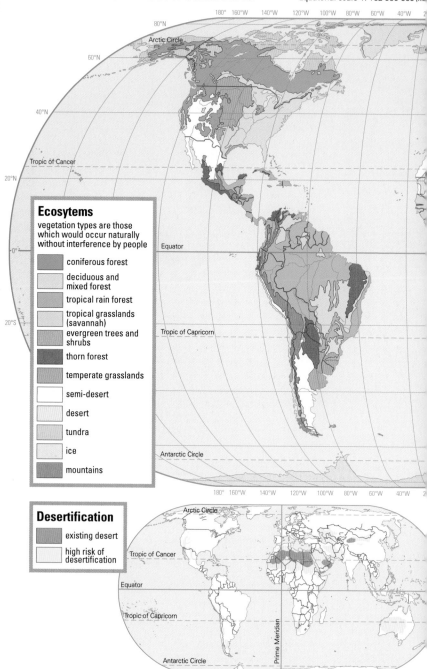

Ecosytems

vegetation types are those
which would occur naturally
without interference by people

- coniferous forest
- deciduous and mixed forest
- tropical rain forest
- tropical grasslands (savannah)
- evergreen trees and shrubs
- thorn forest
- temperate grasslands
- semi-desert
- desert
- tundra
- ice
- mountains

Desertification

- existing desert
- high risk of desertification

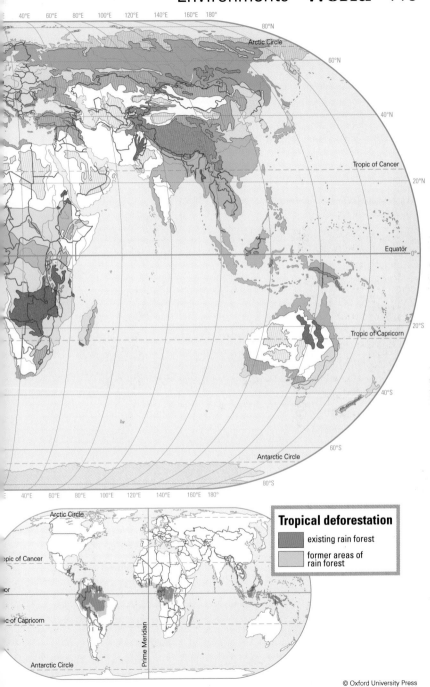

Tropical deforestation

- existing rain forest
- former areas of rain forest

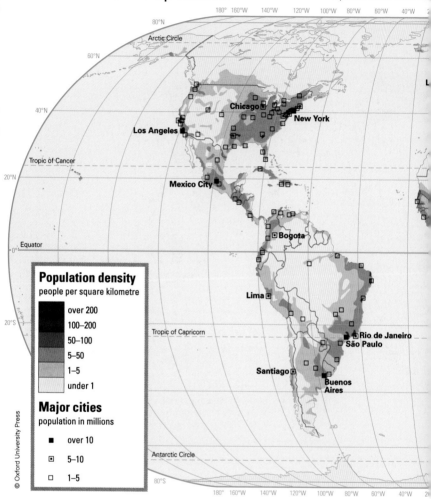

Population density
people per square kilometre

- over 200
- 100–200
- 50–100
- 5–50
- 1–5
- under 1

Major cities
population in millions

- ■ over 10
- ⊡ 5–10
- □ 1–5

World population structure, 2005

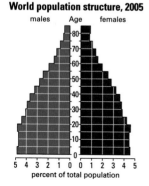

males — Age — females

percent of total population

	Population 2005 (millions)	Natura Increase
WORLD	6 477	1.2
Africa	906	2.3
Asia	3 921	1.3
Central America and the Caribbean	186	1.6
Europe	730	-0.1
North America	329	0.6
Oceania	33	1.0
South America	373	1.5

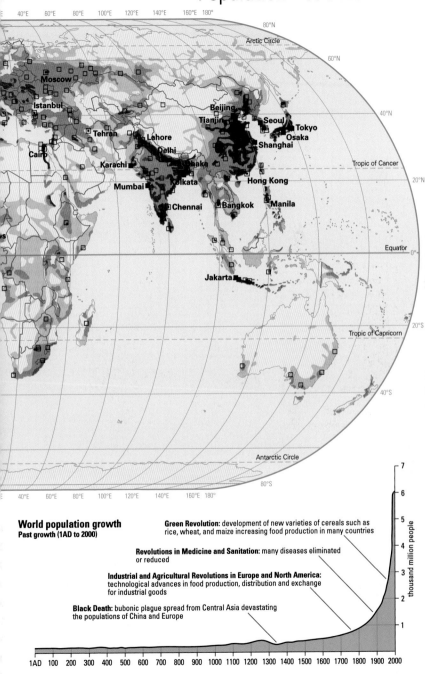

World population growth
Past growth (1AD to 2000)

Green Revolution: development of new varieties of cereals such as rice, wheat, and maize increasing food production in many countries

Revolutions in Medicine and Sanitation: many diseases eliminated or reduced

Industrial and Agricultural Revolutions in Europe and North America: technological advances in food production, distribution and exchange for industrial goods

Black Death: bubonic plague spread from Central Asia devastating the populations of China and Europe

Eckert IV Projection   © Oxford University Press

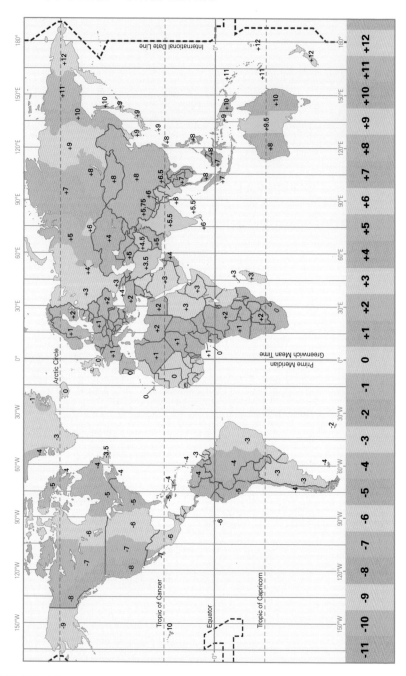

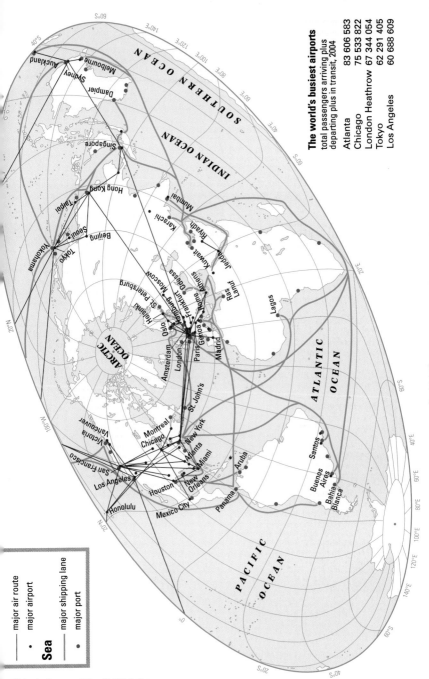

The world's busiest airports
total passengers arriving plus
departing plus in transit, 2004

Atlanta	83 606 583
Chicago	75 533 822
London Heathrow	67 344 054
Tokyo	62 291 405
Los Angeles	60 688 609

— major air route
• major airport

Sea
—— major shipping lane
• major port

ord University Press   Oblique Aitoff Projection

118 **Flags and statistics**

Flags and statistics are shown for the principal countries of the world and the larger territori
They are arranged in alphabetical order and are colour-coded by continent.

☐	Europe	☐	North and Central America
☐	Asia	☐	South America
☐	Africa	☐	Oceania

Flags are used as symbols to represent countries

The area is the total surface area of the country in square kilometres. To convert to square m
multiply by 2.59.

Population figures are the latest available and where necessary, estimates are given. To calc
average population density, divide the number of people in a country by the country's area. I
example, the population density of Afghanistan is 32.75 people per square kilometre.

A country's capital is the most important town or city, usually the seat of government and th
administrative centre. Capital cities are not always the largest settlement in a country. The n
in the statistical tables is that used on the maps in the atlas.

The Gross National Income (GNI) per person is a simple way of measuring how rich or poor
people are. It is the total value of goods and services produced in a country plus the income
received from abroad, divided by the number of people in the country. The figure is shown i
US dollars rather than the local currency, enabling comparisons to be made between countr

The Human Development Index (HDI) is a measure of the relative social and economic prog
of a country. It combines life expectancy, adult literacy, average number of years of schoolin
and purchasing power. Economically more developed countries have an HDI approaching 1.
Economically less developed countries have an HDI approaching 0.

External debt is the total debt owed to other countries and is repayable in foreign currency,
goods or services. The figure is shown in US dollars.

∘∘∘ data not available.

AFGHANISTAN

Area (sq km)	652 090
Population	21 354 000
Capital	Kabul
GNI per person ($US)	∘∘∘
HDI	∘∘∘
External debt ($US)	∘∘∘

ALGERIA

Area (sq km)	2 381 740
Population	32 373 000
Capital	Algiers
GNI per person ($US)	2 280
HDI	0.704
External debt ($US)	23 386 000 000

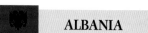

ALBANIA

Area (sq km)	28 750
Population	3 188 000
Capital	Tiranë
GNI per person ($US)	2 080
HDI	0.781
External debt ($US)	1 482 000 000

ANDORRA

Area (sq km)	468
Population	66 000
Capital	Andorra la Vella
GNI per person ($US)	∘∘∘
HDI	∘∘∘
External debt ($US)	∘∘∘

ANGOLA

Area (sq km)	1 246 700
Population	13 963 000
Capital	Luanda
per person ($US)	1 030
HDI	0.381
ternal debt ($US)	9 698 000 000

ANTIGUA AND BARBUDA

Area (sq km)	440
Population	80 000
Capital	St. John's
per person ($US)	10 000
HDI	0.800
ternal debt ($US)	०००

ARGENTINA

Area (sq km)	2 780 400
Population	38 226 000
Capital	Buenos Aires
per person ($US)	3 720
HDI	0.853
ternal debt ($US)	166 207 000 000

ARMENIA

Area (sq km)	29 800
Population	3 050 000
Capital	Yerevan
per person ($US)	1 120
HDI	0.754
ternal debt ($US)	1 127 000 000

AUSTRALIA

Area (sq km)	7 741 220
Population	20 120 000
Capital	Canberra
per person ($US)	26 900
HDI	0.946
ternal debt ($US)	०००

AUSTRIA

Area (sq km)	83 860
Population	8 115 000
Capital	Vienna
per person ($US)	32 300
HDI	0.934
ternal debt ($US)	०००

AZERBAIJAN

Area (sq km)	86 600
Population	8 280 000
Capital	Baku
GNI per person ($US)	950
HDI	0.746
External debt ($US)	1 680 000 000

BAHAMAS, THE

Area (sq km)	13 880
Population	320 000
Capital	Nassau
GNI per person ($US)	14 920
HDI	0.815
External debt ($US)	०००

BAHRAIN

Area (sq km)	710
Population	725 000
Capital	Manama
GNI per person ($US)	12 410
HDI	0.843
External debt ($US)	०००

BANGLADESH

Area (sq km)	144 000
Population	140 494 000
Capital	Dhaka
GNI per person ($US)	440
HDI	0.509
External debt ($US)	18 778 000 000

BARBADOS

Area (sq km)	430
Population	272 000
Capital	Bridgetown
GNI per person ($US)	9 270
HDI	0.888
External debt ($US)	०००

BELARUS

Area (sq km)	207 600
Population	9 832 000
Capital	Minsk
GNI per person ($US)	2 120
HDI	0.790
External debt ($US)	2 692 000 000

BELGIUM

Area (sq km)	30 510
Population	10 405 000
Capital	Brussels
GNI per person ($US)	31 030
HDI	0.942
External debt ($US)	∘∘∘

BOTSWANA

Area (sq km)	581 730
Population	1 727 000
Capital	Gaborone
GNI per person ($US)	4 340
HDI	0.589
External debt ($US)	514 000 000

BELIZE

Area (sq km)	22 960
Population	283 000
Capital	Belmopan
GNI per person ($US)	3 940
HDI	0.737
External debt ($US)	∘∘∘

BRAZIL

Area (sq km)	8 514 880
Population	178 718 000
Capital	Brásília
GNI per person ($US)	3 090
HDI	0.775
External debt ($US)	235 431 000 000

BENIN

Area (sq km)	112 620
Population	6 980 000
Capital	Porto-Novo
GNI per person ($US)	530
HDI	0.421
External debt ($US)	1 828 000 000

BRUNEI

Area (sq km)	5 770
Population	361 000
Capital	Bandar Seri Begaw
GNI per person ($US)	∘∘∘
HDI	0.867
External debt ($US)	∘∘∘

BHUTAN

Area (sq km)	47 000
Population	896 000
Capital	Thimphu
GNI per person ($US)	760
HDI	0.536
External debt ($US)	∘∘∘

BULGARIA

Area (sq km)	110 990
Population	7 780 000
Capital	Sofia
GNI per person ($US)	2 740
HDI	0.796
External debt ($US)	13 289 000 000

BOLIVIA

Area (sq km)	1 098 580
Population	8 986 000
Capital	La Paz
GNI per person ($US)	960
HDI	0.681
External debt ($US)	5 684 000 000

BURKINA

Area (sq km)	274 000
Population	12 387 000
Capital	Ouagadougou
GNI per person ($US)	360
HDI	0.302
External debt ($US)	1 844 000 000

BOSNIA-HERZEGOVINA

Area (sq km)	51 210
Population	3 836 000
Capital	Sarajevo
GNI per person ($US)	2 040
HDI	0.781
External debt ($US)	2 920 000 000

BURUNDI

Area (sq km)	27 830
Population	7 343 000
Capital	Bujumbura
GNI per person ($US)	90
HDI	0.339
External debt ($US)	1 310 000 000

CAMBODIA

Area (sq km)	181 040
Population	13 630 000
Capital	Phnom Penh
I per person ($US)	320
HDI	0.568
external debt ($US)	3 139 000 000

CHILE

Area (sq km)	756 630
Population	15 956 000
Capital	Santiago
GNI per person ($US)	4 910
HDI	0.839
External debt ($US)	43 231 000 000

CAMEROON

Area (sq km)	475 440
Population	16 400 000
Capital	Yaoundé
I per person ($US)	800
HDI	0.501
external debt ($US)	9 189 000 000

CHINA

Area (sq km)	9 598 050
Population	1 296 500 000
Capital	Beijing
GNI per person ($US)	1 290
HDI	0.745
External debt ($US)	193 567 000 000

CANADA

Area (sq km)	9 970 610
Population	31 902 000
Capital	Ottawa
I per person ($US)	28 390
HDI	0.943
external debt ($US)	∘∘∘

COLOMBIA

Area (sq km)	1 138 910
Population	45 300 000
Capital	Bogotá
GNI per person ($US)	2 000
HDI	0.773
External debt ($US)	32 979 000 000

CAPE VERDE

Area (sq km)	4 030
Population	481 000
Capital	Praia
I per person ($US)	170
HDI	0.717
external debt ($US)	∘∘∘

COMOROS

Area (sq km)	2 230
Population	614 000
Capital	Moroni
GNI per person ($US)	530
HDI	0.530
External debt ($US)	∘∘∘

CENTRAL AFRICAN REPUBLIC

Area (sq km)	622 980
Population	3 947 000
Capital	Bangui
I per person ($US)	310
HDI	0.361
external debt ($US)	1 328 000 000

CONGO

Area (sq km)	342 000
Population	3 855 000
Capital	Brazzaville
GNI per person ($US)	770
HDI	0.494
External debt ($US)	5 516 000 000

CHAD

Area (sq km)	1 284 000
Population	8 823 000
Capital	Ndjamena
I per person ($US)	260
HDI	0.379
external debt ($US)	1 499 000 000

CONGO, DEM. REP.

Area (sq km)	2 344 860
Population	54 775 000
Capital	Kinshasa
GNI per person ($US)	120
HDI	0.365
External debt ($US)	11 170 000 000

COSTA RICA

Area (sq km)	51 100
Population	4 061 000
Capital	San José
GNI per person ($US)	4 670
HDI	0.834
External debt ($US)	5 424 000 000

DENMARK

Area (sq km)	43 090
Population	5 397 000
Capital	Copenhagen
GNI per person ($US)	40 650
HDI	0.932
External debt ($US)	∞∞

CÔTE D'IVOIRE

Area (sq km)	322 460
Population	17 142 000
Capital	Yamoussoukro
GNI per person ($US)	770
HDI	0.399
External debt ($US)	12 187 000 000

DJIBOUTI

Area (sq km)	23 200
Population	716 000
Capital	Djibouti
GNI per person ($US)	1 030
HDI	0.454
External debt ($US)	∞∞

CROATIA

Area (sq km)	56 540
Population	4 508 000
Capital	Zagreb
GNI per person ($US)	6 590
HDI	0.830
External debt ($US)	23 452 000 000

DOMINICA

Area (sq km)	750
Population	71 000
Capital	Roseau
GNI per person ($US)	3 650
HDI	0.743
External debt ($US)	∞∞

CUBA

Area (sq km)	110 860
Population	11 365 000
Capital	Havana
GNI per person ($US)	∞∞
HDI	0.809
External debt ($US)	∞∞

DOMINICAN REPUBLIC

Area (sq km)	48 730
Population	8 861 000
Capital	Santo Domingo
GNI per person ($US)	2 080
HDI	0.738
External debt ($US)	6 291 000 000

CYPRUS

Area (sq km)	9 250
Population	776 000
Capital	Nicosia
GNI per person ($US)	17 580
HDI	0.883
External debt ($US)	∞∞

EAST TIMOR

Area (sq km)	14 870
Population	925 000
Capital	Dili
GNI per person ($US)	550
HDI	0.436
External debt ($US)	∞∞

CZECH REPUBLIC

Area (sq km)	78 870
Population	10 183 000
Capital	Prague
GNI per person ($US)	9 150
HDI	0.868
External debt ($US)	34 630 000 000

ECUADOR

Area (sq km)	283 560
Population	13 213 000
Capital	Quito
GNI per person ($US)	2 180
HDI	0.735
External debt ($US)	16 864 000 000

EGYPT

Area (sq km)	1 001 450
Population	68 738 000
Capital	Cairo
per person ($US)	1 310
HDI	0.653
ternal debt ($US)	31 383 000 000

FIJI

Area (sq km)	18 270
Population	848 000
Capital	Suva
GNI per person ($US)	2 690
HDI	0.758
External debt ($US)	ooo

EL SALVADOR

Area (sq km)	21 040
Population	6 658 000
Capital	San Salvador
per person ($US)	2 350
HDI	0.720
ternal debt ($US)	7 080 000 000

FINLAND

Area (sq km)	338 150
Population	5 215 000
Capital	Helsinki
GNI per person ($US)	32 790
HDI	0.935
External debt ($US)	ooo

EQUATORIAL GUINEA

Area (sq km)	28 050
Population	506 000
Capital	Malabo
per person ($US)	ooo
HDI	0.703
ternal debt ($US)	ooo

FRANCE

Area (sq km)	551 500
Population	59 991 000
Capital	Paris
GNI per person ($US)	30 090
HDI	0.932
External debt ($US)	ooo

ERITREA

Area (sq km)	117 600
Population	447 000
Capital	Asmara
per person ($US)	180
HDI	0.439
ternal debt ($US)	635 000 000

FRENCH GUIANA

Area (sq km)	90 000
Population	167 000
Capital	Cayenne
GNI per person ($US)	ooo
HDI	ooo
External debt ($US)	ooo

ESTONIA

Area (sq km)	45 230
Population	1 345 000
Capital	Tallinn
per person ($US)	7 010
HDI	0.853
:ternal debt ($US)	6 972 000 000

GABON

Area (sq km)	267 670
Population	1 374 000
Capital	Libreville
GNI per person ($US)	3 940
HDI	0.648
External debt ($US)	3 792 000 000

ETHIOPIA

Area (sq km)	1 104 300
Population	69 961 000
Capital	Addis Ababa
per person ($US)	110
HDI	0.359
ternal debt ($US)	7 151 000 000

GAMBIA, THE

Area (sq km)	11 300
Population	1 449 000
Capital	Banjul
GNI per person ($US)	290
HDI	0.452
External debt ($US)	629 000 000

GEORGIA

Area (sq km) 69 700
Population 4 521 000
Capital T'bilisi
GNI per person ($US) 1 040
HDI 0.739
External debt ($US) 1 935 000 000

GUATEMALA

Area (sq km) 108 890
Population 12 628 000
Capital Guatemala City
GNI per person ($US) 2 130
HDI 0.649
External debt ($US) 4 981 000 000

GERMANY

Area (sq km) 357 030
Population 82 631 000
Capital Berlin
GNI per person ($US) 30 120
HDI 0.925
External debt ($US) ∘∘∘

GUINEA

Area (sq km) 245 860
Population 8 073 000
Capital Conakry
GNI per person ($US) 460
HDI 0.425
External debt ($US) 3 457 000 000

GHANA

Area (sq km) 238 540
Population 21 053 000
Capital Accra
GNI per person ($US) 380
HDI 0.568
External debt ($US) 7 957 000 000

GUINEA-BISSAU

Area (sq km) 36 120
Population 1 533 000
Capital Bissau
GNI per person ($US) 160
HDI 0.350
External debt ($US) 745 000 000

GREECE

Area (sq km) 131 960
Population 11 075 000
Capital Athens
GNI per person ($US) 16 610
HDI 0.902
External debt ($US) ∘∘∘

GUYANA

Area (sq km) 214 970
Population 772 000
Capital Georgetown
GNI per person ($US) 990
HDI 0.719
External debt ($US) ∘∘∘

GREENLAND

Area (sq km) 410 450
Population 57 000
Capital Nuuk
GNI per person ($US) ∘∘∘
HDI ∘∘∘
External debt ($US) ∘∘∘

HAITI

Area (sq km) 27 750
Population 8 592 000
Capital Port-au-Prince
GNI per person ($US) 390
HDI 0.463
External debt ($US) 1 308 000 000

GRENADA

Area (sq km) 340
Population 106 000
Capital St. George's
GNI per person ($US) 3 760
HDI 0.745
External debt ($US) ∘∘∘

HONDURAS

Area (sq km) 112 090
Population 7 141 000
Capital Tegucigalpa
GNI per person ($US) 1 030
HDI 0.672
External debt ($US) 5 641 000 000

HUNGARY

Area (sq km)	93 030
Population	10 072 000
Capital	Budapest
per person ($US)	8 270
HDI	0.848
ternal debt ($US)	45 785 000 000

IRELAND

Area (sq km)	70 270
Population	4 019 000
Capital	Dublin
GNI per person ($US)	34 280
HDI	0.936
External debt ($US)	°°°

ICELAND

Area (sq km)	103 000
Population	290 000
Capital	Reykjavik
per person ($US)	38 620
HDI	0.941
ternal debt ($US)	°°°

ISRAEL

Area (sq km)	22 140
Population	6 798 000
Capital	Jerusalem
GNI per person ($US)	17 380
HDI	0.908
External debt ($US)	°°°

INDIA

Area (sq km)	3 287 260
Population	1 079 721 000
Capital	New Delhi
per person ($US)	620
HDI	0.595
ternal debt ($US)	113 467 000 000

ITALY

Area (sq km)	301 340
Population	57 573 000
Capital	Rome
GNI per person ($US)	26 120
HDI	0.920
External debt ($US)	°°°

INDONESIA

Area (sq km)	1 904 570
Population	217 588 000
Capital	Jakarta
per person ($US)	1 140
HDI	0.692
ternal debt ($US)	134 389 000 000

JAMAICA

Area (sq km)	10 990
Population	2 665 000
Capital	Kingston
GNI per person ($US)	2 900
HDI	0.764
External debt ($US)	5 584 000 000

IRAN

Area (sq km)	1 648 200
Population	66 928 000
Capital	Tehran
per person ($US)	2 300
HDI	0.732
ternal debt ($US)	11 601 000 000

JAPAN

Area (sq km)	377 890
Population	127 764 000
Capital	Tokyo
GNI per person ($US)	37 180
HDI	0.938
External debt ($US)	°°°

IRAQ

Area (sq km)	438 320
Population	25 261 000
Capital	Baghdad
per person ($US)	°°°
HDI	°°°
ternal debt ($US)	°°°

JORDAN

Area (sq km)	89 210
Population	5 440 000
Capital	Amman
GNI per person ($US)	2 140
HDI	0.750
External debt ($US)	8 337 000 000

KAZAKHSTAN

Area (sq km)	2 724 900
Population	14 958 000
Capital	Astana
GNI per person ($US)	2 260
HDI	0.766
External debt ($US)	22 835 000 000

KENYA

Area (sq km)	580 370
Population	32 447 000
Capital	Nairobi
GNI per person ($US)	460
HDI	0.488
External debt ($US)	6 766 000 000

KIRIBATI

Area (sq km)	730
Population	98 000
Capital	Bairiki
GNI per person ($US)	970
HDI	०००
External debt ($US)	०००

KUWAIT

Area (sq km)	17 820
Population	2 460 000
Capital	Kuwait
GNI per person ($US)	17 970
HDI	0.838
External debt ($US)	०००

KYRGYZSTAN

Area (sq km)	199 900
Population	5 099 000
Capital	Bishkek
GNI per person ($US)	400
HDI	0.701
External debt ($US)	2 021 000 000

LAOS

Area (sq km)	236 800
Population	5 792 000
Capital	Vientiane
GNI per person ($US)	390
HDI	0.534
External debt ($US)	2 846 000 000

LATVIA

Area (sq km)	64 600
Population	2 303 000
Capital	Riga
GNI per person ($US)	5 460
HDI	0.823
External debt ($US)	8 803 000 000

LEBANON

Area (sq km)	10 400
Population	4 554 000
Capital	Beirut
GNI per person ($US)	4 980
HDI	0.758
External debt ($US)	18 598 000 000

LESOTHO

Area (sq km)	30 350
Population	1 809 000
Capital	Maseru
GNI per person ($US)	740
HDI	0.493
External debt ($US)	706 000 000

LIBERIA

Area (sq km)	111 370
Population	3 449 000
Capital	Monrovia
GNI per person ($US)	110
HDI	०००
External debt ($US)	2 568 000 000

LIBYA

Area (sq km)	1 759 540
Population	5 674 000
Capital	Tripoli
GNI per person ($US)	4 450
HDI	0.794
External debt ($US)	०००

LIECHTENSTEIN

Area (sq km)	160
Population	34 000
Capital	Vaduz
GNI per person ($US)	०००
HDI	०००
External debt ($US)	०००

LITHUANIA

Area (sq km) 65 300
Population 3 439 000
Capital Vilnius
GNI per person ($US) 5 740
HDI 0.842
External debt ($US) 8 342 000 000

MALDIVES

Area (sq km) 300
Population 300 000
Capital Male
GNI per person ($US) 2 510
HDI 0.752
External debt ($US) ooo

LUXEMBOURG

Area (sq km) 2 586
Population 450 000
Capital Luxembourg
GNI per person ($US) 56 230
HDI 0.933
External debt ($US) ooo

MALI

Area (sq km) 1 240 190
Population 11 937 000
Capital Bamako
GNI per person ($US) 360
HDI 0.326
External debt ($US) 3 129 000 000

MACEDONIA, FYRO

Area (sq km) 25 710
Population 2 062 000
Capital Skopje
GNI per person ($US) 2 350
HDI 0.793
External debt ($US) 1 837 000 000

MALTA

Area (sq km) 320
Population 384 000
Capital Valletta
GNI per person ($US) 12 250
HDI 0.875
External debt ($US) ooo

MADAGASCAR

Area (sq km) 587 040
Population 17 332 000
Capital Antananarivo
GNI per person ($US) 300
HDI 0.469
External debt ($US) 4 958 000 000

MARSHALL ISLANDS

Area (sq km) 181.3
Population 60 000
Capital Dalap-Uligi-Darrit
GNI per person ($US) 2 710
HDI ooo
External debt ($US) ooo

MALAWI

Area (sq km) 118 480
Population 11 182 000
Capital Lilongwe
GNI per person ($US) 170
HDI 0.388
External debt ($US) 3 134 000 000

MAURITANIA

Area (sq km) 1 025 520
Population 2 906 000
Capital Nouakchott
GNI per person ($US) 420
HDI 0.465
External debt ($US) 2 360 000 000

MALAYSIA

Area (sq km) 329 750
Population 25 209 000
Capital Kuala Lumpur
GNI per person ($US) 4 650
HDI 0.793
External debt ($US) 49 074 000 000

MAURITIUS

Area (sq km) 2 040
Population 1 234 000
Capital Port Louis
GNI per person ($US) 4 640
HDI 0.785
External debt ($US) 2 550 000 000

MEXICO

Area (sq km)	1 958 200
Population	103 795 000
Capital	Mexico City
GNI per person ($US)	6 770
HDI	0.802
External debt ($US)	140 004 000 000

MICRONESIA, FEDERATED STATES

Area (sq km)	702
Population	127 000
Capital	Palikir
GNI per person ($US)	1 990
HDI	∘∘∘
External debt ($US)	∘∘∘

MOLDOVA

Area (sq km)	33 840
Population	4 218 000
Capital	Chişnău
GNI per person ($US)	710
HDI	0.681
External debt ($US)	1 901 000 000

MONACO

Area (sq km)	1.95
Population	33 000
Capital	Monaco-Ville
GNI per person ($US)	∘∘∘
HDI	∘∘∘
External debt ($US)	∘∘∘

MONGOLIA

Area (sq km)	1 566 500
Population	2 515 000
Capital	Ulan Bator
GNI per person ($US)	590
HDI	0.668
External debt ($US)	1 472 000 000

MOROCCO

Area (sq km)	446 550
Population	30 586 000
Capital	Rabat
GNI per person ($US)	1 520
HDI	0.620
External debt ($US)	18 795 000 000

MOZAMBIQUE

Area (sq km)	801 590
Population	19 129 000
Capital	Maputo
GNI per person ($US)	250
HDI	0.354
External debt ($US)	4 930 000 000

MYANMAR

Area (sq km)	676 580
Population	49 910 000
Capital	Yangon
GNI per person ($US)	∘∘∘
HDI	0.551
External debt ($US)	7 318 000 000

NAMIBIA

Area (sq km)	824 290
Population	2 033 000
Capital	Windhoek
GNI per person ($US)	2 370
HDI	0.607
External debt ($US)	∘∘∘

NAURU

Area (sq km)	21
Population	11 000
Capital	Yaren
GNI per person ($US)	∘∘∘
HDI	∘∘∘
External debt ($US)	∘∘∘

NEPAL

Area (sq km)	147 180
Population	25 190 000
Capital	Kathmandu
GNI per person ($US)	260
HDI	0.504
External debt ($US)	3 253 000 000

NETHERLANDS

Area (sq km)	41 530
Population	16 250 000
Capital	Amsterdam
GNI per person ($US)	31 700
HDI	0.942
External debt ($US)	∘∘∘

NEW ZEALAND

Area (sq km)	270 530
Population	4 061 000
Capital	Wellington
per person ($US)	20 310
HDI	0.926
ternal debt ($US)	○○○

NORWAY

Area (sq km)	323 760
Population	4 582 000
Capital	Oslo
GNI per person ($US)	52 030
HDI	0.956
External debt ($US)	○○○

NICARAGUA

Area (sq km)	130 000
Population	5 604 000
Capital	Managua
per person ($US)	790
HDI	0.667
ternal debt ($US)	6 915 000 000

OMAN

Area (sq km)	309 500
Population	2 659 000
Capital	Muscat
GNI per person ($US)	7 890
HDI	0.770
External debt ($US)	3 886 000 000

NIGER

Area (sq km)	1 267 000
Population	12 095 000
Capital	Niamey
per person ($US)	230
HDI	0.292
ternal debt ($US)	2 116 000 000

PAKISTAN

Area (sq km)	796 100
Population	152 061 000
Capital	Islamabad
GNI per person ($US)	600
HDI	0.497
External debt ($US)	36 345 000 000

NIGERIA

Area (sq km)	923 770
Population	139 823 000
Capital	Abuja
per person ($US)	390
HDI	0.466
ternal debt ($US)	34 963 000 000

PALAU

Area (sq km)	460
Population	20 000
Capital	Koror
GNI per person ($US)	6 870
HDI	○○○
External debt ($US)	○○○

NORTHERN MARIANAS

Area (sq km)	477
Population	77 000
Capital	Saipan
per person ($US)	○○○
HDI	○○○
ternal debt ($US)	○○○

PANAMA

Area (sq km)	75 520
Population	3 028 000
Capital	Panama City
GNI per person ($US)	4 450
HDI	0.791
External debt ($US)	8 770 000 000

NORTH KOREA

Area (sq km)	120 540
Population	22 745 000
Capital	Pyongyang
per person ($US)	○○○
HDI	○○○
ternal debt ($US)	○○○

PAPUA NEW GUINEA

Area (sq km)	462 840
Population	5 625 000
Capital	Port Moresby
GNI per person ($US)	580
HDI	0.542
External debt ($US)	2 463 000 000

PARAGUAY

Area (sq km) 406 750
Population 5 782 000
Capital Asunción
GNI per person ($US) 1 170
HDI 0.751
External debt ($US) 3 210 000 000

PERU

Area (sq km) 1 285 220
Population 27 547 000
Capital Lima
GNI per person ($US) 2 360
HDI 0.752
External debt ($US) 29 857 000 000

PHILIPPINES

Area (sq km) 300 000
Population 82 987 000
Capital Manila
GNI per person ($US) 1 170
HDI 0.753
External debt ($US) 62 663 000 000

POLAND

Area (sq km) 312 690
Population 38 160 000
Capital Warsaw
GNI per person ($US) 6 090
HDI 0.850
External debt ($US) 95 219 000 000

PORTUGAL

Area (sq km) 91 980
Population 10 436 000
Capital Lisbon
GNI per person ($US) 14 350
HDI 0.897
External debt ($US) ○○○

QATAR

Area (sq km) 11 000
Population 637 000
Capital Doha
GNI per person ($US) ○○○
HDI 0.833
External debt ($US) ○○○

ROMANIA

Area (sq km) 238 390
Population 21 858 000
Capital Bucharest
GNI per person ($US) 2 920
HDI 0.778
External debt ($US) 21 280 000 000

RUSSIAN FEDERATION

Area (sq km) 17 075 400
Population 142 814 000
Capital Moscow
GNI per person ($US) 3 410
HDI 0.795
External debt ($US) 175 257 000 000

RWANDA

Area (sq km) 26 340
Population 8 412 000
Capital Kigali
GNI per person ($US) 220
HDI 0.431
External debt ($US) 1 540 000 000

ST. KITTS AND NEVIS

Area (sq km) 360
Population 47 000
Capital Basseterre
GNI per person ($US) 7 600
HDI 0.844
External debt ($US) ○○○

ST. LUCIA

Area (sq km) 620
Population 164 000
Capital Castries
GNI per person ($US) 4 310
HDI 0.777
External debt ($US) ○○○

ST. VINCENT AND THE GRENADINES

Area (sq km) 390
Population 108 000
Capital Kingstown
GNI per person ($US) 3 650
HDI 0.751
External debt ($US) ○○○

SAMOA

Area (sq km)	2 840
Population	179 000
Capital	Apia
GNI per person ($US)	1 860
HDI	0.769
External debt ($US)	ooo

SAN MARINO

Area (sq km)	60.5
Population	28 000
Capital	San Marino
GNI per person ($US)	ooo
HDI	ooo
External debt ($US)	ooo

SÃO TOMÉ AND PRÍNCIPE

Area (sq km)	960
Population	161 000
Capital	São Tomé
GNI per person ($US)	370
HDI	0.645
External debt ($US)	ooo

SAUDI ARABIA

Area (sq km)	2 149 690
Population	23 215 000
Capital	Riyadh
GNI per person ($US)	10 430
HDI	0.768
External debt ($US)	ooo

SENEGAL

Area (sq km)	196 720
Population	10 455 000
Capital	Dakar
GNI per person ($US)	670
HDI	0.437
External debt ($US)	4 419 000 000

SERBIA AND MONTENEGRO

Area (sq km)	102 170
Population	8 152 000
Capital	Belgrade
GNI per person ($US)	2 620
HDI	ooo
External debt ($US)	14 885 000 000

SEYCHELLES

Area (sq km)	450
Population	85 000
Capital	Victoria
GNI per person ($US)	8 090
HDI	0.853
External debt ($US)	ooo

SIERRA LEONE

Area (sq km)	71 740
Population	5 436 000
Capital	Freetown
GNI per person ($US)	200
HDI	0.273
External debt ($US)	1 612 000 000

SINGAPORE

Area (sq km)	680
Population	4 335 000
Capital	Singapore
GNI per person ($US)	24 220
HDI	0.902
External debt ($US)	ooo

SLOVAKIA

Area (sq km)	48 845
Population	5 390 000
Capital	Bratislava
GNI per person ($US)	6 480
HDI	0.842
External debt ($US)	18 379 000 000

SLOVENIA

Area (sq km)	20 250
Population	1 995 000
Capital	Ljubljana
GNI per person ($US)	11 870
HDI	0.895
External debt ($US)	ooo

SOLOMON ISLANDS

Area (sq km)	28 900
Population	471 000
Capital	Honiara
GNI per person ($US)	550
HDI	0.624
External debt ($US)	ooo

SOMALIA

Area (sq km)	637 660
Population	9 938 000
Capital	Mogadishu
GNI per person ($US)	०००
HDI	०००
External debt ($US)	2 838 000 000

SOUTH AFRICA

Area (sq km)	1 219 090
Population	45 584 000
Capital	Pretoria
GNI per person ($US)	3 630
HDI	0.666
External debt ($US)	27 807 000 000

SOUTH KOREA

Area (sq km)	99 260
Population	48 142 000
Capital	Seoul
GNI per person ($US)	13 980
HDI	0.888
External debt ($US)	०००

SPAIN

Area (sq km)	505 990
Population	41 286 000
Capital	Madrid
GNI per person ($US)	21 210
HDI	0.922
External debt ($US)	०००

SRI LANKA

Area (sq km)	65 610
Population	19 444 000
Capital	Colombo
GNI per person ($US)	1 010
HDI	0.740
External debt ($US)	10 238 000 000

SUDAN

Area (sq km)	2 505 810
Population	34 356 000
Capital	Khartoum
GNI per person ($US)	530
HDI	0.505
External debt ($US)	17 496 000 000

SURINAME

Area (sq km)	163 270
Population	443 000
Capital	Paramaribo
GNI per person ($US)	2 250
HDI	0.780
External debt ($US)	०००

SWAZILAND

Area (sq km)	17 360
Population	1 120 000
Capital	Mbabane
GNI per person ($US)	1 660
HDI	0.519
External debt ($US)	400 000 000

SWEDEN

Area (sq km)	449 960
Population	8 985 000
Capital	Stockholm
GNI per person ($US)	35 770
HDI	0.946
External debt ($US)	०००

SWITZERLAND

Area (sq km)	41 290
Population	7 382 000
Capital	Bern
GNI per person ($US)	48 230
HDI	0.936
External debt ($US)	०००

SYRIA

Area (sq km)	185 180
Population	17 783 000
Capital	Damascus
GNI per person ($US)	1 190
HDI	0.710
External debt ($US)	21 566 000 000

TAIWAN

Area (sq km)	36 179
Population	21 908 000
Capital	Taipei
GNI per person ($US)	०००
HDI	०००
External debt ($US)	०००

TAJIKISTAN

Area (sq km)	143 100
Population	6 430 000
Capital	Dushanbe
GNI per person ($US)	280
HDI	0.671
External debt ($US)	1 166 000 000

TANZANIA

Area (sq km)	945 090
Population	36 571 000
Capital	Dodoma
GNI per person ($US)	330
HDI	0.407
External debt ($US)	7 516 000 000

THAILAND

Area (sq km)	513 120
Population	62 387 000
Capital	Bangkok
GNI per person ($US)	2 540
HDI	0.768
External debt ($US)	51 793 000 000

TOGO

Area (sq km)	56 790
Population	4 996 000
Capital	Lomé
GNI per person ($US)	380
HDI	0.495
External debt ($US)	1 707 000 000

TONGA

Area (sq km)	750
Population	102 000
Capital	Nuku'alofa
GNI per person ($US)	1 830
HDI	0.787
External debt ($US)	○○○

TRINIDAD AND TOBAGO

Area (sq km)	5 130
Population	1 323 000
Capital	Port of Spain
GNI per person ($US)	8 580
HDI	0.801
External debt ($US)	2 751 000 000

TUNISIA

Area (sq km)	163 610
Population	10 012 000
Capital	Tunis
GNI per person ($US)	2 630
HDI	0.745
External debt ($US)	15 502 000 000

TURKEY

Area (sq km)	774 820
Population	71 727 000
Capital	Ankara
GNI per person ($US)	3 750
HDI	0.751
External debt ($US)	145 662 000 000

TURKMENISTAN

Area (sq km)	488 100
Population	4 931 000
Capital	Ashgabat
GNI per person ($US)	1 340
HDI	0.752
External debt ($US)	○○○

TUVALU

Area (sq km)	25
Population	11 000
Capital	Funafuti
GNI per person ($US)	○○○
HDI	○○○
External debt ($US)	○○○

UGANDA

Area (sq km)	241 040
Population	25 920 000
Capital	Kampala
GNI per person ($US)	270
HDI	0.493
External debt ($US)	4 553 000 000

UKRAINE

Area (sq km)	603 700
Population	48 008 000
Capital	Kiev
GNI per person ($US)	1 260
HDI	0.777
External debt ($US)	16 309 000 000

UNITED ARAB EMIRATES

Area (sq km)	83 600
Population	4 284 000
Capital	Abu Dhabi
GNI per person ($US)	ooo
HDI	0.824
External debt ($US)	ooo

UNITED KINGDOM

Area (sq km)	242 910
Population	59 405 000
Capital	London
GNI per person ($US)	33 940
HDI	0.936
External debt ($US)	ooo

UNITED STATES OF AMERICA

Area (sq km)	9 629 090
Population	293 507 000
Capital	Washington D.C.
GNI per person ($US)	41 400
HDI	0.939
External debt ($US)	ooo

URUGUAY

Area (sq km)	176 220
Population	3 399 000
Capital	Montevideo
GNI per person ($US)	3 950
HDI	0.833
External debt ($US)	11 764 000 000

UZBEKISTAN

Area (sq km)	447 400
Population	25 930 000
Capital	Tashkent
GNI per person ($US)	460
HDI	0.709
External debt ($US)	5 006 000 000

VANUATU

Area (sq km)	12 190
Population	215 000
Capital	Port Vila
GNI per person ($US)	1 340
HDI	0.570
External debt ($US)	ooo

VENEZUELA

Area (sq km)	912 050
Population	26 127 000
Capital	Caracas
GNI per person ($US)	4 020
HDI	0.778
External debt ($US)	34 851 000 000

VIETNAM

Area (sq km)	331 690
Population	82 162 000
Capital	Hanoi
GNI per person ($US)	550
HDI	0.691
External debt ($US)	15 817 000 000

WESTERN SAHAR

Area (sq km)	266 000
Population	275 000
Capital	Laâyoune
GNI per person ($US)	ooo
HDI	ooo
External debt ($US)	ooo

YEMEN REPUBLIC

Area (sq km)	527 970
Population	19 763 000
Capital	Sana
GNI per person ($US)	570
HDI	0.482
External debt ($US)	5 377 000 000

ZAMBIA

Area (sq km)	752 610
Population	10 547 000
Capital	Lusaka
GNI per person ($US)	450
HDI	0.389
External debt ($US)	6 425 000 000

ZIMBABWE

Area (sq km)	390 760
Population	13 151 000
Capital	Harare
GNI per person ($US)	ooo
HDI	0.491
External debt ($US)	4 445 000 000

How to use the index

To find a place on an atlas map use either the grid code or latitude and longitude.

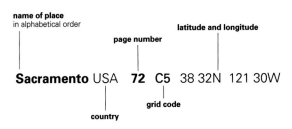

name of place
in alphabetical order

page number

latitude and longitude

Sacramento USA **72** C5 38 32N 121 30W

country

grid code

Grid code

Sacramento USA **72** C5 38 32N 121 30W

Sacramento is in grid square C5

Latitude and longitude

Sacramento USA **72** C5 38 32N 121 30W

Sacramento is at latitude 38 degrees, 32 minutes north and 121 degrees, 30 minutes west

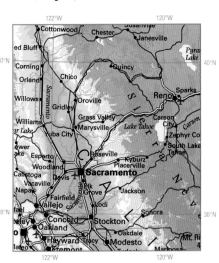

Abbreviations used in the index

admin.	administrative area	PNG	Papua New Guinea
b.	bay or harbour	*r.*	river
Bahamas	The Bahamas	RoI	Republic of Ireland
CAR	Central African Republic	RSA	Republic of South Africa
CDR	Congo Democratic Republic	Russia	Russian Federation
		SM	Serbia and Montenegro
d.	desert	*St.*	Saint
i.	island	*Ste.*	Sainte
is.	islands	*tn.*	town
l.	lake, lakes, lagoon	UAE	United Arab Emirates
mt.	mountain, peak, or spot height	UK	United Kingdom
		USA	United States of America
mts.	mountains	Yemen	Yemen Republic
Philippines	The Philippines		

136 Index

A

Name	Page	Grid	Lat	Long
Aachen Germany	20	B4	50 46N	6 06E
Aba Nigeria	55	C2	5 06N	7 21E
Abādān Iran	38	C3	30 20N	48 15E
Abashiri Japan	44	D3	44 02N	144 17E
Abbeville France	22	D6	50 06N	1 51E
Aberaeron UK	15	A3	52 49N	44 43W
Aberdeen UK	13	C2	57 10N	2 04W
Abergavenny UK	15	B2	51 50N	3 00W
Aberystwyth UK	15	A3	52 25N	4 05W
Abhā Saudi Arabia	38	C1	18 14N	42 31E
Abidjan Côte d'Ivoire	55	B2	5 19N	4 01W
Abilene USA	68	G3	32 27N	99 45W
Abu Dhabi UAE	39	D2	24 28N	54 25E
Abu Hamed Sudan	56	C3	19 32N	33 20E
Abuja Nigeria	55	C2	9 10N	7 11E
Acapulco Mexico	75	E2	16 51N	99 56W
Acayucán Mexico	75	E2	17 59N	95 00W
Accra Ghana	55	B2	5 33N	0 15W
Aconcagua mt. Argentina	84	B3	32 40S	70 02W
A Coruña Spain	24	A5	43 22N	8 24W
Adana Turkey	31	E2	37 00N	35 19E
Ad Dakhla Western Sahara	54	A4	23 50N	15 58W
Ad Dammām Saudi Arabia	38	D2	26 25N	50 06E
Addis Ababa Ethiopia	57	C2	9 03N	38 42E
Adelaide Australia	91	C2	34 56S	138 36E
Aden Yemen	38	C1	12 50N	45 03E
Âdwa Ethiopia	57	C3	14 12N	38 56E
AFGHANISTAN	39	E3		
Afyon Turkey	31	D2	38 46N	30 32E
Agadir Morocco	54	B5	30 30N	9 40W
Agra India	40	C5	27 09N	78 00E
Agri Turkey	31	F2	39 44N	43 04E
Agrigento Italy	26	D2	37 19N	13 35E
Aguilas Spain	25	E2	37 25N	1 35W
Ahmadabad India	40	B4	23 03N	72 40E
Ahvāz Iran	38	C3	31 17N	48 43E
Aïn Sefra Algeria	54	B5	32 45N	0 35W
Airdrie Canada	68	D7	51 20N	114 00W
Aix-en-Provence France	23	F2	43 31N	5 27E
Aizu-wakamatsu Japan	44	C2	37 30N	139 58E
Ajaccio Corsica	23	H1	41 55N	8 43E
Ajmer India	40	B5	26 29N	74 40E
Akashi Japan	45	B1	34 39N	135 00E
Akhtubinsk Russia	30	G4	48 20N	46 10E
Aklavik Canada	66	E4	68 15N	135 02W
Akola India	41	C4	20 49N	77 05E
Akron USA	70	B2	41 04N	81 31W
Aktau Kazakhstan	36	F2	43 37N	51 11E
Aktyubinsk Kazakhstan	36	F3	50 16N	57 13E
Alagoinhas Brazil	83	F1	12 09S	38 21W
Al 'Amārah Iraq	38	C3	31 51N	47 10E
Alamo USA	72	F4	37 23N	115 10W
Alanya Turkey	31	D2	36 32N	32 02E
Al Artāwīyah Saudi Arabia	38	C2	26 31N	45 21E
Alaska state USA	66	B4/D4	63 10N	157 30W
Alaska, Gulf of USA	66	D3	58 00N	147 00W
Albacete Spain	25	E3	39 00N	1 52W
ALBANIA	28/29	B4/C4		
Albany Australia	90	A2	34 57S	117 54E
Albany USA	69	K3	31 37N	84 10W
Al Başrah Iraq	38	C3	30 30N	47 50E
Al Bayda Libya	56	B5	32 00N	21 30E
Albert France	19	B3	50 00N	2 40E
Albertville France	23	G3	45 40N	6 24E
Ålborg Denmark	17	B2	57 05N	9 50E
Albuquerque USA	68	E4	35 05N	106 38W
Albury Australia	91	D2	36 03S	146 54E
Alcamo Italy	26	D2	37 58N	12 58E
Alcañiz Spain	25	E4	41 03N	0 09W
Aldan Russia	37	N3	58 44N	124 22E
Alençon France	22	D5	48 25N	0 05E
Aleppo Syria	38	B3	36 14N	37 10E
Alès France	23	F3	44 08N	4 05E
Alessándria Italy	26	B6	44 55N	8 37E
Alexander Bay tn. RSA	60	B2	28 40S	16 30E
Alexandria Egypt	56	B5	31 13N	29 55E
Alexandria USA	69	H3	31 19N	92 29W
Alexandria Bay tn. USA	71	C2	44 20N	75 55W
Al Fuḩayḩil Kuwait	38	C2	29 07N	47 02E
Algeciras Spain	24	C2	36 08N	5 27W

Name	Page	Grid	Lat	Long
ALGERIA	54	B4/C4		
Algiers Algeria	54	C5	36 50N	3 00E
Al Ḩillah Iraq	38	C3	32 28N	44 29E
Al Ḩufūf Saudi Arabia	38	C2	25 20N	49 34E
Alicante Spain	25	E3	38 21N	0 29W
Alice Springs tn. Australia	91	C3	23 42S	133 52E
Al Jawf Libya	56	B4	24 12N	23 18E
Al Jawf Saudi Arabia	38	B2	29 49N	39 52E
Al Kūt Iraq	38	C3	32 30N	45 51E
Allahabad India	40	D5	25 27N	81 50E
Allende Mexico	74	D4	28 22N	100 50W
Alliance USA	68	F5	42 08N	102 54W
Al Lith Saudi Arabia	38	C2	20 10N	40 20E
Alloa UK	13	C2	56 07N	3 49W
Almada Portugal	24	A3	38 40N	9 09W
Almadén Spain	24	C3	38 47N	4 50W
Almaty Kazakhstan	36	H2	43 19N	76 55E
Almería Spain	25	D2	36 50N	2 26W
Al Mukhā Yemen	38	C1	13 20N	43 16E
Alnwick UK	14	C4	55 25N	1 42W
Alor Setar Malaysia	46	B3	6 07N	100 21E
Alps mts. Europe	23	H4/J4	46 00N	7 30E
Alta Norway	16	E4	69 57N	23 10E
Altamira Brazil	83	D2	3 13S	52 15W
Altay China	42	B4	47 48N	88 07E
Altoona USA	71	C2	40 32N	78 32W
Al Wajh Saudi Arabia	38	B2	26 16N	32 28E
Alwar India	40	C5	27 32N	76 35E
Amapá Brazil	83	D3	2 00N	50 50W
Amarillo USA	68	F4	35 14N	101 50W
Amazon r. Brazil	82/83	C2/D2	2 00S	53 00W
Ambon Indonesia	47	D2	3 41S	128 10E
Amdo China	42	C3	32 22N	91 07E
American Samoa Pacific Ocean	96	F4	15 00S	170 00W
Amherst USA	71	C1	37 35N	79 04W
Amiens France	22	E5	49 54N	2 18E
Amman Jordan	38	B3	31 04N	36 17E
Amravati India	41	C4	20 58N	77 50E
Amritsar India	40	B6	31 35N	74 56E
Amsterdam Netherlands	18	D5	52 22N	4 54E
Amstetten Austria	21	F3	48 08N	14 52E
Anaconda USA	68	D6	46 09N	112 56W
Anadyr' Russia	37	T4	64 50N	178 00E
Anaheim USA	73	E2	33 50N	117 54W
Anápolis Brazil	83	E1	16 19S	48 58W
Anchorage USA	66	D4	61 10N	150 00W
Ancona Italy	26	D5	43 37N	13 31E
Andaman Islands India	41	F2	12 00N	94 00E
Andermatt Switzerland	23	H4	46 38N	8 36E
Andes mts. South America	78/79		10 00S	77 00W
Andizhan Uzbekistan	36	H2	40 40N	72 12E
ANDORRA	25	F5		
Andorra la Vella Andorra	25	F5	42 30N	1 30E
Angers France	22	C4	47 29N	0 32W
Anglesey i. UK	14	A3	53 18N	4 25W
ANGOLA	60	B3		
Angoulême France	22	D3	45 40N	0 10E
Anjó Japan	45	C1	34 56N	137 05E
'Annaba Algeria	54	C5	36 55N	7 47E
An Najaf Iraq	38	C3	31 59N	44 19E
Annapolis USA	71	C1	38 59N	76 30W
Annapurna mt. Nepal	40	D5	28 34N	83 50E
Ann Arbor USA	70	B2	42 18N	83 43W
An Nāsiriyah Iraq	38	C3	31 04N	46 17E
Annecy France	23	G3	45 54N	6 07E
Anniston USA	69	J3	33 38N	85 50W
Anqing China	43	E3	30 46N	119 40E
Anshan China	43	F4	41 05N	122 58E
Antakya Turkey	31	E2	36 12N	36 10E
Antalya Turkey	31	D2	36 53N	30 42E
Antananarivo Madagascar	61	E3	18 52S	47 30E
Antarctica	99			
Antibes France	23	G2	43 35N	7 07E
Antigua Guatemala	76	A2	14 33N	90 42W
ANTIGUA & BARBUDA	77	G3		
Antofagasta Chile	84	B4	23 40S	70 23W
Antrim Mountains UK	12	C3	55 00N	6 10W
Antsiranana Madagascar	61	E3	12 19S	49 17E
Antwerpen Belgium	18	D4	51 13N	4 25E
Anxi China	42	C4	40 32N	95 57E

vang China	43	E3	36 04N	114 20E
mori Japan	44	D3	40 50N	140 43E
sta Italy	26	A6	45 43N	7 19E
arri Philippines	47	D4	18 22N	121 40E
aldoorn Netherlands	18	E5	52 13N	5 57E
palachian Mountains USA	70/71	B1/C2	37 00N	82 00W
pennini mts. Italy	26/27	B6/E4	43 00N	12 30E
aba Jordan	38	B2	29 32N	35 00E
bian Sea Indian Ocean	39	E2	17 00N	60 00E
caju Brazil	83	F1	10 54S	37 07W
cati Brazil	83	F2	4 32S	37 45W
d Romania	28	C7	46 10N	21 19E
k Iran	38	C3	34 05N	49 42E
l Sea l. Asia	36	F2/G2	45 00N	60 00E
l'sk Kazakhstan	36	G2	46 56N	61 43E
ar Saudi Arabia	38	C3	30 58N	41 03E
uca Colombia	82	B3	7 04N	70 41W
il Iraq	38	C3	36 12N	44 01E
roath UK	13	C2	56 34N	2 35W
tic Bay tn. Canada	67	K5	73 05N	85 20W
tic Ocean	98			
labil Iran	38	C3	38 15N	48 18E
lmore USA	68	G3	34 11N	97 08W
res France	19	A3	50 51N	1 59E
rossan UK	13	A2	55 39N	4 40W
quipa Peru	82	B1	16 25S	71 32W
zzo Italy	26	C5	43 28N	11 53E
entan France	22	C5	48 45N	0 01W
enteuil France	19	B1	48 57N	2 15E
GENTINA	84/85	C1/C4		
us Denmark	17	C2	56 15N	10 10E
ca Chile	84	B5	18 30S	70 20W
quemes Brazil	82	C2	9 55S	63 06W
ansas City USA	69	G4	37 03N	97 02W
hangel'sk Russia	36	E3	64 32N	40 40E
low Rol	12	C2	52 48N	6 09W
es France	23	F2	43 41N	4 38E
nagh UK	12	C3	54 21N	6 39W
MENIA	31	F3/G2		
nidale Australia	91	E2	30 32S	151 40E
hem Netherlands	18	E4	52 00N	5 53E
prior Canada	71	C3	45 26N	76 21W
as France	19	B3	50 17N	2 46E
en'yev Russia	44	B3	44 08N	133 26E
em Russia	44	B3	43 23N	132 10E
a Uganda	58	B6	3 02N	30 56E
sha Tanzania	59	E3	3 23S	36 40E
nsol India	40	E4	23 40N	86 59E
bourne Rol	12	C2	53 31N	6 24W
burton New Zealand	93	B2	43 54S	171 45E
neville USA	69	K4	35 35N	82 35W
ford UK	15	D2	51 09N	0 53E
Fork USA	68	D4	35 13N	112 29W
gabat Turkmenistan	36	F1	37 58N	58 24E
ikaga Japan	45	C2	36 21N	139 26E
nland USA	68	B5	42 14N	122 44W
nara Eritrea	57	C3	15 20N	38 58E
sisi Italy	26	D5	43 04N	12 37E
ana Kazakhstan	36	H3	51 10N	71 28E
tara Azerbaijan	31	G2	38 27N	48 53E
i Italy	26	B6	44 54N	8 13E
toria USA	68	B6	46 12N	123 50W
rakhan' Russia	36	E2	46 22N	48 04E
unción Paraguay	84	D4	25 15S	57 40W
wân Egypt	56	C4	24 05N	32 56E
yût Egypt	56	C4	27 14N	31 07E
ara Sudan	57	C3	17 42N	34 00E
abasca, Lake Canada	66	G3/H3	59 10N	109 30W
ens Greece	29	D2	38 00N	23 44E
lone Rol	12	C2	53 25N	7 56W
y Rol	12	C2	52 59N	6 59W
kokan Canada	69	H6	48 45N	91 38W
anta USA	69	K3	33 45N	84 23W
antic Ocean	94			
Ta'if Saudi Arabia	38	C2	21 15N	40 21E
rau Kazakhstan	36	F2	47 08N	51 59E
ckland New Zealand	92	C3	36 51S	174 46E
gsburg Germany	20	D3	48 21N	10 54E
gusta Australia	90	A2	34 19S	115 09E
gusta USA	69	K3	33 29N	82 00W

Aurillac France	22	E3	44 56N	2 26E
Austin USA	68	G3	30 18N	97 47W
AUSTRALIA	90/91			
AUSTRIA	20/21	D2/G3		
Auxerre France	22	E4	47 48N	3 35E
Avallon France	23	E4	47 30N	3 54E
Aveiro Portugal	24	A4	40 38N	8 40W
Avezzano Italy	26	D5	42 02N	13 26E
Aviemore UK	13	C2	57 12N	3 50W
Avignon France	23	F2	43 56N	4 48E
Avila Spain	24	C4	40 39N	4 42W
Avranches France	22	C5	48 42N	1 21W
Awash Ethiopia	57	D2	8 59N	40 10E
Awbari Libya	54	D4	26 35N	12 46E
Ayacucho Peru	82	B1	13 10S	74 15W
Ayaguz Kazakhstan	36	J2	47 59N	80 27E
Aydin Turkey	29	F2	37 51N	27 51E
Ayers Rock mt. Australia	90	C3	25 18S	131 18E
Ayr UK	13	B1	55 28N	4 38W
Ayutthaya Thailand	49	C2	14 20N	100 35E
AZERBAIJAN	31	G2/G3		
Azov, Sea of Asia	31	E4	46 00N	36 00E

B

Baardheere Somalia	59	H6	2 19N	42 18E
Babruysk Belarus	30	C5	53 08N	29 10E
Bacabal Brazil	83	E2	4 15S	44 45W
Bacau Romania	28	F7	46 33N	26 58E
Bac Ninh Vietnam	48	D4	21 10N	106 04E
Bacolod Philippines	47	D4	10 38N	122 58E
Badajoz Spain	24	B3	38 53N	6 58W
Badalona Spain	25	G4	41 27N	2 15E
Bad Ems Germany	19	G3	50 20N	7 43E
Baffin Bay Canada/Greenland	67	K5/M4	72 00N	65 00W
Baffin Island Canada	67	K5/M4	68 30N	70 00W
Baghdad Iraq	38	C3	33 20N	44 26E
BAHAMAS, THE	76/77	E4/D5		
Bahía Blanca Argentina	85	C3	38 45S	62 15W
Bahraich India	40	D5	27 35N	81 36E
BAHRAIN	38	D2		
Baia Mare Romania	28	D7	47 39N	23 36E
Baie-Comeau tn. Canada	69	N6	49 12N	68 10W
Baja Hungary	21	H2	46 11N	18 58E
Baker Lake tn. Canada	67	J4	64 20N	96 10W
Baku Azerbaijan	31	G3	40 22N	49 53E
Balaghat India	40	D4	21 48N	80 16E
Balbriggan Rol	12	C2	53 37N	6 11W
Balearic Islands Spain	25	F3/H3	40 00N	2 00E
Bali i. Indonesia	46	C2	8 30S	115 00E
Balikesir Turkey	31	C2	39 37N	27 51E
Balikpapan Indonesia	46	C2	1 15S	116 50E
Ballarat Australia	91	D2	37 36S	143 58E
Ballina Rol	12	B3	54 07N	9 09W
Ballinasloe Rol	12	B2	53 20N	8 13W
Ballymena UK	12	C3	54 52N	6 17W
Balti Moldova	30	C4	47 44N	28 41E
Baltic Sea Europe	17	D2/E2	55 15N	17 00E
Baltimore USA	71	C1	39 18N	76 38W
Bam Iran	39	D2	29 07N	58 20E
Bamako Mali	55	B3	12 40N	7 59W
Banbury UK	15	C3	52 04N	1 20W
Banda Aceh Indonesia	46	A3	5 30N	95 20E
Bandar-e 'Abbās Iran	39	D2	27 12N	56 15E
Bandar Khomeyní Iran	38	C3	30 40N	49 08E
Bandar Seri Begawan Brunei	46	C3	4 53N	115 00E
Bandon Rol	12	B1	51 45N	8 45W
Bandung Indonesia	46	B2	6 57S	107 34E
Banff Canada	66	G3	51 10N	115 34W
Banff UK	13	C2	57 40N	2 33W
Bangalore India	41	C2	12 58N	77 35E
Bangkok Thailand	49	C2	13 44N	100 30E
BANGLADESH	40	E4/F4		
Bangor UK	14	A3	53 13N	4 08W
Bangor UK	12	D3	54 40N	5 40W
Bangui CAR	57	A2	4 23N	18 37E
Banja Luka Bosnia-Herzegovina	26	F6	44 47N	17 11E
Banjarmasin Indonesia	46	C2	3 22S	114 33E
Banjul The Gambia	55	A3	13 28N	16 39W
Bantry Rol	12	B1	51 41N	9 27W
Baotou China	43	D4	40 38N	109 59E

138 Index

Place	Page	Grid	Lat	Long
BARBADOS	77	H2		
Barcelona Spain	25	G4	41 25N	2 10E
Barcelona Venezuela	82	C4	10 08N	64 43W
Barcelonnette France	23	G3	44 24N	6 40E
Barcs Hungary	21	G1	45 58N	17 30E
Bareilly India	40	C5	28 20N	79 24E
Bari Italy	27	F4	41 07N	16 52E
Barletta Italy	27	F4	41 20N	16 17E
Barnaul Russia	36	J3	53 21N	83 45E
Barnsley UK	14	C3	53 34N	1 28W
Barnstaple UK	15	A2	51 05N	4 04W
Barquisimeto Venezuela	82	C4	10 03N	69 18W
Barrancas Venezuela	77	G1	8 45N	62 13W
Barranquilla Colombia	82	B4	11 10N	74 50W
Barreiras Brazil	83	E1	12 09S	44 58W
Barrow USA	66	C5	71 16N	156 50W
Barrow-in-Furness UK	14	B4	54 07N	3 14W
Barry UK	15	B2	51 24N	3 18W
Bartlesville USA	69	G4	36 44N	95 59W
Barysaw Belarus	30	C5	54 09N	28 30E
Basel Switzerland	24	G4	47 33N	7 36E
Basildon UK	15	D2	51 34N	0 25W
Basingstoke UK	15	C2	51 16N	1 05W
Bassein Myanmar	49	A3	16 46N	94 45E
Bastia France	23	H2	42 14N	9 26E
Bata Equatorial Guinea	55	C2	1 51N	9 49E
Batakan Indonesia	46	C2	4 03S	114 39E
Batang China	42	C3	30 02N	99 01E
Batdâmbâng Cambodia	49	C2	13 06N	103 13E
Bath UK	15	B2	51 23N	2 22W
Bathinda India	40	B6	30 10N	74 58E
Bathurst Australia	91	D2	33 27S	149 35E
Bathurst Canada	69	N6	47 37N	65 40W
Baton Rouge USA	69	H3	30 30N	91 10W
Bat'umi Georgia	31	F3	41 37N	41 36E
Bayeux France	22	C5	49 16N	0 42W
Bayonne France	22	C2	43 30N	1 28W
Bayreuth Germany	20	D3	49 27N	11 35E
Beaumont USA	69	H3	30 04N	94 06W
Beauvais France	22	E5	49 26N	2 05E
Béchar Algeria	54	B5	31 35N	2 17W
Bedford UK	15	C3	52 08N	0 29W
Beersheba Israel	38	B3	31 15N	34 47E
Beihai China	43	D2	21 29N	109 10E
Beijing China	43	E3	39 55N	116 26E
Beira Mozambique	61	D3	19 49S	34 52E
Beirut Lebanon	38	B3	33 52N	35 30E
Beja Portugal	24	B3	38 01N	7 52W
Békéscsaba Hungary	21	J2	46 45N	21 09E
BELARUS	30	C5/D5		
Belém Brazil	83	E2	1 27S	48 29W
Belfast UK	12	D3	54 35N	5 55W
BELGIUM	18/19			
Belgorod Russia	30	E5	50 38N	36 36E
Belgrade SM	28	C6	44 50N	20 30E
BELIZE	76	B3		
Belize Belize	76	B3	17 29N	88 10W
Bellac France	22	D4	46 07N	1 04E
Bellingham USA	68	B4	48 45N	122 29W
Belmopan Belize	76	B3	17 13N	88 48W
Belogorsk Russia	43	F5	50 55N	128 26E
Belo Horizonte Brazil	84	E4	19 54S	43 54W
Bendigo Australia	91	D2	36 48S	144 21E
Benevento Italy	27	E4	41 08N	14 46E
Bengbu China	43	E3	32 56N	117 27E
Benghazi Libya	56	B5	32 07N	20 04E
Benguela Angola	60	B3	12 34S	13 24E
Beni CDR	58	A5	0 30N	29 28E
Beni Abbès Algeria	54	B5	30 11N	2 14W
Beni Mellal Morocco	54	B5	32 22N	6 29W
BENIN	55	C2/C3		
Benin City Nigeria	55	C2	6 19N	5 41E
Beni Suef Egypt	56	C4	29 05N	31 05E
Benjamin Constant Brazil	82	C2	4 23S	69 59W
Ben Nevis mt. UK	13	B2	56 40N	5 00W
Beppu Japan	45	B1	33 18N	131 30E
Bérgamo Italy	26	B6	45 42N	9 40E
Bergen Norway	17	B3	60 23N	5 20E
Bergerac France	22	D3	44 50N	0 29E
Bering Sea Pacific Ocean	96	E7/F8	60 00N	175 00W
Berkeley USA	72	B4	37 53N	122 17W
Berlin Germany	20	E5	52 32N	13
Bern Switzerland	23	G4	46 57N	7
Berwick USA	71	C2	41 04N	76 1
Berwick-upon-Tweed UK	14	C4	55 46N	2 0
Besançon France	23	F4	47 14N	6
Bethel USA	66	B4	60 49N	161 4
Béthune France	22	E6	50 32N	2
Béziers France	22	E2	43 21N	3
Bharatpur India	40	C5	27 14N	77
Bharuch India	40	B4	21 40N	73
Bhopal India	40	C4	23 17N	77
Bhubaneshwar India	41	E4	20 13N	85
BHUTAN	40	F5		
Bialystok Poland	21	K5	53 09N	23
Biarritz France	22	C2	43 29N	1 3
Bida Nigeria	55	C2	9 06N	5
Biel Switzerland	23	G4	46 27N	8
Bielefeld Germany	20	C5	52 02N	8
Bihac Bosnia-Herzegovina	26	E6	44 49N	15
Bikaner India	40	B5	28 01N	73
Bilbao Spain	25	D5	43 15N	2 E
Billings USA	68	E6	45 47N	108 3
Biloxi USA	69	J3	30 24N	88 E
Bintulu Malaysia	46	C3	3 10N	113
Birjand Iran	39	D3	32 55N	59
Birkenhead UK	14	B3	53 24N	3 0
Birmingham UK	15	C3	52 30N	1 E
Birmingham USA	69	J3	33 30N	86 E
Biscay, Bay of Atlantic Ocean	22	B3	45 30N	2 E
Bishkek Kyrgyzstan	36	H2	42 53N	74
Bismarck USA	68	F6	46 50N	100 4
Bissau Guinea-Bissau	55	A3	11 52N	15 3
Bitola FYROM	29	C4	41 01N	21
Bizerte Tunisia	54	C5	37 18N	9
Blackburn UK	14	B3	53 45N	2 2
Blackpool UK	14	B3	53 50N	3 0
Black Sea Europe	31	D3/E3	43 00N	35
Blagoveshchensk Russia	37	N3	50 19N	127
Blairgowrie UK	13	C2	56 36N	3 2
Blantyre Malawi	61	D3	15 46S	35
Blenheim New Zealand	93	C2	41 31S	173
Blida Algeria	54	C5	36 30N	2
Bloemfontein RSA	60	C2	29 07S	26
Bluff New Zealand	93	B1	46 36S	168
Blyth UK	14	C4	55 07N	1 3
Bo Sierra Leone	55	A2	7 58N	11 4
Boa Vista Brazil	82	C3	2 49N	60 4
Bobigny France	19	B1	48 55N	2
Bobo Dioulasso Burkina	55	B3	11 11N	4 1
Bocholt Germany	20	B4	51 49N	6
Boden Sweden	16	E4	65 50N	21
Bodmin UK	15	A2	50 29N	4 3
Bodø Norway	16	C4	67 18N	14
Bognor Regis UK	15	C2	50 47N	0 4
Bogotá Colombia	82	B3	4 38N	74 0
Boise USA	68	C5	43 38N	116 1
Boise City USA	68	F4	36 44N	102 3
Bokaro India	40	E4	23 46N	85
Boké Guinea	55	A3	10 57N	14 1
BOLIVIA	84	C4/C5		
Bologna Italy	26	C6	44 30N	11
Bol'shoy Kamen' Russia	44	B3	43 05N	132
Bolton UK	14	B3	53 35N	2 2
Bolzano Italy	26	C7	46 30N	11 1
Boma CDR	60	B4	5 50S	13
Bom Jesus da Lapa Brazil	83	E1	13 16S	43 2
Bonn Germany	20	B4	50 44N	7
Bonthe Sierra Leone	55	A2	7 32N	12 3
Borås Sweden	17	C2	57 44N	12
Bordeaux France	22	C3	44 50N	0 3
Borgholm Sweden	17	D2	56 51N	16
Borisoglebsk Russia	30	F5	51 23N	42
Borkum Germany	20	F6	53 35N	6
Borneo i. Indonesia/Malaysia	46	B3/C3	1 00N	113
BOSNIA-HERZEGOVINA	26	F6/G5		
Boston UK	15	C3	52 59N	0 0
Boston USA	71	D2	42 20N	71 0
BOTSWANA	60	C2		
Bouaké Côte d'Ivoire	55	B2	7 42N	5 0
Bouârfa Morocco	54	B5	32 30N	1 5
Bougouni Mali	55	B3	11 25N	7 2

© Oxford University Press

Place	Map	Grid	Lat.	Long.
Boulogne-sur-Mer France	22	D6	50 43N	1 37E
Bourges France	22	E4	47 05N	2 23E
Bourke Australia	91	D2	30 09S	145 59E
Bournemouth UK	15	C2	50 43N	1 54W
Bou Saâda Algeria	54	C5	35 10N	4 09E
Bousso Chad	57	A3	10 32N	16 45E
Boyle Rol	12	B2	53 58N	8 18W
Bozeman USA	68	D6	45 40N	111 00W
Bradford UK	14	C3	53 48N	1 45W
Braga Portugal	24	A4	41 32N	8 26W
Brahmaputra r. India/Bangladesh	40	F5	26 40N	93 00E
Braila Romania	28	F6	45 17N	27 58E
Brandenburg Germany	20	E5	52 25N	12 34E
Brandon Canada	66	J2	49 50N	99 57W
Brásília Brazil	83	E1	15 45S	47 57W
Brasov Romania	28	E6	45 39N	25 35E
Bratislava Slovakia	21	G3	48 10N	17 10E
Bratsk Russia	37	L3	56 20N	101 50E
Braunschweig Germany	20	D5	52 15N	10 30E
Bray Rol	12	C2	53 12N	6 06W
BRAZIL	80/81			
Brazzaville Congo	60	B4	4 14S	15 14E
Brecon UK	15	B2	51 57N	3 24W
Brecon Beacons mts. UK	15	B2	51 50N	3 30W
Breda Netherlands	18	D4	51 35N	4 46E
Bregenz Austria	20	C2	47 31N	9 46E
Bremen Germany	20	C5	53 05N	8 48E
Bremerhaven Germany	20	C5	53 33N	8 35E
Bremerton USA	68	B6	47 34N	122 40W
Brescia Italy	26	C6	45 33N	10 13E
Brest Belarus	30	B5	52 08N	23 40E
Brest France	22	A5	48 23N	4 30W
Briançon France	23	G3	44 53N	6 39E
Bridgwater UK	15	B2	51 08N	3 00W
Bridlington UK	14	C4	54 05N	0 12W
Brighton UK	15	C2	50 50N	0 10W
Brindisi Italy	27	F4	40 37N	17 57E
Brisbane Australia	91	E3	27 30S	153 00E
Bristol UK	15	B2	51 27N	2 35W
Bristol Channel UK	15	B2	51 20N	3 50W
Brive-la-Gaillarde France	22	D3	45 09N	1 32E
Brno Czech Republic	21	G3	49 13N	16 40E
Brockton USA	69	D2	42 06N	71 01W
Brodick UK	13	A2	55 35N	5 09W
Bronx USA	71	D2	40 50N	73 50W
Brookings USA	69	C5	44 19N	96 47W
Brooklyn USA	71	D2	40 41N	73 57W
Broome Australia	90	B4	17 58S	122 15E
Bruay-en-Artois France	22	E6	50 29N	2 33E
Brugge Belgium	18	C4	51 13N	3 14E
BRUNEI	46	C3		
Brussels Belgium	19	D3	50 50N	4 21E
Bryansk Russia	30	D5	53 15N	34 09E
Brzeg Poland	21	G4	50 52N	17 27E
Bucaramanga Colombia	82	B3	7 08N	73 10W
Bucharest Romania	28	F6	44 25N	26 07E
Budapest Hungary	21	H2	47 30N	19 03E
Bude UK	15	A2	50 50N	4 33W
Buenaventura Colombia	82	B3	3 54N	77 02W
Buenos Aires Argentina	84	D3	34 40S	58 30W
Buffalo USA	68	E5	44 21N	106 40W
Bujumbura Burundi	58	A3	3 22S	29 19E
Bukama CDR	60	C4	9 13S	25 52E
Bukavu CDR	60	C4	2 30S	28 50E
Bulawayo Zimbabwe	60	C2	20 10S	28 43E
BULGARIA	28/29	D5/F5		
Bumba CDR	57	B2	2 10N	22 30E
Bunbury Australia	90	A2	33 20S	115 34E
Buncrana Rol	12	C3	55 08N	7 27W
Bundaberg Australia	91	E3	24 50S	152 21E
Bunia CDR	57	C2	1 33N	30 13E
Buôn Mê Thuôt Vietnam	49	D2	12 41N	108 02E
Buraydah Saudi Arabia	38	C2	26 20N	43 59E
Burdur Turkey	31	D2	37 44N	30 17E
Burgas Bulgaria	28	F5	42 30N	27 29E
Burgos Spain	24	D5	42 21N	3 41W
BURKINA	55	B3/C3		
Burnley UK	14	B3	53 48N	2 14W
Bursa Turkey	31	C3	40 12N	29 04E
Bûr Safâga Egypt	56	C4	25 43N	33 55E
Burton upon Trent UK	15	C3	52 48N	1 36W
BURUNDI	58	A3/B3		
Bury St. Edmunds UK	15	D3	52 15N	0 43E
Bûshehr Iran	38	D2	28 57N	50 52E
Busia Uganda	58	D5	0 28N	34 06E
Busto Arsizio Italy	26	B6	45 37N	8 51E
Butare Rwanda	58	A3	2 35S	29 44E
Butte USA	68	D6	46 00N	112 31W
Butterworth Malaysia	49	C1	5 26N	100 24E
Butuan Philippines	47	D3	8 56N	125 31E
Bydgoszcz Poland	21	G5	53 16N	18 00E
Bytom Poland	21	H4	50 21N	18 51E

C

Place	Map	Grid	Lat.	Long.
Cabinda admin. Angola	60	B4	5 30S	12 20E
Cáceres Brazil	82	D1	16 05S	57 40W
Cadiz Philippines	47	D4	10 57N	123 18E
Cádiz Spain	24	B2	36 32N	6 18W
Caen France	22	C5	49 11N	0 22W
Caernarfon UK	14	A3	53 08N	4 16W
Caerphilly UK	15	B2	51 35N	3 14W
Cagayan de Oro Philippines	47	D3	8 29N	124 40E
Cágliari Italy	27	B3	39 13N	9 08E
Cairngorms mts. UK	13	C2	57 07N	3 40W
Cairns Australia	91	D4	16 51S	145 43E
Cairo Egypt	56	C4	30 00N	31 15E
Cakovec Croatia	26	F7	46 24N	16 26E
Calais France	22	D6	50 57N	1 52E
Caldwell USA	68	C5	43 39N	116 40W
Calgary Canada	66	G3	51 05N	114 05W
Cali Colombia	82	B3	3 24N	76 30W
Calicut India	41	C2	11 15N	75 45E
California state USA	72/73			
CAMBODIA	49	C2/D2		
Cambrai France	22	E6	50 10N	3 14E
Cambria USA	73	C3	35 34N	121 05W
Cambrian Mountains UK	15	B3	52 15N	3 45W
Cambridge UK	15	D3	52 12N	0 07E
CAMEROON	55	D2		
Campbell River tn. Canada	68	A6	50 00N	125 18W
Campbeltown UK	13	B1	55 26N	5 36W
Campeche Mexico	75	F2	19 50N	90 30W
Câmpina Romania	28	E6	45 08N	25 44E
Campina Grande Brazil	83	F2	7 15S	35 50W
Campinas Brazil	84	E4	22 54S	47 06W
CANADA	66/67			
Canakkale Turkey	31	C3	40 09N	26 25E
Canary Islands Spain	54	A4	28 30N	15 10W
Canberra Australia	91	D2	35 18S	149 08E
Cancún Mexico	75	G3	21 09N	86 45W
Cannanore India	41	C2	11 53N	75 23E
Cannes France	23	G2	43 33N	7 00E
Canterbury UK	15	D2	51 17N	1 05E
Can Tho Vietnam	49	D2	10 03N	105 46E
Cape Town RSA	60	B1	33 56S	18 28E
CAPE VERDE	94	E5		
Caracas Venezuela	82	C4	10 35N	66 56W
Caravelas Brazil	83	F1	17 45S	39 15W
Carcassonne France	22	E2	43 13N	2 21E
Cardiff UK	15	B2	51 30N	3 13W
Cardigan UK	15	A3	52 06N	4 40W
Cardigan Bay UK	15	A3	52 30N	4 30W
Caribbean Sea Central America	76/77	D3/F3	15 00N	75 00W
Carlisle UK	14	B4	54 54N	2 55W
Carlow Rol	12	C2	52 50N	6 55W
Carlsbad USA	68	F3	32 25N	104 14W
Carmarthen UK	15	A2	51 51N	4 20W
Carnarvon Australia	90	A3	24 51S	113 45E
Carnoustie UK	13	C2	56 30N	2 44W
Carpathians mts. Europe	21	H3/K3	49 00N	22 00E
Carrantoohill mt. Rol	12	B1	52 00N	9 45W
Carrick-on-Shannon Rol	12	B2	53 57N	8 05W
Carrick-on-Suir Rol	12	C2	52 21N	7 25W
Cartagena Colombia	82	B4	10 24N	75 33W
Cartagena Spain	25	E2	37 36N	0 59W
Casablanca Morocco	54	B5	33 39N	7 35W
Casa Grande USA	68	D3	32 52N	111 46W
Cashel Rol	12	C2	52 31N	7 53W
Casper USA	68	E5	42 50N	106 20W
Caspian Sea Asia	36	F1/F2	41 00N	50 00E

140 Index

Name	Page	Grid	Lat	Long
Castellane France	23	G2	43 50N	6 30E
Castelvetrano Italy	27	D2	37 41N	12 47E
Castlebar Rol	12	B2	53 52N	9 17W
Castle Douglas UK	13	C1	54 57N	3 56W
Castleford UK	14	C3	53 44N	1 21W
Castres France	22	E2	43 36N	2 14E
Castries St. Lucia	77	G2	14 02N	60 59W
Castrovillari Italy	27	F3	39 48N	16 12E
Catanzaro Italy	27	F3	38 54N	16 36E
Caucasus mts. Asia	31	F3/G3	43 00N	43 00E
Cavan Rol	12	C3	53 58N	7 21W
Caxias do Sul Brazil	84	D4	29 14S	51 10W
Cayenne French Guiana	83	D3	4 55N	52 18W
Cebu Philippines	47	D4	10 17N	123 56E
Cedar Rapids tn. USA	69	H5	41 59N	91 39W
Cegléd Hungary	21	H2	47 10N	19 47E
Celle Germany	20	D5	52 37N	10 05E
CENTRAL AFRICAN REPUBLIC	57	A2/B2		
Ceuta territory Spain	24	C1	35 53N	5 19W
CHAD	56/57	A3/B3		
Chalkída Greece	29	D3	38 28N	23 36E
Chambéry France	23	F3	45 34N	5 55E
Chamonix France	23	G3	45 55N	6 52E
Chandigarh India	40	C6	30 44N	76 54E
Changchun China	43	F4	43 53N	125 20E
Chang Jiang r. China	43	D3/E3	31 00N	110 00E
Changsha China	43	E2	28 10N	113 00E
Channel Islands British Isles	11	E1	49 30N	2 30W
Chanthaburi Thailand	49	C2	12 35N	102 08E
Chardzhev Turkmenistan	36	G1	39 09N	63 34E
Charleroi Belgium	19	D3	50 25N	4 27E
Charleston USA	69	L3	32 48N	79 58W
Charleville-Mézières France	23	F5	49 46N	4 43E
Charlotte USA	69	K4	35 03N	80 50W
Châteaubriant France	22	C4	47 43N	1 22W
Châteauroux France	22	D4	46 49N	1 41E
Chattanooga USA	69	J4	35 02N	85 18W
Chaumont France	23	F5	48 07N	5 08E
Cheb Czech Republic	20	E4	50 08N	12 28E
Cheboksary Russia	30	G6	56 08N	47 12E
Chelm Poland	21	K4	51 08N	23 29E
Chelmsford UK	15	D2	51 44N	0 28E
Cheltenham UK	15	B2	51 54N	2 04W
Chelyabinsk Russia	36	G3	55 12N	61 25E
Chemnitz Germany	20	E4	50 50N	12 55E
Chengdu China	43	D3	30 37N	104 06E
Chennai India	41	D2	13 05N	80 18E
Cherbourg France	22	C5	49 38N	1 37W
Cherepovets Russia	30	E6	59 09N	37 50E
Cherkasy Ukraine	30	D4	49 27N	32 04E
Chernivtsi Ukraine	28	E8	48 19N	25 52E
Chesapeake USA	69	L4	36 45N	76 15W
Chester UK	14	B3	53 12N	2 54W
Chesterfield UK	14	C3	53 15N	1 25W
Cheyenne USA	68	F5	41 08N	104 50W
Chiang Mai Thailand	48	B3	18 48N	98 59E
Chiang Rai Thailand	48	B3	19 56N	99 51E
Chiba Japan	45	D2	35 38N	140 07E
Chibougamau Canada	67	L2	49 56N	74 24W
Chicago USA	70	A2	41 50N	87 45W
Chiclayo Peru	82	B2	6 47S	79 47W
Chihuahua Mexico	74	C4	28 40N	106 06W
CHILE	84/85	B5/C1		
Chillán Chile	85	B3	36 37S	72 10W
Chimborazo mt. Ecuador	82	B2	1 29S	78 52W
CHINA	42/43	A3/G4		
Chinju South Korea	43	F3	35 10N	128 06E
Chisasibi Canada	67	L3	53 50N	79 01W
Chisinau Moldova	31	C4	47 00N	28 50E
Chita Russia	37	M3	52 03N	113 35E
Chittagong Bangladesh	40	F4	22 20N	91 48E
Chongqing China	43	D2	29 30N	106 35E
Christchurch New Zealand	93	C2	43 32S	172 38E
Chumphon Thailand	49	B2	10 30N	99 11E
Chunchon South Korea	43	F3	37 56N	127 40E
Cirebon Indonesia	46	B2	6 46S	108 33E
Citlaltépetl mt. Mexico	74	E2	19 00N	97 18W
Ciucea Romania	28	D7	46 58N	22 50E
Ciudad Bolívar Venezuela	82	C3	8 06N	63 36W
Ciudad Guayana Venezuela	82	C3	8 22N	62 37W
Ciudad Juárez Mexico	74	C5	31 42N	106 29W
Ciudad Obregon Mexico	74	C4	27 28N	109 59W
Ciudad Rodrigo Spain	24	B4	40 36N	6 33W
Civitavecchia Italy	26	C5	42 05N	11 47E
Clarksville USA	69	J4	36 31N	87 21W
Clermont-Ferrand France	22	E3	45 47N	3 05E
Cleveland USA	70	B2	41 30N	81 41W
Clonakilty Rol	12	B1	51 37N	8 54W
Cloncurry Australia	91	D3	20 41S	140 30E
Clonmel Rol	12	C2	52 21N	7 42W
Clovis USA	68	F3	34 14N	103 13W
Cluj-Napoca Romania	28	D7	46 47N	23 37E
Clyde r. UK	13	C1	55 50N	3 55W
Clydebank UK	13	B1	55 54N	4 24W
Clyde River tn. Canada	67	M5	70 30N	68 30W
Coatbridge UK	13	C1	55 52N	4 01W
Cobh Rol	12	B1	51 51N	8 17W
Coburg Germany	20	D4	50 15N	10 58E
Cochin India	41	C1	9 56N	76 15E
Cockermouth UK	14	B4	54 40N	3 21W
Codó Brazil	83	E2	4 28S	43 51W
Cognac France	22	C3	45 42N	0 19W
Coimbatore India	41	C2	11 00N	76 57E
Coimbra Portugal	24	A4	40 12N	8 25W
Colchester UK	15	D2	51 54N	0 54E
Coleraine UK	12	C3	55 08N	6 40W
Colima Mexico	74	D2	19 14N	103 41W
Collingwood New Zealand	92	C2	40 41S	172 41E
Colmar France	23	G5	48 05N	7 21E
Cologne Germany	20	B4	50 56N	6 57E
COLOMBIA	82	B3		
Colombo Sri Lanka	41	C1	6 55N	79 52E
Colorado r. North America	68	D3	33 00N	114 00W
Colorado Springs tn. USA	68	F4	38 50N	104 50W
Columbia r. North America	68	B6/C6	46 00N	120 00W
Columbia USA	69	K3	34 00N	81 00W
Columbus USA	69	K3	32 28N	84 59W
Colwyn Bay tn. UK	14	B3	53 18N	3 43W
Comanesti Romania	28	F7	46 25N	26 29E
Como Italy	26	B6	45 48N	9 05E
COMOROS	61	E3		
Conakry Guinea	55	A2	9 30N	13 43W
Concepción Chile	85	B3	36 50S	73 03W
Concepción Mexico	74	D3	24 38N	101 25W
Concordia Argentina	84	D3	31 25S	58 00W
Condom France	22	D2	43 58N	0 23E
Congo r. Congo/CDR	57	A1/B2	2 00S	17 00E
CONGO	60	B4		
Constanta Romania	28	G6	44 12N	28 40E
Cook, Mount New Zealand	93	B2	43 36S	170 09E
Cooktown Australia	91	D4	15 29S	145 15E
Copenhagen Denmark	17	C2	55 43N	12 34E
Coquimbo Chile	84	B4	29 57S	71 25W
Córdoba Argentina	84	C3	31 25S	64 11W
Córdoba Mexico	75	E2	18 55N	96 55W
Córdoba Spain	24	C2	37 53N	4 46W
Cordova USA	66	D4	60 29N	145 52W
Corfu Greece	29	H3	39 38N	19 55E
Cork Rol	12	B1	51 54N	8 28W
Corpus Christi USA	68	G2	27 47N	97 26W
Corrientes Argentina	84	D4	27 30S	58 48W
Corsica i. France	23	H1/H2	42 00N	9 00E
Corumbá Brazil	84	D5	19 00S	57 35W
Cosenza Italy	27	F3	39 17N	16 16E
COSTA RICA	76	B2/C1		
CÔTE D'IVOIRE	55	B2		
Cotonou Benin	55	C2	6 24N	2 31E
Cotopaxi mt. Ecuador	82	B2	0 40S	78 28W
Cottbus Germany	20	F4	51 43N	14 21E
Coventry UK	15	C2	52 25N	1 30W
Cox's Bazar Bangladesh	40	F4	21 25N	91 59E
Craiova Romania	28	D6	44 18N	23 47E
Crawley UK	15	C2	51 07N	0 12W
Cremona Italy	26	C6	45 08N	10 01E
Crewe UK	14	B3	53 05N	2 27W
Crianlarich UK	13	B2	56 23N	4 37W
CROATIA	26	E6/F6		
Cromer UK	15	D3	52 56N	1 18E
Crotone Italy	27	F3	39 05N	17 08E
Croydon UK	15	C2	51 23N	0 06W
Cruzeiro do Sul Brazil	82	B2	7 40S	72 39W

CUBA	**76/77**	**C4/E4**		
Cúcuta Colombia	82	B3	7 55N	73 31W
Cuddalore India	41	C2	11 43N	79 46E
Cuenca Ecuador	82	B2	2 54S	79 00W
Cuenca Spain	25	D4	40 04N	2 07W
Cuiabá Brazil	83	D1	15 32S	56 05W
Cumberland USA	71	C1	39 40N	78 47W
Cumbernauld UK	13	C1	55 57N	4 00W
Cuneo Italy	26	A6	44 24N	7 33E
Cunnamula Australia	91	D3	28 04S	145 40E
Curicó Chile	85	B3	35 00S	71 15W
Curitiba Brazil	84	E4	25 25S	49 25W
Curvelo Brazil	84	E5	18 45S	44 27W
Cuttack India	41	E4	20 26N	85 56E
Cuzco Peru	82	B1	13 32S	71 59W
Cwmbran UK	15	B2	51 39N	3 00W
CYPRUS	31	D1/D2		
CZECH REPUBLIC	20/21	E3/G3		
Czestochowa Poland	21	H4	50 49N	19 07E

D

Dabola Guinea	55	A3	10 48N	11 02W
Dachau Germany	26	C8	48 15N	11 26E
Dafang China	48	D5	27 07N	105 33E
Dagupan Philippines	47	D4	16 02N	120 21E
Dahuk Iraq	31	F2	36 52N	43 00E
Dakar Senegal	55	A3	14 38N	17 27W
Da Lat Vietnam	49	D2	11 56N	108 25E
Dalby Australia	91	E3	27 11S	151 12E
Dali China	42	D2	25 33N	100 09E
Dalian China	43	F3	38 53N	121 37E
Dallas USA	69	G3	32 47N	96 48W
Dal'negorsk Russia	44	C3	44 28N	135 30E
Daly Waters tn. Australia	91	C4	16 13S	133 20E
Daman India	41	B4	20 15N	72 58E
Damascus Syria	38	B3	33 30N	36 19E
Damävand mt. Iran	38	D3	35 56N	52 08E
Damietta Egypt	56	C5	31 24N	31 48E
Dampier Australia	90	A3	20 45S	116 48E
Da Näng Vietnam	49	D3	16 04N	108 14E
Dandong China	43	F4	40 08N	124 24E
Danville USA	69	L4	36 34N	79 25W
Daqing China	43	F4	46 28N	125 01E
Dar es Salaam Tanzania	61	D4	6 51S	39 18E
Dargaville New Zealand	92	C2	35 56S	173 52E
Darjiling India	40	E5	27 02N	88 20E
Darling r. Australia	91	D2	30 30S	144 00E
Darlington UK	14	C4	54 31N	1 34W
Darmstadt Germany	20	C3	49 52N	8 39E
Darnah Libya	56	B5	32 46N	22 39E
Dartford UK	15	D2	51 27N	0 13E
Dartmoor UK	15	A2/B2	50 35N	3 50W
Darwin Australia	90	C4	12 23S	130 44E
Dashkhovuz Turkmenistan	36	F2	41 49N	59 58E
Datong China	43	E4	40 02N	113 33E
Daugavpils Latvia	17	F2	55 52N	26 31E
Dauphin Canada	66	H3	51 09N	100 05W
Davangere India	41	C2	14 30N	75 52E
Davao Philippines	47	D3	7 05N	125 38E
Davenport USA	69	H5	41 32N	90 36W
Davis Inlet tn. Canada	67	M3	55 51N	60 52W
Davis Strait Canada/Greenland	67	M4/N4	69 00N	60 00W
Davos Switzerland	23	H4	46 47N	9 50E
Dawson Canada	66	E4	64 04N	139 24W
Dawson Creek tn. Canada	66	F3	55 44N	120 15W
Dax France	22	C2	43 43N	1 03W
Dayr az Zawr Syria	38	C3	35 20N	40 02E
Daytona Beach tn. USA	69	K2	29 11N	81 01W
Dead Sea Israel/Jordan	38	B3	31 35N	35 30E
Dease Lake tn. Canada	66	E3	58 05N	130 04W
Death Valley USA	73	E4	36 00N	117 00W
Debrecen Hungary	21	J2	47 30N	21 37E
Debre Tabor Ethiopia	57	C3	11 50N	38 06E
Dehra Dun India	40	C6	30 19N	78 03E
Dej Romania	28	D7	47 08N	23 55E
Dekese CDR	60	C4	3 28S	21 24E
Delaware USA	70	E3	39 00N	75 30W
Delft Netherlands	18	D5	52 00N	4 22E
Delhi India	40	C5	28 40N	77 14E
Delice Turkey	31	D2	39 56N	34 02E
Deming USA	68	E3	32 17N	107 46W

DEMOCRATIC REPUBLIC OF CONGO	**60/61**	**B4/C4**		
Dendermonde Belgium	19	D4	51 02N	4 06E
Denizli Turkey	31	C2	37 46N	29 05E
DENMARK	17	B2/C2		
Denpasar Indonesia	46	C2	8 40S	115 14E
Denver USA	68	E4	39 45N	105 00W
Dera Ghazi Khan Pakistan	39	F3	30 05N	70 44E
Dera Ismail Khan Pakistan	39	F3	31 51N	70 56E
Derbent Russia	31	G3	42 03N	48 18E
Derby Australia	90	B4	17 19S	123 38E
Derby UK	15	C3	52 55N	1 30W
Dese Ethiopia	57	C3	11 05N	39 40E
Deseado Argentina	85	C2	47 44S	65 56W
Desierto de Atacama d. Chile	84	B4/C5	22 30S	70 00W
Des Moines USA	69	H5	41 35N	93 35W
Dessau Germany	20	E4	51 51N	12 15E
Detroit USA	70	B2	42 23N	83 05W
Devonport Australia	91	D1	41 09S	146 16E
Dezfül Iran	38	C3	32 23N	48 28E
Dezhou China	43	E3	37 29N	116 11E
Dhaka Bangladesh	40	F4	23 42N	90 22E
Dhamär Yemen	38	C1	14 33N	44 30E
Dhanbad India	40	E4	23 47N	86 32E
Dharwad India	41	C3	15 30N	75 04E
Dibrugarh India	40	F5	27 29N	95 00E
Dickinson USA	68	F6	46 54N	102 48W
Diên Biên Vietnam	48	C3	21 24N	103 04E
Diepholz Germany	20	C5	52 37N	8 22E
Dieppe France	22	B5	49 55N	1 05E
Dijon France	23	F4	47 20N	5 02E
Dili East Timor	47	D2	8 33S	125 34E
Dimitrovgrad Bulgaria	28	E5	42 03N	25 34E
Dimitrovgrad Russia	30	G5	54 14N	49 37E
Dinajpur Bangladesh	40	E5	25 38N	88 44E
Dinan France	22	B5	48 27N	2 02W
Dinard France	22	B5	48 38N	2 03W
Dingle Rol	12	A2	52 08N	10 15W
Dingwall UK	13	B2	57 35N	4 29W
Dire Dawa Ethiopia	57	D2	9 35N	41 50E
Dispur India	40	F5	26 07N	91 48E
Diu India	41	B4	20 41N	71 03E
Divinópolis Brazil	84	E4	20 08S	44 55W
Divrigi Turkey	31	E2	39 23N	38 06E
Diyarbakir Turkey	31	F2	37 55N	40 14E
Djambala Congo	60	B4	2 32S	14 43E
DJIBOUTI	57	D3		
Djibouti Djibouti	57	D3	11 35N	43 11E
Djougou Benin	55	C2	9 40N	1 47E
Dnipropetrovs'k Ukraine	30	D4	48 29N	35 00E
Doboj Bosnia-Herzegovina	26	G6	44 44N	18 05E
Dobrich Bulgaria	28	F5	43 34N	27 51E
Dodge City USA	68	F4	37 45N	100 02W
Dodoma Tanzania	61	D4	6 10S	35 40E
Doha Qatar	38	D2	25 15N	51 36E
Dolbeau Canada	69	M6	48 52N	72 15W
Dôle France	23	F4	47 05N	5 30E
Dolgellau UK	15	B3	52 44N	3 53W
DOMINICA	77	G3		
DOMINICAN REPUBLIC	77	E3/F3		
Doncaster UK	14	C3	53 32N	1 07W
Donegal Rol	12	B3	54 39N	8 07W
Donets'k Ukraine	30	E4	48 00N	37 50E
Dongchuan China	43	D2	26 07N	103 05E
Dongfang China	48	D3	19 03N	108 39E
Dông Hôi Vietnam	48	D3	17 32N	106 35E
Dongola Sudan	56	C3	19 10N	30 27E
Dongou Congo	57	A2	2 02N	18 02E
Dorchester UK	15	B2	50 43N	2 26W
Dordrecht Netherlands	18	D4	51 48N	4 40E
Dornbirn Austria	20	C2	47 25N	9 46E
Dorohoi Romania	28	F8	47 57N	26 31E
Dortmund Germany	20	B4	51 32N	7 27E
Dothan USA	69	J3	31 12N	85 25W
Douai France	22	E6	50 22N	3 05E
Douala Cameroon	55	C2	4 04N	9 43E
Douarnenez France	22	A5	48 05N	4 20W
Douglas Isle of Man	14	A4	54 09N	4 29W
Dourados Brazil	84	D4	22 09S	54 52W
Dover UK	15	D2	51 08N	1 19E
Downpatrick UK	12	D3	54 20N	5 43W

Drammen Norway	17	C2	59 45N 10 15E
Dresden Germany	20	E4	51 03N 13 45E
Dreux France	22	D5	48 44N 1 23E
Drobeta-Turnu-Severin Romania			
	28	D6	44 36N 22 39E
Drogheda RoI	12	C2	53 43N 6 21W
Droichead Nua RoI	12	C2	53 11N 6 45W
Dubai UAE	39	D2	25 14N 55 17E
Dubbo Australia	91	D2	32 16S 148 41E
Dublin RoI	12	C2	53 20N 6 15W
Dubrovnik Croatia	26	G5	42 40N 18 07E
Dudley UK	15	B3	52 30N 2 05W
Duisburg Germany	20	B4	51 26N 6 45E
Duluth USA	69	H6	46 45N 92 10W
Dumbarton UK	13	A2	55 57N 4 35W
Dumfries UK	13	C1	55 04N 3 37W
Dunaújváros Hungary	21	H2	47 00N 18 55E
Dundalk RoI	12	C3	54 01N 6 25W
Dundee UK	13	C2	56 28N 3 00W
Dunedin New Zealand	93	B1	45 53S 170 30E
Dunfermline UK	13	C2	56 04N 3 29W
Dungannon UK	12	C3	54 31N 6 46W
Dungarvan RoI	12	C2	52 05N 7 37W
Dunkerque France	22	E6	51 02N 2 23E
Dunkirk USA	70	C2	42 29N 79 21W
Dún Laoghaire RoI	12	C2	53 17N 6 08W
Durango Mexico	74	D3	24 01N 104 40W
Durango USA	68	E4	37 16N 107 53W
Durban RSA	61	D2	29 53S 31 00E
Durgapur India	40	E4	24 47N 87 44E
Durg-Bhilai India	41	D4	21 12N 81 20E
Durham UK	14	C4	54 47N 1 34W
Durrës Albania	29	B4	41 19N 19 27E
Dushanbe Tajikistan	36	G1	38 38N 68 51E
Düsseldorf Germany	20	B4	51 13N 6 47E

E

Eagle Pass tn. USA	68	F2	28 44N 100 31W
Eastbourne UK	15	D2	50 46N 0 17E
East Kilbride UK	13	B1	55 46N 4 10W
East London RSA	60	C1	33 00S 27 54E
EAST TIMOR	47	D2	
Eau Claire tn. USA	69	H5	44 50N 91 30W
Eberswalde-Finow Germany	20	E5	52 50N 13 53E
Ebolowa Cameroon	55	D2	2 56N 11 11E
Ech Cheliff Algeria	54	C5	36 05N 1 15E
ECUADOR	82	B3	
Ed Damer Sudan	57	C3	17 37N 33 59E
Edessa Greece	29	D4	40 48N 22 03E
Edinburgh UK	13	C1	55 57N 3 13W
Edirne Turkey	31	C3	41 40N 26 34E
Edmonton Canada	66	G3	53 34N 113 25W
Edremit Turkey	29	F3	39 34N 27 01E
EGYPT	56	B4/C4	
Eindhoven Netherlands	18	E4	51 26N 5 30E
Eisenach Germany	20	D4	50 59N 10 19E
Eisenstadt Austria	21	G2	47 51N 16 31E
Elat Israel	38	B2	29 33N 34 57E
Elâziğ Turkey	31	E2	38 41N 39 14E
El Bayadh Algeria	54	C5	33 40N 1 00E
Elbląg Poland	21	H6	54 10N 19 25E
Elburg Netherlands	18	E5	52 27N 5 50E
Elche Spain	25	E3	38 16N 0 41W
Elda Spain	25	E3	38 29N 0 47W
El Dorado USA	75	F5	33 12N 92 40W
Eldoret Kenya	58	D5	0 31N 35 17E
El Faiyûm Egypt	56	C4	29 19N 30 50E
El Fasher Sudan	57	B3	13 37N 25 22E
El Fuerte Mexico	74	C4	26 28N 108 35W
Elgin UK	13	C2	57 39N 3 20W
El Gîza Egypt	56	C4	30 01N 31 12E
Elista Russia	31	F4	46 18N 44 14E
Elizabeth Australia	91	C2	34 45S 138 39E
Elk Poland	21	K5	53 51N 22 20E
El Khârga Egypt	56	C4	25 27N 30 32E
Ellesmere Port UK	14	B3	53 17N 2 54W
El Minya Egypt	56	C4	28 06N 30 45E
El Muglad Sudan	57	B3	11 01N 27 50E
El Obeid Sudan	57	C3	13 11N 30 10E
El Paso USA	68	E3	31 45N 106 30W
El Progreso Honduras	76	B3	15 20N 87 50W

El Salto Mexico	74	C3	23 47N 105 22W
EL SALVADOR	76	B2	
El Tigre Venezuela	82	C3	8 44N 64 18W
Eluru India	41	D3	16 45N 81 10E
Elvas Portugal	24	B3	38 53N 7 10W
Ely UK	15	D3	52 24N 0 16E
Ely USA	68	D4	39 15N 114 53W
Emämrüd Iran	39	D3	36 15N 54 59E
Emba Kazakhstan	36	F2	48 47N 58 05E
Embu Kenya	59	E4	0 31S 37 26E
Emden Germany	20	B5	53 23N 7 13E
Empalme Mexico	74	B4	28 00N 110 49W
Emporia USA	69	G4	38 24N 96 10W
Encarnación Paraguay	84	D4	27 20S 55 50W
Engel's Russia	30	G5	51 30N 46 07E
England country UK	14/15		53 00N 2 00W
English Channel UK/France	11	E1/G2	50 00N 2 30W
Enid USA	68	G4	36 24N 97 54W
Enna Italy	27	E2	37 34N 14 16E
En Nahud Sudan	57	B3	12 41N 28 28E
Ennis RoI	12	B2	52 50N 8 59W
Enniscorthy RoI	12	C2	52 30N 6 34W
Enniskillen UK	12	C3	54 21N 7 38W
Ennistimon RoI	12	B2	52 57N 9 15W
Enschede Netherlands	18	F5	52 13N 6 55E
Entebbe Uganda	58	C5	0 04N 32 27E
Enugu Nigeria	55	C2	6 20N 7 29E
Epe Netherlands	18	E5	52 21N 5 59E
Épernay France	23	E5	49 02N 3 58E
Épinal France	23	G5	48 10N 6 28E
EQUATORIAL GUINEA	55	C2/D2	
Erding Germany	26	C8	48 17N 11 56E
Erechim Brazil	84	D4	27 35S 52 15W
Erenhot China	43	E4	43 50N 112 00E
Erfurt Germany	20	D4	50 58N 11 02E
Erie, Lake Canada/USA	70/71	B2/C2	42 15N 81 00W
ERITREA	57	C3/D3	14 40N 40 15E
Erlangen Germany	20	D3	49 36N 11 02E
Erzincan Turkey	31	E2	39 44N 39 30E
Erzurum Turkey	31	F2	39 57N 41 17E
Esbjerg Denmark	17	B2	55 20N 8 20E
Esfahán Iran	38	D3	32 41N 51 41E
Eskilstuna Sweden	17	D2	59 22N 16 31E
Eskimo Point tn. Canada	67	J4	61 10N 84 15W
Eskisehir Turkey	31	D2	39 46N 30 30E
Esmeraldas Ecuador	82	B3	0 56N 79 40W
Esperance Australia	90	B2	33 49S 121 52E
Espoo Finland	17	E3	60 10N 24 40E
Esquel Argentina	85	B2	42 55S 71 20W
Esquimalt Canada	68	B6	48 25N 123 29W
Essen Germany	20	B4	51 27N 6 57E
Estância Brazil	83	F1	11 15S 37 28W
Estevan Canada	66	H2	49 09N 103 00W
ESTONIA	17	E2/F2	
Étampes France	22	E5	48 26N 2 10E
ETHIOPIA	57	C2/D2	
Etna, Mount Italy	27	E2	37 45N 15 00E
Eucla Australia	90	B2	31 40S 128 51E
Eugene USA	68	B5	44 03N 123 04W
Everest, Mount China/Nepal	40	E5	27 59N 86 56E
Évora Portugal	24	B3	38 46N 7 41W
Evreux France	22	D5	49 03N 1 11E
Evry France	19	B1	48 38N 2 26E
Exeter UK	15	B2	50 43N 3 31W
Exmoor UK	15	B2	51 08N 3 40W
Exmouth Australia	90	A3	21 54S 114 10E
Exmouth UK	15	B2	50 37N 2 39W

F

Fairbanks USA	66	D4	64 50N 147 50W
Faisalabad Pakistan	39	F3	31 25N 73 09E
Faizabad India	40	D5	26 46N 82 08E
Fakfak Indonesia	47	E2	2 55S 132 17E
Falkirk UK	12	C2	55 59N 3 48W
Falkland Islands Atlantic Ocean			
	85	C1/D1	52 30S 60 00W
Famagusta Cyprus	31	D2	35 07N 33 57E
Farafangana Madagascar	61	E2	22 50S 47 50E
Faráh Afghanistan	39	E3	32 22N 62 07E
Fargo USA	69	G6	46 52N 96 49W
Farmington USA	68	E4	36 43N 108 12W

Name	Page	Grid	Lat	Long
ro Portugal	24	B2	37 01N	7 56W
tehgarh India	40	C5	27 22N	79 38E
yetteville USA	69	H4	36 03N	94 10W
yetteville USA	69	L4	35 03N	78 53W
camp France	22	D5	49 45N	0 23E
DERATED STATES OF MICRONESIA	96	D5		
ilding New Zealand	92	C2	40 14S	175 34E
ira de Santana Brazil	83	F1	12 17S	38 53W
dkirch Austria	20	C2	47 15N	9 38E
lixstowe UK	15	D2	51 58N	1 20E
ngfeng China	43	E3	37 00N	114 00E
rgus Falls tn. USA	69	G6	46 18N	96 07W
rmo Italy	26	D5	43 09N	13 44E
rmoy Rol	12	B2	52 08N	8 16W
rrara Italy	26	C6	44 50N	11 38E
s Morocco	54	B5	34 05N	5 00W
yzābād Afghanistan	39	F3	37 06N	70 34E
anarantsoa Madagascar	61	E2	21 27S	47 05E
denza Italy	26	C6	44 52N	10 04E
jeac France	22	E3	44 32N	2 01E
queira da Foz Portugal	24	A4	40 09N	8 51W
queres Spain	25	G5	42 16N	2 57E
jI	96	E4	17 00S	178 00E
NLAND	16/17	E3/F4		
hguard UK	15	A2	51 59N	4 59W
ensburg Germany	20	C6	54 47N	9 27E
ers France	22	C5	48 45N	0 34W
n Flon Canada	66	H3	54 50N	102 00W
nt USA	70	B2	43 03N	83 40W
prence Italy	26	C5	43 47N	11 15E
prencia Colombia	82	B3	1 37N	75 37W
pres Guatemala	76	B3	16 58N	89 50W
priano Brazil	83	E2	6 45S	43 00W
prianópolis Brazil	84	E4	27 35S	48 31W
prø Norway	17	B3	61 36N	5 04E
csani Romania	28	F6	45 41N	27 12E
ggia Italy	27	E4	41 28N	15 33E
ix France	22	D2	42 57N	1 35E
lkestone UK	15	D2	51 05N	1 11E
ntainebleau France	22	E5	48 24N	2 42E
nte Boa Brazil	82	C2	2 33S	65 59W
rfar UK	13	C2	56 38N	2 54W
rlì Italy	26	D6	44 13N	12 02E
RMER YUGOSLAV REPUBLIC OF MACEDONIA (FYROM)	28/29	C4/D4		
rmosa Argentina	84	D4	26 07S	58 14W
rmosa Brazil	83	E1	15 30S	47 22W
rtaleza Brazil	83	F2	3 45S	38 35W
rt Bragg USA	72	B5	39 29N	123 46W
rt Chipewyan Canada	66	G3	58 46N	111 09W
rt Collins USA	68	E5	40 35N	105 05W
rt Frances Canada	69	H6	48 37N	93 23W
rt Good Hope Canada	66	F4	66 16N	128 37W
rth r. UK	13	B2	56 10N	4 05W
rt Liard Canada	66	F4	60 14N	123 28W
rt McMurray Canada	66	G3	56 45N	111 27W
rt McPherson Canada	66	F4	67 29N	134 50W
rt Myers USA	69	K2	26 39N	81 51W
rt Nelson Canada	66	F3	58 48N	122 44W
rt Portal Uganda	58	B5	0 40N	30 17E
rt Providence Canada	66	G4	61 03N	117 40W
rt Resolution Canada	66	G4	61 10N	113 39W
rt St. John Canada	66	F3	56 14N	120 55W
rt Saskatchewan Canada	66	G3	53 42N	113 16W
rt Severn Canada	67	K3	56 00N	87 40W
rt Simpson Canada	66	F4	61 46N	121 15W
rt Smith Canada	66	G4	60 01N	111 55W
rt Smith USA	69	H4	35 22N	94 27W
rt William UK	13	B2	56 49N	5 07W
rt Worth USA	68	G3	32 45N	97 20W
rt Yukon USA	66	D4	66 35N	145 20W
shan China	43	E2	23 03N	113 08E
ugères France	22	C5	48 21N	1 12W
umban Cameroon	55	D2	5 43N	10 50E
z do Iguaçu Argentina	84	D4	25 33S	54 31W
ANCE	22/23			
ancistown Botswana	60	C2	21 11S	27 32E
ankfurt am Main Germany	20	C4	50 06N	8 41E
aserburgh UK	13	D2	57 42N	2 00W
edericksburg USA	71	C1	38 18N	77 30W
Freetown Sierra Leone	55	A2	8 30N	13 17W
Fréjus France	23	G2	43 26N	6 44E
Fremantle Australia	90	A2	32 07S	115 44E
French Guiana territory France	83	D3	5 00N	53 00W
Fresnillo Mexico	74	D3	23 10N	102 54W
Fresno USA	73	D4	36 41N	119 47W
Frobisher Bay Canada	67	M4	62 15N	65 00W
Frontera Mexico	75	F2	18 32N	92 39W
Fuji Japan	45	C2	35 10N	138 37E
Fuji-san mt. Japan	45	C2	35 23N	138 42E
Fukui Japan	45	C2	36 04N	136 12E
Fukuoka Japan	45	B1	33 39N	130 21E
Fukushima Japan	44	D2	37 44N	140 28E
Fukuyama Japan	45	B1	34 29N	133 21E
Funchal Madeira	54	A5	32 40N	16 55W
Fushun China	43	F4	41 50N	123 54E
Fuxin China	43	F4	42 04N	121 39E
Fuzhou China	43	E2	26 09N	119 17E

G

Name	Page	Grid	Lat	Long
Gabès Tunisia	54	D5	33 52N	10 06E
GABON	55	D1		
Gaborone Botswana	60	C2	24 45S	25 55E
Gadsden USA	69	J3	34 00N	86 00W
Gaeta Italy	27	D4	41 13N	13 36E
Gafsa Tunisia	54	C5	34 28N	8 43E
Gainesville USA	69	K2	29 37N	82 21W
Galashiels UK	13	C1	55 37N	2 49W
Galati Romania	28	G6	45 27N	28 02E
Galle Sri Lanka	41	D1	6 01N	80 13E
Gallipoli Italy	27	G4	40 03N	17 59E
Galveston USA	69	H2	29 17N	94 48W
Galway Rol	12	B2	53 16N	9 03W
GAMBIA, THE	55	A3		
Gäncä Azerbaijan	31	G3	40 39N	46 20E
Gander Canada	67	N2	49 00N	54 15W
Ganga r. India	40	C5	25 00N	83 30E
Ganzhou China	43	E2	25 45N	114 51E
Gao Mali	55	B3	16 19N	0 09W
Gap France	23	G3	44 33N	6 05E
Garda Italy	26	C6	45 34N	10 43E
Garden City USA	68	F4	37 57N	100 54W
Gardēz Afghanistan	40	A6	33 37N	69 07E
Garissa Kenya	59	F4	0 27S	39 39E
Garland USA	69	G3	32 55N	96 37W
Garzón Colombia	82	B3	2 14N	75 37W
Gaspé Canada	67	M2	48 50N	64 30W
Gateshead UK	14	C4	54 58N	1 35W
Gatineau Canada	71	C3	45 29N	75 40W
Gävle Sweden	17	D3	60 41N	17 10E
Gaya India	40	E4	24 48N	85 00E
Gaziantep Turkey	31	E2	37 04N	37 21E
Gbarnga Liberia	55	B2	7 02N	9 26W
Gdansk Poland	21	H6	54 22N	18 41E
Gdynia Poland	21	H6	54 31N	18 30E
Gedaref Sudan	57	C3	14 01N	35 24E
Geelong Australia	91	D2	38 10S	144 26E
Gejiu China	43	D2	23 25N	103 05E
Geldrop Netherlands	18	E4	51 25N	5 34E
Gelibolu Turkey	29	F4	40 25N	26 41E
Gendringen Netherlands	18	F4	51 53N	6 24E
Geneva Switzerland	23	G4	46 13N	6 09E
Genoa Italy	26	B6	44 24N	8 56E
Gent Belgium	19	C4	51 02N	3 42E
Georgetown Guyana	82	D3	6 46N	58 10W
George Town Malaysia	36	B3	5 25N	100 20E
GEORGIA	31	F3/G3		
Geraldton Australia	90	A3	28 49S	144 36E
GERMANY	20/21			
Gerona Spain	25	G4	41 59N	2 49E
Getafe Spain	24	D4	40 18N	3 44W
Gettysburg USA	71	C1	39 50N	77 16W
Ghadamis Libya	54	C5	30 08N	9 30E
GHANA	55	B2		
Ghanzi Botswana	60	C2	21 42S	21 39E
Gharyan Libya	56	A5	32 10N	13 01E
Ghat Libya	54	D4	24 58N	10 11E
Ghazni Afghanistan	39	E3	33 33N	68 26E
Gibraltar territory UK	24	C2	36 09N	5 21W
Gien France	22	E4	47 41N	2 37E

Place	Page	Grid	Lat.	Long.
Gifu Japan	45	C2	35 27N	136 46E
Gijón Spain	24	C5	43 32N	5 40W
Gilgit Jammu and Kashmir	39	F3	35 54N	74 20E
Gillette USA	68	E5	44 18N	105 30W
Gillingham UK	15	D2	51 02N	2 17W
Girvan UK	13	A2	55 15N	4 51W
Gisborne New Zealand	92	D3	38 40S	178 01E
Gladstone Australia	91	E3	23 52S	151 16E
Glasgow UK	13	B1	55 53N	4 15W
Glenrothes UK	13	C2	56 12N	3 10W
Gliwice Poland	21	H4	50 20N	18 40E
Głogów Poland	21	G4	51 40N	16 06E
Gloucester Canada	71	C3	45 16N	75 39W
Gloucester UK	15	B2	51 53N	2 14W
Gniezno Poland	21	G5	52 32N	17 32E
Gobi Desert Mongolia	42/43	C4/D4	48 30N	100 00E
Godhra India	40	B4	22 49N	73 40E
Gödöllő Hungary	21	H2	47 36N	19 20E
Goiânia Brazil	83	E1	16 43S	49 18W
Goiás Brazil	83	D1	15 57S	50 07W
Gold Coast tn. Australia	91	E3	27 59S	153 22E
Golmud China	42	C3	36 22N	94 55E
Good Hope, Cape of RSA	60	B1	34 30S	19 00E
Goodland USA	68	F4	39 20N	101 43W
Gorakhpur India	40	D5	26 45N	83 23E
Gore Ethiopia	57	C2	8 10N	35 29E
Gorey RoI	12	C2	52 40N	6 18W
Gore New Zealand	93	B1	46 06S	168 56E
Gorgān Iran	39	D3	36 50N	54 29E
Gorizia Italy	26	D6	45 57N	13 37E
Görlitz Germany	21	F4	51 09N	15 00E
Gort RoI	12	B2	53 04N	8 50W
Gorzów Wielkopolski Poland	21	F5	52 42N	15 12E
Gostivar FYROM	28	C4	41 47N	20 55E
Göteborg Sweden	17	C2	57 45N	12 00E
Gotha Germany	20	D4	50 57N	10 43E
Göttingen Germany	20	C4	51 32N	9 57E
Gouda Netherlands	18	D5	52 00N	4 42E
Governador Valadares Brazil	84	E5	18 51S	41 57W
Grafton Australia	91	E3	29 40S	152 56E
Grahamstown RSA	60	C1	33 18S	26 32E
Grampian Mountains UK	13	B2/C2	56 45N	4 00W
Granada Nicaragua	76	B2	11 58N	85 59W
Granada Spain	24	D2	37 10N	3 35W
Grande Prairie tn. Canada	66	G3	55 10N	118 52W
Grand Forks USA	69	G6	47 57N	97 05W
Grand Junction tn. USA	68	E4	39 04N	108 33W
Grand Rapids tn. Canada	66	J3	53 12N	99 19W
Grangemouth UK	13	C2	56 01N	3 44W
Grantham UK	15	C3	52 55N	0 39W
Grasse France	23	G2	43 40N	5 56E
Grayling USA	70	B2	44 40N	84 43W
Graz Austria	21	F2	47 05N	15 22E
Great Dividing Range mts. Australia	91	D2/D4	35 00S	148 00E
Great Falls tn. USA	68	D6	47 30N	111 16W
Great Yarmouth UK	15	D3	52 37N	1 44E
GREECE	29			
Greeley USA	68	F5	40 26N	104 43W
GREENLAND	67	M5/S4		
Greenock UK	13	B1	55 57N	4 45W
Greensboro USA	69	L4	36 03N	79 50W
Greenville USA	69	K3	34 52N	82 25W
GRENADA	77	G2		
Grenoble France	23	F3	45 11N	5 43E
Greymouth New Zealand	93	B2	42 27S	171 12E
Grimsby UK	14	C3	53 35N	0 05W
Groningen Netherlands	18	F6	53 13N	6 35E
Grootfontein Namibia	60	B3	19 32S	18 05E
Groznyy Russia	36	E2	43 21N	45 42E
Guadalajara Mexico	74	D3	20 40N	103 20W
Guadalajara Spain	24	D4	40 37N	3 10W
GUAM	96	D5		
Guangzhou China	43	E2	23 08N	113 20E
Guantánamo Cuba	77	D4	20 09N	75 14W
Guarapuava Brazil	84	D4	25 22S	51 28W
Guarda Portugal	24	B4	40 32N	7 17W
GUATEMALA	76	A3/B2		
Guatemala City Guatemala	76	A2	14 38N	90 22W
Guayaquil Ecuador	82	A2	2 13S	79 54W
Guaymas Mexico	74	B4	27 59N	110 54W
Guelph Canada	70	B2	43 34N	80 16
Guernsey i. Channel Islands	11	E1	46 27N	2 35
Guildford UK	15	C2	51 14N	0 35
Guilin China	43	E2	25 21N	110 1
GUINEA	55	A3/B2		
GUINEA-BISSAU	55	A3		
Güines Cuba	76	C4	22 50N	82 02
Guise France	19	C2	49 54N	3 3
Guiyang China	43	D2	26 35N	106 4
Gujranwala Pakistan	39	F3	32 06N	74 1
Gujrat Pakistan	40	B6	32 35N	74 0
Gulf, The Middle East	38/39	C2/D2	27 20N	51 0
Güstrow Germany	20	E5	53 48N	12 1
Guthrie USA	68	G4	35 53N	97 26
Guwahati India	40	F5	26 10N	91 4
GUYANA	82	D3		
Gwalior India	40	C5	26 12N	78 0
Gweru Zimbabwe	61	C3	19 27S	29 4
Gyangze China	40	E5	28 52N	89 3
Gympie Australia	91	E3	26 10S	152 3
Gyöngyös Hungary	21	H2	47 46N	20 0
Győr Hungary	21	G2	47 41N	17 4
Gyumri Armenia	31	F3	40 47N	43 5

H

Place	Page	Grid	Lat.	Long.
Haarlem Netherlands	18	D5	52 23N	4 3
Habbān Yemen	38	C1	14 21N	47 0
Haboro Japan	44	D3	44 23N	141 4
Hachinohe Japan	44	D3	40 30N	141 3
Haddington UK	13	C1	55 58N	2 4
Hadīboh Yemen	39	D1	12 36N	53 5
Haeju North Korea	43	F3	38 04N	125 4
Ha Giang Vietnam	48	C4	22 50N	105 0
Haifa Israel	38	B3	32 49N	34 5
Haikou China	43	E1	20 00N	110 2
Hā'il Saudi Arabia	38	C2	27 31N	41 4
Hailar China	43	E4	49 15N	119 4
Hai Phong Vietnam	48	D4	20 50N	106 4
HAITI	77	E3		
Hakodate Japan	44	D3	41 46N	140 4
Halifax UK	14	C3	53 44N	1 52
Halifax Canada	67	M2	44 38N	63 35
Halls Creek tn. Australia	90	B4	18 17S	127 3
Halmstad Sweden	17	C2	56 41N	12 5
Hamada Japan	45	B1	34 56N	132 0
Hamadān Iran	38	C3	34 46N	48 3
Hamah Syria	31	E2	35 10N	36 4
Hamamatsu Japan	45	C1	34 42N	137 4
Hamar Norway	17	C3	60 57N	10 5
Hamburg Germany	20	D5	53 33N	10 0
Hamhung North Korea	43	F3	39 54N	127 3
Hami China	42	C4	42 37N	93 3
Hamilton Canada	70	C2	43 15N	79 5
Hamilton New Zealand	92	C3	37 47S	175 1
Hamilton UK	13	C1	55 47N	4 03
Hamilton USA	70	B1	39 23N	84 33
Hamm Germany	20	B4	51 40N	7 4
Hammerfest Norway	16	E5	70 40N	23 4
Hampton USA	69	L4	37 02N	76 23
Hangzhou China	43	F3	30 18N	120 0
Hanna Canada	68	D7	51 38N	111 56
Hannover Germany	20	C5	52 23N	9 4
Hanoi Vietnam	48	D4	21 01N	105 5
Hanover Canada	70	B2	44 10N	81 03
Haora India	40	B2	22 35N	88 1
Happy Valley-Goose Bay tn. Canada	67	M3	53 15N	60 20
Haql Saudi Arabia	38	B2	29 14N	34 5
Harad Saudi Arabia	38	C2	24 12N	49 1
Harare Zimbabwe	61	D3	17 50S	31 0
Harbin China	43	F4	45 45N	126 4
Harbor Beach tn. USA	70	B2	43 51N	83 4
Harer Ethiopia	57	D2	9 20N	42 1
Hargeysa Somalia	57	D2	9 31N	44 0
Harlingen Netherlands	18	E6	53 10N	5 2
Harlow UK	15	D2	51 47N	0 0
Harrisburg USA	71	C2	40 17N	76 54
Harrisville USA	70	B2	44 41N	83 19
Harrogate UK	14	C3	54 00N	1 33
Hartford USA	71	D2	41 00N	72 0
Hartlepool UK	14	C4	54 41N	1 13

Name				
ᴧrwich UK	15	D2	51 57N	1 17E
ᴧssi Messaoud Algeria	54	C5	31 52N	5 43E
ᴧstings New Zealand	92	D3	39 39S	176 51E
ᴧstings UK	15	D2	50 51N	0 36E
ᴧ Tinh Vietnam	48	D3	18 18N	105 55E
ᴧttiesburg USA	69	J3	31 20N	89 19W
ᴧt Yai Thailand	49	C1	7 00N	100 25E
ᴧugesund Norway	17	B2	59 25N	5 16E
ᴧvana Cuba	76	C4	23 07N	82 25W
ᴧverfordwest UK	15	A2	51 49N	4 58W
ᴧvre USA	68	E6	48 34N	109 40W
ᴧwaiian Islands Pacific Ocean	96	F6	25 00N	166 00W
ᴧwera New Zealand	92	C3	39 35S	174 17E
ᴧwick UK	13	C1	55 25N	2 47W
ᴧy River tn. Canada	66	G4	60 51N	115 42W
ᴧchuan China	43	D3	30 02N	106 5E
ᴧfei China	43	E3	31 55N	117 18E
ᴧgang China	43	G4	47 36N	130 30E
ᴧidelberg Germany	20	C3	49 25N	8 42E
ᴧilbronn Germany	20	C3	49 08N	9 14E
ᴧkou China	43	D2	22 30N	104 00E
ᴧlena USA	68	D6	46 35N	112 00W
ᴧlmond Netherlands	18	E4	51 28N	5 40E
ᴧlmsdale UK	13	C3	58 07N	3 40W
ᴧlsingborg Sweden	17	C2	56 03N	12 43E
ᴧlsinki Finland	17	E3	60 08N	25 00E
ᴧmel Hempstead UK	15	C2	51 46N	0 28W
ᴧngelo Netherlands	18	F5	52 16N	6 46E
ᴧngyang China	43	E2	26 58N	112 31E
ᴧpu China	48	D4	21 38N	109 14E
ᴧrāt Afghanistan	39	E3	34 20N	62 12E
ᴧreford UK	15	B3	52 04N	2 43W
ᴧrmosillo Mexico	74	B4	29 15N	110 59W
ᴧrne Mexico	75	E3	24 16N	99 20W
ᴧgh Wycombe UK	15	C2	51 38N	0 46W
ᴧdesheim Germany	20	C5	52 09N	9 58E
ᴧllsboro USA	70	B1	39 12N	83 37W
ᴧmalaya mts. Asia	40	C6/E5	28 00N	85 00E
ᴧrosaki Japan	44	D3	40 34N	140 28E
ᴧroshima Japan	45	B1	34 23N	132 27E
ᴧsar India	40	C5	29 10N	75 45E
ᴧtachi Japan	45	D2	36 35N	140 40E
ᴧa Binh Vietnam	48	D4	20 49N	105 20E
ᴧobart Australia	91	D1	42 54S	147 18E
ᴧ Chi Minh Vietnam	49	D2	10 46N	106 43E
ᴧdeida Yemen	38	C1	14 50N	42 58E
ᴧof Germany	20	D4	50 19N	11 56E
ᴧfn Iceland	16	K6	64 16N	15 10W
ᴧfu China	45	B1	34 02N	131 34E
ᴧhhot China	43	E4	40 49N	111 37E
ᴧi An Vietnam	49	D3	15 52N	108 18E
ᴧkitika New Zealand	93	B2	42 43S	170 58E
ᴧkkaidō i. Japan	44	D3	43 30N	143 00E
ᴧlguín Cuba	76	D4	20 54N	76 15W
ᴧlyhead UK	14	A3	53 19N	4 38W
ᴧoms Syria	38	B3	34 42N	36 40E
ᴧomyel' Belarus	30	D5	52 25N	31 00E
ᴧONDURAS	76	B2/B3		
ᴧong Kong China	43	E2	23 00N	114 00E
ᴧoniton UK	15	B2	50 48N	3 13W
ᴧonshū i. Japan	44/45	B1/D3	37 15N	139 00E
ᴧoofdorp Netherlands	18	D5	52 18N	4 41E
ᴧorsham Australia	91	D2	36 45S	142 15E
ᴧospitalet Spain	25	G4	41 21N	2 06E
ᴧotan China	42	A3	37 07N	79 57E
ᴧoting Sweden	16	D3	64 08N	16 15E
ᴧouayxay Laos	48	C4	20 15N	100 29E
ᴧouston USA	69	G2	29 45N	95 25W
ᴧovd Mongolia	42	C4	48 00N	91 43E
ᴧradec Králové Czech Republic	21	F4	50 13N	15 50E
ᴧrodna Belarus	30	B5	53 40N	23 50E
ᴧua Hin Thailand	49	B2	12 33N	99 59E
ᴧuainan China	43	E3	32 41N	117 06E
ᴧuajuápan de León Mexico	75	E2	17 50N	97 48W
ᴧuambo Angola	60	B3	12 44S	15 47E
ᴧuancayo Peru	82	B1	12 05S	75 12W
ᴧuanuco Peru	82	B2	9 55S	76 11W
ᴧuddersfield UK	14	C3	53 39N	1 47W
Hudson Bay Canada	67	K3/K4	60 00N	89 00W
Huê Vietnam	49	D3	16 28N	107 35E
Huelva Spain	24	B2	37 15N	6 56W
Huesca Spain	25	E5	42 08N	0 25W
Huizhou China	43	E2	23 08N	114 28E
Hull Canada	71	C3	45 26N	75 45W
Humaitá Brazil	82	C2	7 33S	63 01W
Humboldt USA	72	D6	40 35N	118 16W
Hunedoara Romania	28	D6	45 45N	22 54E
Huntly New Zealand	92	C3	37 34S	175 10E
Huntly UK	13	C2	57 27N	2 47W
Huntsville USA	69	J3	34 44N	86 35W
Hurghada Egypt	56	C4	27 17N	33 47E
Huron, Lake Canada/USA	70	B2/B3	45 00N	83 00W
Hutchinson USA	68	G4	38 03N	97 56W
Hwange Zimbabwe	60	C3	18 22S	26 29E
Hyderabad India	41	C3	17 22N	78 26E
Hyderabad Pakistan	39	E2	25 23N	68 24E
I				
Ianca Romania	28	F6	45 06N	27 29E
Iasi Romania	28	F7	47 09N	27 38E
Ibadan Nigeria	55	C2	7 23N	3 56E
Ibagué Colombia	82	B3	4 25N	75 20W
Ibarra Ecuador	82	B3	0 23N	78 05W
Ibb Yemen	38	C1	14 03N	44 10E
Ibi Nigeria	55	C2	8 11N	9 44E
Ibiza i. Spain	25	F3	39 00N	1 20E
Ica Peru	82	B1	14 02S	75 48W
ICELAND	16	J7/L6		
Ichinomiya Japan	45	C2	35 18N	136 48E
Idaho Falls tn. USA	68	D5	43 30N	112 01W
Idfu Egypt	56	C4	24 58N	32 50E
Ieper Belgium	19	B3	50 51N	2 53E
Iguala Mexico	75	E2	18 21N	99 31W
Iguatu Brazil	83	F2	6 22S	39 20W
Iida Japan	45	C2	35 32N	137 48E
Ilagan Philippines	47	D4	17 07N	121 53E
Ilebo CDR	60	C4	4 20S	20 35E
Ilesa Nigeria	55	C2	7 39N	4 38E
Ilfracombe UK	15	A2	51 13N	4 08W
Ilhéus Brazil	83	F1	14 50S	39 06W
Iligan Philippines	47	D3	8 12N	124 13W
Iloilo Philippines	47	D4	10 41N	122 33E
Imi Ethiopia	57	D2	6 28N	42 10E
Imola Italy	26	C6	44 22N	11 43E
Imperatriz Brazil	83	E2	5 32S	47 28W
Imperia Italy	26	B5	43 53N	8 03E
Impfondo Congo	57	A2	1 36N	18 00E
Imphal India	40	F4	24 47N	93 55E
Inchon South Korea	43	F3	37 30N	126 38E
INDIA	40/41	A4/G4		
Indiana USA	71	C2	40 39N	79 11W
Indianapolis USA	70	A1	39 45N	86 10W
Indian Ocean	95			
INDONESIA	46/47	A3/F2		
Indore India	40	C4	22 42N	75 54E
Indus r. Pakistan	39	E2/F3	28 00N	69 00E
Ingolstadt Germany	20	D3	48 46N	11 27E
Inner Hebrides is. UK	13	A2	56 45N	6 45W
Innisfail Australia	91	D4	17 30S	146 00E
Innsbruck Austria	20	D2	47 17N	11 25E
Inongo CDR	60	B4	1 55S	18 20E
Inowroclaw Poland	21	H5	52 49N	18 12E
In Salah Algeria	54	C4	27 20N	2 03E
Interlaken Switzerland	23	G4	46 42N	7 52E
Inukjuak Canada	67	L3	58 40N	78 15W
Inuvik Canada	66	E4	68 16N	133 40W
Inveraray UK	13	B2	56 13N	5 05W
Invercargill New Zealand	93	B1	46 25S	168 22E
Invergarry UK	13	B2	57 02N	4 47W
Inverness UK	13	B2	57 27N	4 15W
Inverurie UK	13	C2	57 17N	2 23W
Ioánnina Greece	29	C3	39 40N	20 51E
Ipatinga Brazil	84	E5	19 32S	42 30W
Ipiales Colombia	82	B3	0 52N	77 38W
Ipoh Malaysia	46	B3	4 36N	101 05E
Ipswich UK	15	D3	52 04N	1 10E
Iqaluit Canada	67	M4	63 45N	68 30W
Iquique Chile	84	B4	20 15S	70 08W
Iquitos Peru	82	B2	3 51S	73 13W

© Oxford University Press

146 Index

Name	Page	Grid	Lat	Long
Iráklion Greece	29	E1	35 20N	25 08E
IRAN	38/39	C3/D3		
IRAQ	38	C3		
Irian Jaya admin. Indonesia	47	E2	3 00S	133 00E
Iringa Tanzania	61	D4	7 49S	35 39E
Irish Sea British Isles	11	D3	53 30N	5 30W
Irkutsk Russia	37	L3	52 18N	104 15E
Irrawaddy r. Myanmar	48	B3/B4	20 00N	95 00E
Irún Spain	25	E5	43 20N	1 48W
Irvine UK	13	A2	55 37N	4 40W
Irving USA	69	G3	32 49N	96 57W
Ise Japan	45	C1	34 29N	136 41E
Iseyin Nigeria	55	C2	7 59N	3 40E
Ishinomaki Japan	44	D2	38 25N	141 18E
Isiolo Kenya	59	E5	0 22N	37 38E
Isiro CDR	57	B2	2 50N	27 40E
Iskenderun Turkey	31	E2	36 37N	36 08E
Isla Grande de Tierra del Fuego i. Chile/Argentina				
	85	C1	54 00S	67 30W
Islamabad Pakistan	39	F3	33 40N	73 08E
Islas Galápagos i. Ecuador	97	K4	0 05S	90 00W
Isle of Man British Isles	14	A4	54 15N	4 15W
Isle of Wight UK	15	C2	50 40N	1 20W
Ismâ'îliya Egypt	56	C5	30 36N	32 16E
Isoka Zambia	61	D3	10 09S	32 39E
ISRAEL	38	B3		
Issoire France	22	E3	45 33N	3 15E
Istanbul Turkey	31	C3	41 02N	28 57E
Istres France	23	F2	43 30N	4 59E
Itabuna Brazil	83	F1	14 48S	39 18W
Itaituba Brazil	83	D2	4 15S	55 56W
Itajaí Brazil	84	E4	26 50S	48 39W
ITALY	26/27			
Itzehoe Germany	20	C5	53 56N	9 32E
Ivano-Frankivs'k Ukraine	30	B4	48 40N	24 40E
Ivanovo Russia	30	F6	57 00N	41 00E
Ivdel' Russia	36	G4	60 45N	60 30E
Ivujivik Canada	67	L4	62 25N	77 54W
Iwaki Japan	45	D2	37 03N	140 58E
Iwakuni Japan	45	B1	34 10N	132 09E
Iwamizawa Japan	44	D3	43 12N	141 47E
Ixtepec Mexico	75	E2	16 32N	95 10W
Izmayil Ukraine	28	G6	45 20N	28 48E
Izmir Turkey	31	C2	38 25N	27 10E

J

Name	Page	Grid	Lat	Long
Jabalpur India	40	C4	23 10N	79 59E
Jablonec Czech Republic	21	F4	50 44N	15 10E
Jackson USA	69	H3	32 20N	90 11W
Jacksonville USA	69	K3	30 20N	81 40W
Jacmel Haiti	77	E3	18 18N	72 32W
Jacobina Brazil	83	E1	11 13S	40 30W
Jaén Spain	24	D2	37 46N	3 48W
Jaffna Sri Lanka	41	D1	9 40N	80 01E
Jagdalpur India	41	D3	19 04N	82 05E
Jaipur India	40	C5	26 53N	75 50E
Jakarta Indonesia	46	B2	6 08S	106 45E
Jakobstad Finland	17	E3	63 40N	22 42E
Jalālābād Afghanistan	40	B6	34 26N	70 25E
Jalapa Enríquez Mexico	75	E2	19 32N	96 56W
Jalgaon India	41	C4	21 01N	75 39E
JAMAICA	76	D3		
Jamestown USA	68	G6	46 54N	98 42W
Jamiltepec Mexico	75	E2	16 18N	97 51W
Jammu India	40	B6	32 43N	74 54E
Jamnagar India	40	B4	22 28N	70 06E
Januária Brazil	84	E5	15 28S	44 23W
JAPAN	44/45	A1/E3		
Jāsk Iran	39	D2	25 40N	57 46E
Jaslo Poland	21	J3	49 45N	21 28E
Jasper Canada	68	C7	52 55N	118 05W
Jastrowie Poland	21	G5	53 25N	16 50E
Jaunpur India	40	D5	25 44N	82 41E
Jawa i. Indonesia	46	B2/C2	7 00S	110 00E
Jayapura Indonesia	47	F2	2 37S	140 39E
Jedburgh UK	13	C1	55 29N	2 34W
Jedda Saudi Arabia	38	B2	21 30N	39 10E
Jefferson City USA	69	H4	38 33N	92 10W
Jeffersonville USA	70	A1	38 16N	85 45W
Jelenia Góra Poland	21	F4	50 55N	15 45E
Jequié Brazil	83	E1	13 52S	40 06W
Jerez de la Frontera Spain	24	B2	36 41N	6 08
Jerez de los Caballeros Spain	24	B3	38 20N	6 45
Jersey i. Channel Islands	11	E1	49 13N	2 07
Jersey City USA	71	D2	40 44N	74 06
Jerusalem Israel/West Bank	38	B3	31 47N	35 1
Jhansi India	40	C5	25 27N	78 3
Jhelum Pakistan	40	B6	32 56N	73 4
Jiamusi China	43	G4	46 59N	130 2
Ji'an China	43	E2	27 08N	115 0
Jiangmen China	43	E2	22 40N	113 0
Jilin China	43	F4	43 53N	126 3
Jima Ethiopia	57	C2	7 39N	36 4
Jinan China	43	E3	36 41N	117 0
Jinhua China	43	E2	29 06N	119 44
Jining China	43	E4	40 58N	113 0
Jinja Uganda	58	C5	0 27N	33 1
Jinxi China	43	F4	40 46N	120 4
Jinzhou China	43	F4	41 07N	121 0
Jixi China	43	G4	45 17N	131 0
João Pessoa Brazil	83	F2	7 06S	34 53
Jodhpur India	40	B5	26 18N	73 0
Jōetsu Japan	45	C2	37 06N	138 1
Johannesburg RSA	60	C2	26 10S	28 0
John o'Groats UK	13	C3	58 38N	3 05
Johnson City USA	69	K4	36 20N	82 23
Johor Bahru Malaysia	46	B3	1 27N	103 48
Joinville Brazil	84	E4	26 20S	48 55
Jönköping Sweden	17	C2	57 45N	14 10
Joplin USA	69	H4	37 04N	94 31
JORDAN	38	B3		
Jos Nigeria	55	C2	9 54N	8 5
Juàzeiro Brazil	83	E2	9 25S	40 30
Juàzeiro do Norte Brazil	83	F2	7 10S	39 18
Juba Sudan	57	C2	4 50N	31 3
Juchitán Mexico	75	E2	16 27N	95 05
Juiz de Fora Brazil	84	E4	21 47S	43 23
Juliaca Peru	82	B1	15 29S	70 09
Juneau USA	66	E3	58 20N	134 20W
Jyväskylä Finland	17	F3	62 16N	25 5

K

Name	Page	Grid	Lat	Long
Kabale Uganda	58	A4	1 15S	29 5
Kābul Afghanistan	39	E3	34 30N	69 1
Kabwe Zambia	60	C3	14 29S	28 2
Kadoma Zimbabwe	61	C3	18 21S	29 5
Kaduna Nigeria	55	C3	10 28N	7 2
Kaesong North Korea	43	F3	37 59N	126 3
Kafue Zambia	60	C3	15 44S	28 1
Kagoshima Japan	45	B1	31 37N	130 3
Kaiserslautern Germany	20	B3	49 27N	7 4
Kalahari Desert Southern Africa				
	60	C2	23 30S	23 0
Kalamáta Greece	29	D2	37 02N	22 0
Kalémié CDR	61	C4	5 57S	29 1
Kalgoorlie Australia	90	B2	30 49S	121 2
Kaliningrad Russia	17	E1	54 40N	20 3
Kalispell USA	68	D6	48 12N	114 19
Kalmar Sweden	17	D2	56 39N	16 2
Kálymnos Greece	29	F2	36 57N	26 5
Kamaishi Japan	44	D2	39 18N	141 52
Kamensk-Shakhtinskiy Russia	30	F4	48 19N	40 16
Kamina CDR	60	C4	8 46S	25 0
Kamloops Canada	67	F3	50 39N	120 24
Kampala Uganda	58	C5	0 19N	32 3
Kamphaeng Phet Thailand	49	B3	16 27N	99 3
Kâmpóng Cham Cambodia	49	D2	11 59N	105 2
Kâmpóng Spoe Cambodia	49	C2	11 23N	104 3
Kampot Cambodia	49	C2	10 37N	104 1
Kananga CDR	60	C4	5 53S	22 2
Kanchanaburi Thailand	49	B2	13 59N	99 3
Kandahār Afghanistan	39	E3	31 35N	65 4
Kandi Benin	55	C3	11 05N	2 5
Kandla India	39	F2	23 03N	70 1
Kandy Sri Lanka	41	D1	7 17N	80 4
Kangān Iran	39	D2	27 51N	52 0
Kangar Malaysia	46	B3	6 27N	100 1
Kangnung South Korea	43	F3	37 48N	127 52
Kano Nigeria	55	C3	12 00N	8 3
Kanpur India	40	D5	26 27N	80 14
Kansas City USA	69	H4	39 02N	94 33W
Kansk Russia	37	K3	56 11N	95 48

Place	Page	Grid	Lat	Long
Kaohsiung Taiwan	**43**	F2	22 36N	120 17E
Kaolack Senegal	**55**	A3	14 09N	16 08W
Kaposvár Hungary	**21**	G2	46 21N	17 49E
Kapsabet Kenya	**58**	D5	0 10N	35 07E
Kapuskasing Canada	**67**	K2	49 25N	82 26W
Karachi Pakistan	**39**	E2	24 51N	67 02E
Karbalā' Iraq	**38**	C3	32 37N	44 03E
Karlovac Croatia	**26**	E6	45 30N	15 34E
Karlovy Vary Czech Republic	**20**	E4	50 13N	12 52E
Karlsruhe Germany	**20**	C3	49 00N	8 24E
Karlstad Sweden	**17**	C2	59 24N	13 32E
Karshi Uzbekistan	**39**	E3	38 52N	65 48E
Karwar India	**41**	B2	14 50N	74 09E
Kasese Uganda	**58**	B5	0 10N	30 06E
Kāshān Iran	**38**	D3	33 59N	51 35E
Kashi China	**42**	A3	39 29N	76 02E
Kashiwazaki Japan	**45**	C2	37 22N	138 33E
Kassala Sudan	**57**	C3	15 24N	36 30E
Kassel Germany	**20**	C4	51 18N	9 30E
Kastoriá Greece	**29**	C4	40 33N	21 15E
Kasur Pakistan	**40**	B6	31 07N	74 30E
Katerini Greece	**29**	D4	40 15N	22 30E
Katha Myanmar	**48**	B4	24 11N	96 20E
Katherine Australia	**90**	C4	14 29S	132 20E
Kathmandu Nepal	**40**	E5	27 42N	85 19E
Katowice Poland	**21**	H4	50 15N	18 59E
Katsina Nigeria	**55**	C3	13 00N	7 32E
Kaunas Lithuania	**17**	E1	54 52N	23 55E
Kavaratti India	**41**	B2	10 33N	72 39E
Kawagoe Japan	**45**	C2	35 55N	139 30E
Kawasaki Japan	**45**	C2	35 30N	139 45E
Kawerau New Zealand	**92**	D3	38 05S	176 42E
Kayseri Turkey	**31**	E2	38 42N	35 28E
Kazach'ye Russia	**37**	P5	70 46N	136 15E
KAZAKHSTAN	**36**	E2/J2		
Kazan' Russia	**36**	E3	55 45N	49 10E
Kearney USA	**68**	G5	40 42N	99 04W
Kecskemét Hungary	**21**	H2	46 56N	19 43E
Kediri Indonesia	**46**	C2	7 45S	112 01E
Keflavik Iceland	**16**	J6	64 01N	22 35W
Kells Rol	**12**	C2	53 44N	6 53W
Kelowna Canada	**66**	G2	49 50N	119 29W
Kelsey Bay tn. Canada	**67**	A7	50 22N	125 29W
Kemi Finland	**16**	E4	65 46N	24 34E
Kempten Germany	**20**	D2	47 44N	10 19E
Kenai USA	**66**	C4	60 35N	151 19W
Kendal UK	**14**	B4	54 20N	2 45W
Kendari Indonesia	**47**	D2	3 57S	122 36E
Keningau Malaysia	**46**	C3	5 21N	116 11E
Kénitra Morocco	**54**	B5	34 20N	6 34W
Kenmare Rol	**12**	B1	51 53N	8 57W
Kenora Canada	**67**	J2	49 47N	94 26W
Kenton USA	**70**	B2	40 38N	83 38W
KENYA	**58/59**	D5/G5		
Kenya, Mount Kenya	**59**	E4	0 08S	37 18E
Kerch' Ukraine	**31**	E4	45 22N	36 27E
Kermān Iran	**39**	D3	30 18N	57 05E
Kermānshāh Iran	**38**	C3	34 19N	47 04E
Ketapang Indonesia	**46**	C2	1 50S	110 00E
Ketrzyn Poland	**21**	J6	54 05N	21 24E
Kettering UK	**15**	C3	52 24N	0 44W
Key West USA	**69**	K1	24 34N	81 48W
Khammam India	**41**	D3	17 15N	80 11E
Khandwa India	**40**	C4	21 49N	76 23E
Kharagpur India	**40**	E4	22 23N	87 22E
Kharan Pakistan	**39**	E2	28 32N	65 26E
Kharkiv Ukraine	**30**	E4	50 00N	36 15E
Khartoum Sudan	**57**	C3	15 33N	32 35E
Khāsh Iran	**39**	E2	28 14N	61 15E
Khatanga Russia	**37**	L5	71 59N	102 31E
Khemisset Morocco	**54**	B5	33 50N	6 03W
Khemmarat Thailand	**49**	D3	16 00N	105 12E
Kherson Ukraine	**31**	D4	46 39N	32 38E
Khmel'nyts'kyy Ukraine	**30**	C4	49 25N	26 59E
Khon Kaen Thailand	**49**	C3	16 25N	102 50E
Khorog Tajikistan	**36**	G1	37 22N	71 32E
Khorramābād Iran	**38**	C3	33 29N	48 21E
Khulna Bangladesh	**40**	E4	22 49N	89 34E
Kibale Uganda	**58**	B5	0 47N	31 07E
Kibombo CDR	**60**	C4	3 58S	25 54E
Kibwezi Kenya	**59**	E3	2 25S	37 58E
Kidderminster UK	**15**	B3	52 23N	2 14W
Kiel Germany	**20**	D6	54 20N	10 08E
Kielce Poland	**21**	J4	50 51N	20 39E
Kiev Ukraine	**30**	D5	50 25N	30 30E
Kigali Rwanda	**58**	B4	1 56S	30 04E
Kigoma Tanzania	**58**	A2	4 52S	29 36E
Kikwit CDR	**60**	B4	5 02S	18 51E
Kildare Rol	**12**	C2	53 10N	6 55W
Kilimanjaro, Mount Tanzania	**59**	E3	3 04S	37 22E
Kilkee Rol	**12**	B2	52 41N	9 38W
Kilkenny Rol	**12**	C2	52 39N	7 15W
Kilkis Greece	**29**	D4	40 59N	22 52E
Killarney Rol	**12**	B2	52 03N	9 30W
Killeen USA	**68**	G3	31 08N	97 44W
Killimer Rol	**12**	B2	52 37N	9 24W
Kilmarnock UK	**13**	B1	55 36N	4 30W
Kilyos Turkey	**29**	G4	41 14N	29 02E
Kimberley RSA	**60**	C2	28 45S	24 46E
Kimchaek North Korea	**43**	F4	40 41N	129 12E
Kingman USA	**68**	D4	35 12N	114 02W
King's Lynn UK	**15**	D3	52 45N	0 24E
Kingston Canada	**71**	C2	44 14N	76 30W
Kingston Jamaica	**76**	D3	17 58N	76 48W
Kingston USA	**71**	D2	41 55N	74 00W
Kingston upon Hull UK	**14**	C3	53 45N	0 20W
Kingsville Canada	**70**	B2	42 02N	82 44W
Kinkala Congo	**60**	B4	4 18S	14 49E
Kinleith New Zealand	**92**	C3	38 15S	175 56E
Kinshasa CDR	**60**	B4	4 18S	15 18E
Kipili Tanzania	**61**	D4	7 30S	30 39E
KIRIBATI	**96/97**	E4/G4		
Kirikkale Turkey	**31**	D2	39 51N	33 32E
Kirkcaldy UK	**13**	C2	56 07N	3 10W
Kirkcudbright UK	**13**	B1	54 50N	4 03W
Kirkland Lake tn. Canada	**67**	K2	48 10N	80 02W
Kirkūk Iraq	**38**	C3	35 28N	44 26E
Kirkwall UK	**13**	C2	58 59N	2 58W
Kirov Russia	**36**	E3	58 00N	49 38E
Kirovohrad Ukraine	**30**	D4	48 31N	32 15E
Kiryū Japan	**45**	C2	36 26N	139 18E
Kisangani CDR	**57**	B2	0 33N	25 14E
Kismaayo Somalia	**57**	D1	0 25S	42 31E
Kisumu Kenya	**58**	D4	0 08S	34 47E
Kita-Kyūshu Japan	**45**	B1	33 52N	130 49E
Kitale Kenya	**58**	D5	1 01N	35 00E
Kitami Japan	**44**	D3	43 51N	143 54E
Kitchener Canada	**70**	B2	43 27N	80 30W
Kitgum Uganda	**58**	C6	3 19N	32 53E
Kitimat Canada	**67**	F3	54 05N	128 38W
Kitwe Zambia	**60**	C3	0 08S	30 30E
Kitzbühel Austria	**20**	E2	47 27N	12 23E
Klagenfurt Austria	**20**	F2	46 38N	14 20E
Klaipeda Lithuania	**17**	E2	55 43N	21 07E
Klamath Falls tn. USA	**68**	B5	42 14N	121 47W
Klerksdorp RSA	**60**	C2	26 52S	26 39E
Kleve Germany	**18**	F4	51 47N	6 08E
Knokke-Heist Belgium	**18**	C4	51 21N	3 19E
Knoxville USA	**69**	K4	36 00N	83 57W
Kōbe Japan	**45**	C1	34 40N	135 12E
Koblenz Germany	**20**	B4	50 21N	7 36E
Kobryn Belarus	**21**	L5	52 16N	24 22E
Kocaeli Turkey	**31**	C3	40 47N	29 55E
Kōchi Japan	**45**	B1	33 33N	133 32E
Kodiak USA	**66**	C3	57 49N	152 30W
Kōfu Japan	**45**	C2	35 42N	138 34E
Kohat Pakistan	**40**	B6	33 37N	71 30E
Kokkola Finland	**16**	E3	62 45N	30 06E
Kolhapur India	**41**	B3	16 40N	74 20E
Kolkata India	**40**	E4	22 30N	88 20E
Komatsu Japan	**45**	C2	36 25N	136 27E
Komotiní Greece	**29**	E4	41 06N	25 25E
Kongolo CDR	**60**	C4	5 20S	27 00E
Kongwa Tanzania	**59**	E1	6 12S	36 25E
Konin Poland	**21**	H5	52 12N	18 12E
Konstanz Germany	**20**	C2	47 40N	9 10E
Konya Turkey	**31**	D2	37 51N	32 30E
Koper Slovenia	**26**	D6	45 31N	13 44E
Korbach Germany	**20**	C4	51 16N	8 53E
Korçë Albania	**29**	C4	40 37N	20 47E
Kórinthos Greece	**29**	D2	37 56N	22 55E
Kōriyama Japan	**44**	D2	37 23N	140 22E

Place				
Koror Palau	47	E3	7 21N	134 28E
Korosten' Ukraine	30	C5	51 00N	28 30E
Kosciusko, Mount Australia	91	D2	36 28S	148 17E
Kosice Slovakia	21	J3	48 44N	21 15E
Kosovska Mitrovica SM	28	C5	42 54N	20 52E
Koszalin Poland	21	G6	54 10N	16 10E
Kota India	40	C5	25 11N	75 58E
Kota Bharu Malaysia	46	B3	6 08N	102 14E
Kota Kinabalu Malaysia	46	C3	5 59N	116 04E
Kotlas Russia	36	E4	61 15N	46 35E
Koudougou Burkina	55	B3	12 15N	2 23W
Koulikoro Mali	55	B3	12 55N	7 31W
Kouvola Finland	17	F3	60 54N	26 45E
Kovel' Ukraine	30	B5	51 12N	24 48E
Kovrov Russia	30	F6	56 23N	41 21E
Kozáni Greece	29	C4	40 18N	21 48E
Krâchéh Cambodia	49	D2	12 30N	106 03E
Kragujevac SM	28	C5	44 01N	20 55E
Kraków Poland	21	H4	50 03N	19 55E
Kranj Slovenia	26	E7	46 15N	14 20E
Krasnodar Russia	36	D2	45 02N	39 00E
Krasnovodsk Turkmenistan	36	F1	40 01N	53 00E
Krefeld Germany	20	B4	51 20N	6 32E
Krems Austria	21	F3	48 25N	15 36E
Kribi Cameroon	55	C2	2 56N	9 56E
Kristiansand Norway	17	B2	58 08N	8 01E
Kristianstad Sweden	17	C2	56 02N	14 10E
Kristiansund Norway	17	B3	63 06N	7 58E
Kríti i. Greece	29	E1	35 00N	25 00E
Krotoszyn Poland	21	G4	51 41N	17 27E
Kryvyy Rih Ukraine	30	D4	47 55N	33 24E
Kuala Lumpur Malaysia	46	B3	3 09N	101 42E
Kuching Malaysia	46	C3	1 35N	110 21E
Kugluktuk Canada	66	G4	67 49N	115 12W
Kumamoto Japan	45	B1	32 50N	130 42E
Kumi Uganda	58	C5	1 28N	33 55E
Kundat Malaysia	46	C3	6 54N	116 50E
Kunlun Shan mts. China	42	B3	36 30N	85 00E
Kunming China	42	D2	25 04N	102 41E
Kununurra Australia	90	B4	15 42S	128 50E
Kupang Indonesia	47	D1	10 13S	123 38E
Kurashiki Japan	45	B1	34 36N	133 43E
Kurgan Russia	36	G3	55 30N	65 20E
Kursk Russia	36	D3	51 45N	36 14E
Kushiro Japan	44	D3	42 58N	144 24E
Kuujjuaq Canada	67	M3	58 25N	68 55W
Kuusamo Finland	16	F4	65 57N	29 15E
Kuvango Angola	60	B3	14 27S	16 20E
KUWAIT	38	C2		
Kuwait Kuwait	38	C2	29 20N	48 00E
Kuytun China	42	B4	44 30N	85 00E
Kwangju South Korea	43	F3	35 07N	126 52E
Kyōto Japan	45	C2	35 02N	135 45E
KYRGYZSTAN	36	H2		
Kyūshū i. Japan	45	B1	32 20N	131 00E
Kyzyl Russia	37	K3	51 45N	94 28E
Kyzylorda Kazakhstan	36	G2	44 25N	65 28E
L				
La Asunción Venezuela	77	G2	11 02N	63 51W
Laâyoune Western Sahara	54	A4	27 10N	13 11W
Labé Guinea	55	A3	11 17N	12 11W
Labrador City Canada	67	M3	52 54N	66 50W
La Crosse USA	69	H5	43 48N	91 04W
Ladysmith Canada	68	B6	48 57N	123 50W
Ladysmith RSA	60	C2	28 34S	29 47E
Lafayette USA	69	H3	30 12N	92 18W
Lago de Maracaibo l. Venezuela	82	B3/B4	9 50N	71 30W
Lagos Nigeria	55	C2	6 27N	3 28E
Lagos Portugal	24	A2	37 05N	8 40W
Lago Titicaca l. Peru/Bolivia	82	B1/C1	16 00S	69 30W
La Grande USA	68	C6	45 21N	118 05W
Lagunillas Venezuela	82	B4	10 07N	71 16W
Lahore Pakistan	39	F3	31 34N	74 22E
Lake Charles tn. USA	69	H3	30 13N	93 13W
La Línea de la Concepción Spain	24	C2	36 10N	5 21W
Lalitpur India	40	C4	24 42N	78 24E
La Maddalena Italy	27	B4	41 13N	9 25E
Lamar USA	68	F4	38 04N	102 37W
Lamego Portugal	24	B4	41 05N	7 49W
Lamía Greece	29	D3	38 55N	22 26E
Lampang Thailand	48	B3	18 16N	99 30E
Lamu Kenya	59	G3	2 17S	40 54E
Lancaster UK	14	B4	54 03N	2 48W
Langon France	22	C3	44 33N	0 14W
Langres France	23	F4	47 53N	5 20E
Lang Son Vietnam	48	D4	21 48N	106 47E
Lannion France	22	B5	48 44N	3 27W
Lansing USA	70	B2	42 44N	85 34W
Lanzhou China	43	D3	36 01N	103 45E
Laoag Philippines	47	D4	18 14N	120 36E
Lao Cai Vietnam	48	C4	22 30N	103 57E
LAOS	48/49	C4/D2		
La Paz Bolivia	84	C5	16 30S	68 10W
La Paz Mexico	74	B3	24 10N	110 17W
La Plata Argentina	84	D3	34 52S	57 55W
Lapua Finland	17	E3	62 57N	23 00E
Laramie USA	68	E5	41 20N	105 38W
Laredo USA	68	G2	27 32N	99 22W
La Rioja Argentina	84	C4	29 26S	66 50W
Lárisa Greece	29	D3	39 38N	22 25E
Larnaca Cyprus	31	D1	34 54N	33 29E
Larne UK	12	D3	54 51N	5 49W
la Rochelle France	22	C4	46 10N	1 10W
Las Cruces USA	68	E3	32 18N	106 47W
Las Palmas Canary Islands	54	A4	28 08N	15 27W
La Spézia Italy	26	B6	44 07N	9 48E
Las Vegas USA	73	F4	36 10N	115 10W
Latakia Syria	38	B3	35 31N	35 47E
LATVIA	17	E2/F2		
Launceston Australia	91	D1	41 25S	147 07E
Laurel USA	69	J3	31 41N	89 09W
Lausanne Switzerland	23	G4	46 32N	6 39E
Laval France	22	C5	48 04N	0 45W
Laverton Australia	90	B3	28 49S	122 25E
La Victoria Venezuela	77	F2	10 16N	67 21W
Lawrence USA	71	D2	42 16N	71 12W
Lawton USA	68	G3	34 36N	98 25W
Laylá Saudi Arabia	38	C2	22 16N	46 45E
Laytonville USA	72	B5	39 41N	123 29W
LEBANON	38	B3		
Lebu Chile	85	B3	37 38S	73 43W
Lecce Italy	27	G4	40 21N	18 11E
Leeds UK	14	C3	53 50N	1 35W
Leer Germany	20	B5	53 15N	7 28E
Leganés Spain	24	D4	40 20N	3 46W
Leh India	40	C6	34 09N	77 36E
le Havre France	22	D5	49 30N	0 06E
Leicester UK	15	C3	52 38N	1 05W
Leiden Netherlands	18	D5	52 10N	4 30E
Leipzig Germany	20	E4	51 20N	12 25E
Leiria Portugal	24	A3	39 45N	8 49W
le Mans France	22	D4	48 00N	0 12E
Leninogorsk Kazakhstan	36	J3	50 23N	83 32E
Lens France	22	E6	50 26N	2 50E
Lensk Russia	37	M4	60 48N	114 55E
León Mexico	74	D3	21 10N	101 42W
León Nicaragua	76	B2	12 24N	86 52W
León Spain	24	C5	42 35N	5 34W
le Puy France	23	E3	45 03N	3 53E
Lerwick UK	13	C1	60 09N	1 09W
Leskovac SM	28	C5	43 00N	21 57E
LESOTHO	60	C2		
Lesser Antilles is. West Indies	77	F2/G3	18 00N	65 00W
Leszno Poland	21	G4	51 51N	16 35E
Lethbridge Canada	66	G2	49 43N	112 48W
le Touquet-Paris-Plage France	15	D2	50 13N	1 36E
le Tréport France	22	D6	50 04N	1 22E
Letterkenny RoI	12	C3	54 57N	7 44W
Levanto Italy	26	B6	44 10N	9 37E
Lewes USA	71	C1	38 47N	75 09W
Lewistown USA	68	E6	47 04N	109 26W
Lexington USA	70	B1	38 03N	84 30W
Lhasa China	42	C2	29 41N	91 10E
Lhaze China	42	B2	29 08N	87 43E
Libenge CDR	57	A2	3 39N	18 39E
Liberec Czech Republic	21	F4	50 48N	15 05E
LIBERIA	55	A2/B2		
Liberty USA	71	D2	41 47N	74 46W
Libourne France	22	C3	44 55N	0 14W

Name				
▪reville Gabon	55	C2	0 30N	9 25E
BYA	56	A4/B4		
▪da Belarus	30	C5	53 50N	25 19E
ECHTENSTEIN	23	H4		
▪ge Belgium	19	E3	50 38N	5 35E
▪enz Austria	20	E2	46 51N	12 50E
▪epaja Latvia	17	E2	56 30N	21 00E
▪iang China	48	C5	26 54N	100 16E
▪kasi CDR	60	C3	10 58S	26 47E
▪le France	22	E6	50 39N	3 05E
▪lehammer Norway	17	C3	61 06N	10 27E
▪ongwe Malawi	61	D3	13 58S	33 49E
▪ma Peru	82	B1	12 04S	77 03W
▪massol Cyprus	31	D1	34 04N	33 03E
▪mburg Germany	20	C4	50 23N	8 04E
▪merick RoI	12	B2	52 04N	8 38W
▪moges France	22	D3	45 50N	1 15E
▪moux France	22	E2	43 03N	2 13E
▪nares Spain	24	D3	38 05N	3 38W
▪ncang China	48	C4	23 52N	100 07E
▪ncoln UK	14	C3	53 14N	0 33W
▪ncoln USA	69	G5	40 49N	96 41W
▪ngen Germany	20	B5	52 32N	7 19E
▪nhares Brazil	84	F5	19 22S	40 04W
▪nköping Sweden	17	D2	58 25N	15 35E
▪nsell Sweden	17	C3	62 10N	13 50E
▪nton USA	68	F6	46 17N	100 14W
▪nxia China	43	D3	35 31N	103 08E
▪nz Austria	20	F3	48 19N	14 18E
▪petsk Russia	30	E5	52 37N	39 36E
▪sbon Portugal	24	A3	38 44N	9 08W
▪sburn UK	12	C3	54 31N	6 03W
▪smore Australia	91	E3	28 48S	153 17E
▪stowel RoI	12	B2	52 27N	9 29W
▪thgow Australia	91	E2	33 30S	150 09E
THUANIA	17	E1/E2		
▪ttle Aden Yemen	38	C1	12 47N	44 55E
▪ttle Rock USA	69	H3	34 42N	92 17W
▪uzhou China	43	D2	24 17N	109 15E
▪verpool UK	14	B3	53 25N	2 55W
▪vingston UK	13	C1	55 53N	3 32W
▪vingstone Zambia	60	C3	17 52S	25 52E
▪vorno Italy	26	C5	43 33N	10 18E
▪wale Tanzania	61	D4	9 47S	38 00E
▪ubljana Slovenia	26	E7	46 04N	14 30E
▪andrindod Wells UK	15	B3	52 15N	3 23W
▪anelli UK	15	A2	51 42N	4 10W
▪anes Spain	24	C5	43 25N	4 45W
▪eida Spain	25	F4	41 37N	0 38E
▪ydminster Canada	66	H3	53 18N	110 00W
▪carno Switzerland	23	H4	46 10N	8 48E
▪chboisdale UK	13	A2	57 09N	7 19W
▪chgilphead UK	13	B2	56 03N	5 26W
▪chmaddy UK	13	A2	57 36N	7 08W
▪ckerbie UK	13	C1	55 07N	3 22W
▪dz Poland	21	H4	51 49N	19 28E
▪groño Spain	24	D5	42 28N	2 26W
▪ire r. France	22	C4	47 20N	1 20W
▪koja Nigeria	55	C2	7 49N	6 44E
▪mé Togo	55	C2	6 10N	1 21E
▪mela CDR	57	B1	2 19S	23 15E
▪mmel Belgium	18	E4	51 14N	5 19E
▪ndon Canada	70	B2	42 58N	81 15W
▪ndon UK	15	C2	51 30N	0 10W
▪ndonderry UK	12	C3	54 59N	7 19W
▪ndrina Brazil	84	D4	23 18S	51 13W
▪ngford RoI	12	C2	53 44N	7 47W
▪ngreach Australia	91	D3	23 30S	144 15E
▪nguyon France	23	F5	49 27N	5 36E
▪ngview USA	69	H3	32 20N	94 45W
▪ngwy France	23	F5	49 32N	5 46E
▪rain USA	70	B2	41 28N	82 11W
▪rca Spain	25	E2	37 40N	1 41W
▪rica Colombia	76	D1	9 13N	75 50W
▪rient France	22	B4	47 45N	3 21W
▪s Angeles USA	73	D3	34 00N	118 15W
▪s Mochis Mexico	74	C4	25 48N	109 00W
▪s Teques Venezuela	82	C4	10 25N	67 01W
▪uangphrabang Laos	48	C3	19 53N	102 10E
▪ubomo Congo	60	B4	4 09S	12 47E
▪udéac France	22	B5	48 11N	2 45W

Name				
Loughborough UK	15	C3	52 47N	1 11W
Lough Neagh l. UK	12	C3	54 35N	6 30W
Louisville USA	70	A1	38 13N	85 48W
Lourdes France	22	C2	43 06N	0 02W
Louth UK	14	D3	53 22N	0 01W
Lowestoft UK	15	D3	52 29N	1 45E
Łowicz Poland	21	H5	52 06N	19 55E
Lowville USA	71	C2	43 47N	75 30W
Loznica SM	28	B6	44 31N	19 14E
Luanda Angola	60	B4	8 50S	13 15E
Lubango Angola	60	B3	14 55S	13 30E
Lubbock USA	68	F3	33 35N	101 53W
Lübeck Germany	20	D5	53 52N	10 40E
Lublin Poland	21	K4	51 18N	22 31E
Lubumbashi CDR	60	C3	11 41S	27 29E
Lucca Italy	26	C5	43 50N	10 30E
Lucena Spain	24	C2	37 25N	4 29W
Lucknow India	40	D5	26 50N	80 54E
Lüderitz Namibia	60	B2	26 38S	15 10E
Ludhiana India	40	C6	30 56N	75 52E
Ludvika Sweden	17	D3	60 08N	15 14E
Ludwigshafen Germany	20	C3	49 29N	8 27E
Luena Angola	60	B3	11 47S	19 52E
Lugano Switzerland	23	H3	46 01N	8 57E
Lugo Spain	24	B5	43 00N	7 33W
Luhans'k Ukraine	30	E3	48 35N	39 20E
Łuków Poland	21	K4	51 57N	22 21E
Luleå Sweden	16	E4	65 35N	22 10E
Lumphat Cambodia	49	D2	13 30N	107 00E
Lund Sweden	17	C2	55 42N	13 10E
Lüneburg Germany	20	D5	53 15N	10 24E
Lunéville France	23	G5	48 35N	6 30E
Luoshan China	43	E3	31 12N	114 30E
Luoyang China	43	E3	34 47N	112 26E
Lupanshui China	48	C5	26 40N	104 48E
Lurgan UK	12	C3	54 28N	6 20W
Lusaka Zambia	60	C3	15 26S	28 20E
Lusambo CDR	60	C4	4 59S	23 26E
Luton UK	15	C2	51 53N	0 25W
Luts'k Ukraine	30	C4	50 42N	25 15E
Luuq Somalia	57	D2	2 52N	42 34E
LUXEMBOURG	19	E2/F2		
Luxembourg Luxembourg	19	F2	49 37N	6 08E
Luxor Egypt	56	C4	25 41N	32 24E
Luzern Switzerland	23	H4	47 03N	8 17E
Luzhou China	43	D2	28 55N	105 25E
Luziânia Brazil	83	E1	16 16S	47 57W
L'viv Ukraine	30	B4	49 50N	24 00E
Lynchburg USA	69	L4	37 24N	79 09W
Lynn Lake tn. Canada	66	H3	56 51N	101 01W
Lyons France	23	F3	45 46N	4 50E
Lyttelton New Zealand	93	C2	43 36S	172 42E

M

Name				
Ma'ān Jordan	38	B3	30 11N	35 43E
Maastricht Netherlands	19	E3	50 51N	5 42E
Mabalane Mozambique	61	D2	23 51S	32 38E
McAlester USA	69	G3	34 56N	95 46W
McAllen USA	68	G2	26 13N	98 15W
Macao China	43	E2	22 10N	113 40E
Macapá Brazil	83	D3	0 04N	51 04W
Macarata Italy	26	D5	43 18N	13 27E
Macclesfield UK	14	B3	53 16N	2 07W
Maceió Brazil	83	F2	9 40S	35 44W
Mackay Australia	91	D3	21 10S	149 10E
Mackinaw City USA	70	B3	45 47N	84 43W
McKinley, Mount USA	66	C4	62 02N	151 01W
Mâcon France	23	F4	46 18N	4 50E
Macon USA	69	K3	32 49N	83 37W
Macroom RoI	12	B1	51 54N	8 57W
MADAGASCAR	61	E2/E3		
Madeira Islands Portugal	54	A5	32 45N	17 00W
Madison USA	69	J5	43 04N	89 22W
Madiun Indonesia	46	C2	7 37S	111 33E
Madrid Spain	24	D4	40 25N	3 43W
Madurai India	41	C1	9 55N	78 07E
Maebashi Japan	45	C2	36 24N	139 04E
Mae Hong Son Thailand	48	B3	19 17N	97 58E
Mae Sot Thailand	49	B3	16 38N	98 36E
Magadan Russia	37	R3	59 38N	150 50E
Magadi Kenya	59	E4	1 52S	36 19E

Place	Page	Grid	Lat.	Long.
Magdeburg Germany	20	D5	52 08N	11 37E
Magnitogorsk Russia	36	F3	53 28N	59 06E
Magwe Myanmar	48	A4	20 08N	94 55E
Mahajanga Madagascar	61	E3	15 40S	46 20E
Mahilyow Belarus	30	D5	53 54N	30 20E
Mahón Spain	25	H3	39 54N	4 15E
Maidstone UK	15	D2	51 17N	0 32E
Mainz Germany	20	C3	50 00N	8 16E
Maiquetía Venezuela	77	F2	10 38N	66 59W
Maitland Australia	91	E2	32 33S	151 33E
Maji Ethiopia	57	C2	6 12N	35 32E
Makeni Sierra Leone	55	A2	8 57N	12 02W
Makhado RSA	61	C2	23 01S	29 43E
Makkovik Canada	67	N3	55 09N	59 10W
Makó Hungary	21	J2	46 11N	20 30E
Makokou Gabon	55	D2	0 38N	12 47E
Malabo Equatorial Guinea	55	C2	3 45N	8 48E
Málaga Spain	24	C2	36 43N	4 25W
Malatya Turkey	31	E2	38 22N	38 18E
MALAWI	61	D3		
MALAYSIA	46	B3/C3		
Malbork Poland	21	H6	54 02N	19 01E
MALDIVES	95	D5		
MALI	54/55	B3/B4		
Malindi Kenya	59	G3	3 14S	40 06E
Mallaig UK	13	B2	57 00N	5 50W
Mallorca i. Spain	25	G3	39 50N	2 30E
Mallow RoI	12	B2	52 08N	8 39W
Malmédy Belgium	19	F3	50 26N	6 02E
Malmesbury RSA	60	B1	33 28S	18 43E
Malmö Sweden	17	C2	55 35N	13 00E
MALTA	27	E1/E2		
Mambasa CDR	57	B2	1 20N	29 05E
Manacor Spain	25	G3	39 35N	3 12E
Managua Nicaragua	76	B2	12 06N	86 18W
Manama Bahrain	38	D2	26 12N	50 38E
Manaus Brazil	82	D2	3 06S	60 00W
Manchester UK	14	B3	53 30N	2 15W
Manchester USA	71	D2	42 59N	71 28W
Mandal Norway	17	B2	58 02N	7 30E
Mandalay Myanmar	48	B4	21 57N	96 04E
Mangalia Romania	28	G5	43 48N	28 36E
Mangalore India	41	B2	12 54N	74 51E
Mangui China	43	F5	52 05N	122 17E
Manhattan USA	71	D2	40 48N	73 58W
Manica Mozambique	61	D3	18 56S	32 52E
Manicoré Brazil	82	C2	5 48S	61 16W
Manicouagan Canada	69	N7	50 40N	68 45W
Manila Philippines	47	D4	14 37N	120 58E
Manistique USA	70	A3	45 58N	86 17W
Manitowoc USA	70	A2	44 04N	87 40W
Manizales Colombia	82	B3	5 03N	75 32W
Mannheim Germany	20	C3	49 30N	8 28E
Mansa Zambia	60	C3	11 10S	28 52E
Mansfield USA	70	B2	40 46N	82 31W
Manta Ecuador	82	A2	0 59S	80 44W
Mantua Italy	26	C6	45 10N	10 47E
Manukau New Zealand	92	C3	37 00S	174 52E
Manzanares Spain	24	D3	39 00N	3 23W
Manzanillo Mexico	74	D2	19 00N	104 20W
Manzhouli China	43	E4	46 36N	117 28E
Maoming China	43	E2	21 50N	110 56E
Mapi Indonesia	47	E2	7 06S	139 23E
Maputo Mozambique	61	D2	25 58S	32 35E
Marabá Brazil	83	E2	5 23S	49 10W
Maracaibo Venezuela	82	B4	10 44N	71 37W
Maracay Venezuela	82	C4	10 20N	67 28W
Marbella Spain	24	C2	36 31N	4 53W
Margate UK	15	D2	51 24N	1 24E
Maribor Slovenia	26	E7	46 34N	15 38E
Mariehamn Finland	17	D3	60 05N	19 55E
Marietta USA	70	B1	39 26N	81 27W
Marijampole Lithuania	17	E1	54 31N	23 20E
Marilia Brazil	84	D4	22 13S	49 58W
Maringá Brazil	84	D4	23 26S	52 02W
Marion USA	70	B2	40 35N	83 08W
Mariscal Estigarribia Paraguay	84	C4	22 03S	60 35W
Mariupol' Ukraine	31	E4	47 05N	37 34E
Markovo Russia	37	T4	64 40N	170 24E
Marl Germany	18	G4	51 40N	7 06E
Marrakesh Morocco	54	B5	31 49N	8 00W
Marsabit Kenya	59	F6	2 20N	37 5?E
Marsala Italy	26	D2	37 48N	12 2?
Marseilles France	23	F2	43 18N	5 2?
MARSHALL ISLANDS	96	E5		
Martigny Switzerland	23	G4	46 07N	7 0?
Martinsville USA	70	A1	39 25N	86 25?
Marvejois France	22	E3	44 33N	3 1?
Maryborough Australia	91	E3	25 32S	152 3?
Marysville USA	72	C5	39 10N	121 34?
Masaka Uganda	58	B4	0 20S	31 4?
Masan South Korea	43	F3	35 10N	128 3?
Maseru Lesotho	60	C2	29 19S	27 2?
Mashhad Iran	39	D3	36 16N	59 3?
Masindi Uganda	58	B5	1 41N	31 4?
Massena USA	71	D2	44 56N	74 5?
Massif Central mts. France	22	E3	45 00N	3 3?
Masterton New Zealand	93	C2	40 57S	175 3?
Matadi CDR	60	B4	5 50S	13 3?
Matagami Canada	67	L2	49 45N	77 4?
Matamoros Mexico	75	E4	25 50N	97 3?
Mataram Indonesia	46	C2	8 36S	116 0?
Matehuala Mexico	74	D3	23 40N	100 4?
Matsumoto Japan	45	C2	36 18N	137 5?
Matsuyama Japan	45	B1	33 50N	132 4?
MAURITANIA	54/55	A3/B4		
MAURITIUS	95	C3/C4		
Mayen Germany	19	G3	50 19N	7 1?
Maykop Russia	31	F3	44 37N	40 4?
Mayo Canada	66	E4	63 34N	135 5?
Maysville USA	70	B1	38 38N	83 4?
Mazär-e Sharif Afghanistan	39	E1	36 42N	67 0?
Mazatlán Mexico	74	C3	23 11N	106 2?
Mbabane Swaziland	61	D2	26 20S	31 0?
Mbandaka CDR	57	A2	0 03N	18 2?
Mbeya Tanzania	61	D4	8 54S	33 2?
Mbuji-Mayi CDR	60	C4	6 10S	23 3?
Meadville USA	70	B2	41 38N	80 1?
Meaux France	22	E5	48 58N	2 5?
Mecca Saudi Arabia	38	B2	21 26N	39 4?
Medan Indonesia	46	A3	3 35N	98 3?
Medellín Colombia	82	B3	6 15N	75 3?
Medford USA	68	B5	42 20N	122 5?
Medias Romania	28	E7	46 10N	24 2?
Medicine Hat Canada	66	G3	50 03N	110 4?
Medina Saudi Arabia	38	B2	24 30N	39 3?
Medinipur India	40	E4	22 25N	87 2?
Mediterranean Sea	6/7		35 00N	15 0?
Meekatharra Australia	90	A3	26 30S	118 3?
Meerut India	40	C5	29 00N	77 4?
Mega Ethiopia	57	C2	4 02N	38 1?
Mekele Ethiopia	57	C3	13 32N	39 3?
Meknès Morocco	54	B5	33 53N	5 3?
Mekong r. Asia	48	C3	16 00N	105 0?
Melaka Malaysia	46	B3	2 11N	102 1?
Melbourne Australia	91	D2	37 45S	144 5?
Melbourne USA	69	K2	28 04N	80 3?
Melfort Canada	66	H3	52 52N	104 3?
Melilla territory Spain	24	D1	35 17N	2 5?
Melitopol' Ukraine	31	E4	46 51N	35 2?
Melville Canada	68	F7	50 57N	102 4?
Memmingen Germany	20	D2	47 59N	10 1?
Memphis USA	69	J4	35 10N	90 0?
Mendoza Argentina	84	C3	32 48S	68 5?
Menominee USA	70	A3	45 07N	87 3?
Menorca i. Spain	25	G4/H3	39 45N	4 1?
Merauke Indonesia	47	F2	8 30S	140 2?
Mercedes Argentina	84	C3	33 41S	65 2?
Mergui Myanmar	49	B2	12 26N	98 3?
Mérida Mexico	75	G3	20 59N	89 3?
Mérida Spain	24	B3	38 55N	6 2?
Mérida Venezuela	82	B3	8 24N	71 0?
Meridian USA	69	J3	32 21N	88 4?
Mersey r. UK	14	B3	53 20N	2 5?
Mersin Turkey	31	D2	36 47N	34 3?
Merthyr Tydfil UK	15	B2	51 46N	3 2?
Meru Kenya	59	E5	0 05N	37 3?
Mesa USA	68	D3	33 25N	115 5?
Mesquite USA	73	F4	36 48N	114 0?
Messina Italy	27	E3	38 13N	15 3?
Metković Bosnia-Herzegovina	26	F5	43 02N	17 3?
Metz France	23	G5	49 07N	6 1?

150 Index

Place	Page	Grid	Lat	Long
Mexicali Mexico	**74**	A5	32 36N	115 30W
MEXICO	**74/75**	A5/G3		
Mexico City Mexico	**75**	E2	19 25N	99 10W
Mexico, Gulf of Mexico	**75**	F3/G3	25 00N	90 00W
Mezen' Russia	**36**	E4	65 50N	44 20E
Miami USA	**69**	K2	25 45N	80 15W
Michigan City USA	**70**	A2	41 43N	86 54W
Michigan, Lake USA	**70**	A2/A3	44 00N	87 00W
Michipicoten Canada	**67**	K2	47 57N	84 55W
Middlesbrough UK	**14**	C4	54 35N	1 14W
Midland USA	**70**	B2	43 38N	84 14W
Midleton RoI	**12**	B1	51 55N	8 10W
Mikhaylovka Russia	**30**	F5	50 04N	43 15E
Milan Italy	**26**	B6	45 28N	9 12E
Milas Turkey	**29**	F2	37 19N	27 48E
Mildura Australia	**91**	D2	34 14S	142 13E
Miles City USA	**68**	E6	46 24N	105 48W
Milford Haven UK	**15**	A2	51 44N	5 02W
Milford Sound tn. New Zealand	**93**	A1	44 41S	167 56E
Milton Keynes UK	**15**	C3	52 02N	0 42W
Milwaukee USA	**70**	A2	43 03N	87 56W
Minamata Japan	**45**	B1	32 13N	130 23E
Minas Uruguay	**84**	D3	34 20S	55 15W
Minden Germany	**20**	C5	52 18N	8 54E
Minneapolis USA	**69**	H5	45 00N	93 15W
Minot USA	**68**	F6	48 16N	101 19W
Minsk Belarus	**30**	C5	53 51N	27 30E
Miram Shah Pakistan	**40**	B6	32 59N	70 07E
Miri Malaysia	**46**	C3	4 23N	114 00E
Mirpur Khas Pakistan	**40**	A5	25 33N	69 05E
Mirzapur India	**40**	D5	25 09N	82 34E
Misawa Japan	**44**	D3	40 42N	141 26E
Miskolc Hungary	**21**	J3	48 07N	20 47E
Misratah Libya	**56**	A5	32 23N	15 00E
Mississippi r. USA	**69**	H3	35 00N	90 00W
Missoula USA	**68**	D6	46 52N	114 00W
Missouri r. USA	**68**	G5	43 00N	98 00W
Mitchell USA	**68**	G5	43 40N	98 01W
Mito Japan	**45**	D2	36 22N	140 29E
Massawa Eritrea	**57**	C3	15 42N	39 25E
Miyako Japan	**44**	D2	39 38N	141 59E
Miyazaki Japan	**45**	B1	31 56N	131 27E
Mlawa Poland	**21**	J5	53 08N	20 20E
Mobaye CAR	**57**	B2	4 19N	21 11E
Mobile USA	**69**	J3	30 40N	88 05W
Moçambique Mozambique	**61**	E3	15 03S	40 45E
Módena Italy	**26**	C6	44 39N	10 55E
Modesto USA	**72**	C4	37 37N	121 00W
Mogadishu Somalia	**57**	D2	2 02N	45 21E
Mojave USA	**73**	D3	35 02N	118 11W
Mokau New Zealand	**92**	C3	38 42S	174 37E
Mokolo Cameroon	**55**	D3	10 49N	13 54E
Mokp'o South Korea	**43**	F3	34 50N	126 25E
MOLDOVA	**30/31**	C4		
Mombasa Kenya	**59**	F2	4 04S	39 40E
MONACO	**23**	G2		
Monaghan RoI	**12**	C3	54 15N	6 58W
Mönchengladbach Germany	**20**	B4	51 12N	6 25E
Monclova Mexico	**74**	D4	26 55N	101 25W
Mondovì Italy	**26**	A6	44 23N	7 49E
Móng Cai Vietnam	**48**	D4	21 30N	107 59E
MONGOLIA	**42/43**	C4/E4		
Mongu Zambia	**60**	C3	15 13S	23 09E
Monopoli Italy	**27**	F4	40 57N	17 18E
Monroe USA	**69**	H3	32 31N	92 06W
Monrovia Liberia	**55**	A2	6 20N	10 46W
Mons Belgium	**19**	C3	50 28N	3 58E
Montauban France	**22**	D3	44 01N	1 20E
Montbéliard France	**23**	G4	47 31N	6 48E
Mont Blanc mt. France/Italy	**23**	G3	45 50N	6 52E
Montdidier France	**19**	B2	49 39N	2 35E
Monte Carlo Monaco	**23**	G2	43 44N	7 25E
Montego Bay tn. Jamaica	**76**	D3	18 27N	77 56W
Montélimar France	**23**	F3	44 33N	4 45E
Montepulciano Italy	**26**	C5	43 05N	11 46E
Monterey USA	**73**	C4	36 35N	121 55W
Monterrey Mexico	**74**	D4	25 40N	100 20W
Montes Claros tn. Brazil	**84**	E5	16 45S	43 52W
Montevideo Uruguay	**84**	D3	34 55S	56 10W
Montgomery USA	**69**	J3	32 22N	86 20W
Montmagny Canada	**71**	D3	46 50N	70 33W
Montpellier France	**23**	E2	43 36N	3 53E
Montréal Canada	**71**	D3	45 32N	73 36W
Montreux Switzerland	**23**	G4	46 27N	6 55E
Montrose UK	**13**	C2	56 43N	2 29W
Monywa Myanmar	**48**	B4	22 05N	95 12E
Monza Italy	**26**	B6	45 35N	9 16E
Moora Australia	**90**	A2	30 40S	116 01E
Moorhead USA	**69**	G6	46 51N	96 44W
Moose Jaw Canada	**66**	H3	50 23N	105 35W
Moosonee Canada	**67**	K3	51 18N	80 39W
Mopti Mali	**55**	B3	14 29N	4 10W
Morecambe UK	**14**	B4	54 04N	2 53W
Moree Australia	**91**	D3	29 29S	149 53E
Mori Japan	**44**	D3	42 07N	140 33E
MOROCCO	**54**	A4/B5		
Morogoro Tanzania	**61**	D4	6 49S	37 40E
Morón Cuba	**76**	D4	22 08N	78 39W
Moroni Comoros	**61**	E3	11 40S	43 16E
Moroto Uganda	**58**	D6	2 32N	34 41E
Moscow Russia	**36**	D3	55 45N	37 42E
Moscow USA	**68**	C6	46 44N	117 00W
Moshi Tanzania	**59**	E3	3 21S	37 19E
Mostar Bosnia-Herzegovina	**26**	F5	43 20N	17 50E
Móstoles Spain	**24**	D4	40 19N	3 53W
Mosul Iraq	**38**	C3	36 21N	43 08E
Motherwell UK	**13**	C1	55 48N	3 59W
Moulins France	**22**	E4	47 00N	3 48E
Moulmein Myanmar	**49**	B3	16 30N	97 39E
Mount Cook tn. New Zealand	**93**	B2	43 44S	170 06E
Mount Gambier tn. Australia	**91**	D2	37 51S	140 50E
Mount Isa tn. Australia	**91**	C3	20 50S	139 29E
Mount Magnet tn. Australia	**90**	A3	28 06S	117 50E
Mount Pleasant tn. USA	**70**	B2	43 36N	84 46W
Mount Vernon tn. USA	**70**	B2	40 30N	82 30W
Moyale Ethiopia	**59**	F6	3 32N	39 04E
MOZAMBIQUE	**61**	D2/E3		
Mpanda Tanzania	**61**	D4	6 21S	31 01E
Mtwara Tanzania	**61**	E3	10 17S	40 11E
Mudanjiang China	**43**	F4	44 36N	129 42E
Mulhouse France	**23**	G4	47 45N	7 21E
Mullingar RoI	**12**	C2	53 32N	7 20W
Multan Pakistan	**39**	B3	30 10N	71 36E
Mumbai India	**41**	B3	18 56N	72 51E
Munich Germany	**20**	D3	48 08N	11 35E
Münster Germany	**20**	B4	51 58N	7 37E
Murchison New Zealand	**93**	C2	41 50S	172 20E
Murcia Spain	**25**	E2	37 59N	1 08W
Murmansk Russia	**36**	D4	68 59N	33 08E
Muroran Japan	**44**	D3	42 21N	140 59E
Muroto Japan	**45**	B1	33 13N	134 11E
Murray r. Australia	**91**	D2	35 30S	144 00E
Murupara New Zealand	**92**	D3	38 27S	176 42E
Murwara India	**40**	D4	23 49N	80 28E
Muscat Oman	**39**	D2	23 37N	58 38E
Mutare Zimbabwe	**61**	D3	18 58S	32 40E
Mutomo Kenya	**59**	F4	1 50S	38 15E
Mutsu Japan	**44**	D3	41 18N	141 15E
Muzaffarpur India	**40**	E5	26 07N	85 23E
Mwanza Tanzania	**58**	C3	2 31S	32 56E
Mwaya Tanzania	**61**	D4	9 33S	33 56E
Mwenga CDR	**58**	A3	3 03S	28 23E
MYANMAR	**48/49**	B2/B5		
Mykolayiv Ukraine	**31**	D4	46 57N	32 00E
Mysore India	**41**	C2	12 18N	76 37E
My Tho Vietnam	**49**	D2	10 21N	106 21E
Mytilíni Greece	**29**	F3	39 06N	26 34E
Mzuzu Malawi	**61**	D3	11 31S	34 00E

N

Naas RoI	**12**	C2	53 13N	6 39W
Naberezhnyye Chelny Russia	**30**	H6	55 42N	52 19E
Nadym Russia	**36**	H4	65 25N	72 40E
Naga Philippines	**47**	D4	13 36N	123 12E
Nagaon India	**40**	F5	26 20N	92 41E
Nagasaki Japan	**45**	A1	32 45N	129 52E
Nagato Japan	**45**	B1	34 22N	131 11E
Nagpur India	**41**	C4	21 10N	79 12E
Nairobi Kenya	**59**	E4	1 17S	36 50E
Nakamura Japan	**45**	B1	33 02N	132 58E
Nakatsu Japan	**45**	B1	33 37N	131 11E

© Oxford University Press

Name	Page	Grid	Lat	Long
Nakhodka Russia	37	P2	42 53N	132 54E
Nakhon Ratchasima Thailand	49	C2	14 59N	102 06E
Nakhon Si Thammarat Thailand	49	B1	8 24N	99 58E
Nakuru Kenya	59	E4	0 16S	36 05E
Nal'chik Russia	31	F3	43 31N	43 38E
Nam Dinh Vietnam	48	D4	20 25N	106 12E
NAMIBIA	60	B2		
Nampa USA	68	C5	43 35N	116 34W
Nampo North Korea	43	F3	38 51N	125 10E
Nampula Mozambique	61	D3	15 09S	39 14E
Nanaimo Canada	66	F2	49 08N	123 58W
Nanchang China	43	E2	28 33N	115 58E
Nancy France	23	G5	48 42N	6 12E
Nanjing China	43	E3	32 03N	118 47E
Nanning China	43	D2	22 50N	108 19E
Nanping China	43	E2	26 40N	118 07E
Nantes France	22	C4	47 14N	1 35W
Nantong China	43	F3	32 06N	121 04E
Nanyang China	43	E3	33 06N	112 31E
Nanyuki Kenya	59	E5	0 01N	37 05E
Napier New Zealand	92	D3	39 30S	176 54E
Naples Italy	27	E4	40 50N	14 15E
Narbonne France	22	E2	43 11N	3 00E
Narva Estonia	17	F2	59 22N	28 17E
Narvik Norway	16	D4	68 26N	17 25E
Nar'yan Mar Russia	36	F4	67 37N	53 02E
Nashik India	41	B4	20 00N	73 52E
Nashville USA	69	J4	36 10N	86 50W
Nassau Bahamas	76	D5	25 05N	77 20W
Nässjö Sweden	17	C2	57 40N	14 40E
Natal Brazil	83	F2	5 46S	35 15W
Natchez USA	69	H3	31 32N	91 24W
NAURU	96	E4		
Navan RoI	12	C2	53 39N	6 41W
Nazca Peru	82	B1	14 53S	74 54W
Ndélé CAR	57	B2	8 25N	20 38E
Ndjamena Chad	57	A3	12 10N	14 59E
Ndola Zambia	60	C3	13 00S	28 39E
Neath UK	15	B3	51 40N	3 48W
Nebitdag Turkmenistan	39	D3	39 31N	54 24E
Needles USA	73	F3	34 51N	114 36W
Neijiang China	43	D2	29 32N	105 03E
Neiva Colombia	82	B3	2 58N	75 15W
Nellore India	41	D2	14 29N	80 00E
Nelson Canada	68	C6	49 29N	117 17W
Nelson New Zealand	93	C2	41 16S	173 17E
Nemuro Japan	44	E3	43 22N	145 36E
Nenagh RoI	12	B2	52 52N	8 12W
Nenana USA	66	D4	64 35N	149 20W
Nenjiang China	43	F4	49 10N	125 15E
NEPAL	40	D5/E5		
Nerchinsk Russia	43	E5	52 02N	116 38E
NETHERLANDS	18/19			
Netzahualcóyotl Mexico	75	E2	19 24N	99 02W
Neubrandenburg Germany	20	E5	53 33N	13 16E
Neuchâtel Switzerland	23	G4	46 55N	6 56E
Neufchâteau Belgium	19	E2	49 51N	5 26E
Neustrelitz Germany	20	E5	53 22N	13 05E
Nevers France	22	E4	47 00N	3 09E
Newark USA	71	D2	40 44N	74 24W
Newbury UK	15	C2	51 25N	1 20W
Newcastle Australia	91	E2	32 55S	151 46E
Newcastle upon Tyne UK	14	C4	54 59N	1 35W
Newcastle West RoI	12	B2	52 27N	9 03W
New Delhi India	40	C5	28 37N	77 14E
Newfoundland i. Canada	67	N2	48 15N	57 00W
New Guinea i. Pacific Ocean	86/87		5 00S	141 00E
New Orleans USA	69	H2	30 00N	90 03W
New Plymouth New Zealand	92	C3	39 04S	174 04E
Newport UK	15	B2	51 35N	3 00W
Newport UK	15	C2	50 42N	1 18W
Newport News USA	69	L4	36 59N	76 26W
Newquay UK	15	A2	50 25N	4 43W
New Ross RoI	12	C2	52 24N	6 56W
Newry UK	12	C3	54 11N	6 20W
Newton Stewart UK	13	A2	54 57N	4 29W
Newtown UK	15	B3	52 32N	3 19W
Newtownabbey UK	12	D3	54 40N	5 54W
New Westminster Canada	68	B6	49 10N	122 58W
New York USA	71	D2	40 40N	73 50W
NEW ZEALAND	92/93			
Neyrīz Iran	39	D2	29 14N	54 18E
Neyshābūr Iran	39	D3	36 13N	58 49E
Ngaoundéré Cameroon	55	D2	7 19N	13 34E
Nguru Nigeria	55	D3	12 53N	10 30E
Nha Trang Vietnam	49	D2	12 15N	109 10E
Niagara Falls tn. Canada	71	C2	43 05N	79 06W
Niagara Falls tn. USA	71	C2	43 06N	79 04W
Niamey Niger	55	C3	13 32N	2 05E
NICARAGUA	76	B2/C2		
Nice France	23	G2	43 42N	7 16E
Nicosia Cyprus	31	D2	35 11N	33 23E
Nienburg Germany	20	C5	52 38N	9 13E
NIGER	54/55	C3/D4		
NIGERIA	55	C2/D3		
Niigata Japan	44	C2	37 58N	139 02E
Nikol'sk Russia	30	G6	59 32N	45 27E
Nikopol' Ukraine	30	D4	45 34N	34 25E
Niksic SM	28	B5	42 48N	18 56E
Nile r. Sudan/Egypt	56/57	C3/C4	27 30N	31 40E
Nîmes France	23	F2	43 50N	4 21E
Nimule Sudan	57	C2	3 35N	32 03E
Ningbo China	43	F2	29 54N	121 33E
Ninh Binh Vietnam	48	D4	20 14N	106 00E
Nis SM	28	C5	43 20N	21 54E
Nizhneangarsk Russia	37	L3	55 48N	109 35E
Nizhniy Novgorod Russia	36	E3	56 20N	44 00E
Nizhniy Tagil Russia	36	G3	58 00N	59 58E
Noatak USA	66	B4	67 33N	163 10W
Nome USA	66	B4	64 30N	165 30W
Nonthaburi Thailand	49	C2	13 48N	100 11E
Nordhausen Germany	20	D4	51 31N	10 48E
Nordvik Russia	37	M5	74 01N	111 30E
Norfolk USA	69	L4	36 54N	76 18W
Noril'sk Russia	36	J4	69 21N	88 02E
Normanton Australia	91	D4	17 40S	141 05E
Norman Wells tn. Canada	66	F4	65 19N	126 46W
Norrköping Sweden	17	D2	58 35N	16 10E
Northallerton UK	14	C4	54 20N	1 26W
Northam Australia	90	A2	31 40S	116 40E
Northampton Australia	90	A3	28 27S	114 37E
Northampton UK	15	C3	52 14N	0 54W
North Battleford Canada	66	H3	52 47N	108 17W
Northern Ireland country UK	12	C3/D3	54 40N	7 00W
NORTHERN MARIANAS	96	D5		
North Island New Zealand	92/93	C2/C4	39 00S	176 00E
NORTH KOREA	43	F3/F4		
North Platte USA	68	F5	41 09N	100 45W
North River tn. Canada	67	J3	58 55N	94 30W
North Sea Europe	6		61 00N	1 00E
Northwest Highlands UK	13	B2/B3	58 00N	5 00W
NORWAY	16/17	B2/G5		
Norwich UK	15	D3	52 38N	1 18E
Norwich USA	71	D2	41 32N	72 05W
Nottingham UK	15	C3	52 58N	1 10W
Nouadhibou Mauritania	54	A4	20 54N	17 01W
Nouakchott Mauritania	55	A3	18 09N	15 58W
Nova Iguaçu Brazil	84	E4	22 46S	43 23W
Novara Italy	26	B6	45 27N	8 37E
Novgorod Russia	36	D3	58 30N	31 20E
Novi Sad SM	28	B6	45 15N	19 51E
Novokuznetsk Russia	36	J3	53 45N	87 12E
Novorossiysk Russia	36	D2	44 44N	37 46E
Novosibirsk Russia	36	J3	55 04N	83 05E
Novvy Port Russia	36	H4	67 38N	72 33E
Nowy Sacz Poland	21	J3	49 39N	20 40E
Nuevo Laredo Mexico	75	E4	27 39N	99 30W
Nuneaton UK	15	C3	52 32N	1 28W
Nuremberg Germany	20	D3	49 27N	11 05E
Nutak Canada	67	M3	57 30N	61 59W
Nuuk Greenland	67	N4	64 10N	51 40W
Nyköping Sweden	17	D2	58 45N	17 03E

O

Oamaru New Zealand	93	B1	45 06S	170 58E
Oaxaca Mexico	75	E2	17 05N	96 41W
Oban UK	13	B2	56 25N	5 29W
Ocean City USA	71	C1	38 21N	75 06W
Ocotlán Mexico	74	D3	20 21N	102 42W
Ōda Japan	45	B2	35 10N	132 29E

Place	Page	Grid	Lat	Long
Odate Japan	44	D3	40 18N	140 32E
Odawara Japan	45	C2	35 15N	139 08E
Odense Denmark	17	C2	55 24N	10 25E
Odessa Ukraine	31	D4	46 30N	30 46E
Odessa USA	68	F3	31 50N	102 23W
Offenburg Germany	20	B3	48 29N	7 57E
Ōgaki Japan	45	C2	35 22N	136 36E
Ogbomoso Nigeria	55	C2	8 05N	4 11E
Ogden USA	68	D5	41 14N	111 59W
Ōhata Japan	44	D3	41 22N	141 11E
Ōita Japan	45	B1	33 15N	131 36E
Okayama Japan	45	B1	34 40N	133 54E
Okehampton UK	15	B2	50 44N	4 00W
Okhotsk Russia	37	Q3	59 20N	143 15E
Oklahoma City USA	68	G4	35 28N	97 33W
Oktyabr'skiy Russia	37	R3	52 43N	156 14E
Oldenburg Germany	20	C5	53 08N	8 13E
Oldenzaal Netherlands	18	F5	52 19N	6 55E
Oldham UK	14	B3	53 33N	2 07W
Olenek Russia	37	M4	68 28N	112 18E
Olsztyn Poland	21	J5	53 48N	20 29E
Olympia USA	68	B6	47 03N	122 53W
Omagh UK	12	C3	54 36N	7 18W
Omaha USA	68	G5	41 15N	96 00W
OMAN	39	D1/D2		
Omboué Gabon	55	C1	1 38S	9 20E
Omdurman Sudan	57	C3	15 37N	32 29E
Omsk Russia	36	H3	55 00N	73 22E
Ōmuta Japan	45	B1	33 02N	130 26E
Onesti Romania	28	F7	46 15N	26 45E
Onitsha Nigeria	55	C2	6 10N	6 47E
Ontario, Lake Canada/USA	70/71	C2	43 45N	78 00W
Oostende Belgium	18	B4	51 13N	2 55E
Opava Czech Republic	21	G3	49 58N	17 55E
Oporto Portugal	24	A4	41 09N	8 37W
Opotiki New Zealand	92	D3	38 01S	177 17E
Oradea Romania	28	C7	47 03N	21 55E
Oran Algeria	54	B5	35 45N	0 38W
Ordu Turkey	31	E3	41 00N	37 52E
Örebro Sweden	17	D2	59 17N	15 13E
Oregon City USA	68	B6	45 21N	122 36W
Orël Russia	36	D3	52 58N	36 04E
Orenburg Russia	36	F3	51 50N	55 00E
Orense Spain	24	B5	42 20N	7 52W
Orinoco r. Venezuela	82	C3	8 00N	64 00W
Oristano Italy	27	B3	39 54N	8 36E
Orkney Islands is. UK	13	C3	59 00N	3 00W
Orlando USA	69	K2	28 33N	81 21W
Orléans France	22	D4	47 54N	1 54E
Orsk Russia	36	F3	51 13N	58 35E
Orümiyeh Iran	38	C3	37 40N	45 00E
Oruro Bolivia	84	C5	17 59S	67 08W
Orvieto Italy	26	D5	42 43N	12 06E
Ōsaka Japan	45	C1	34 40N	135 30E
Osijek Croatia	26	G6	45 33N	18 41E
Oslo Norway	17	C2	59 56N	10 45E
Osnabrück Germany	20	C5	52 17N	8 03E
Östersund Sweden	17	C3	63 10N	14 40E
Östervall Sweden	17	D3	62 20N	15 20E
Ostrava Czech Republic	21	H3	49 50N	18 15E
Ostróda Poland	21	H5	53 42N	19 59E
Otaki New Zealand	93	C2	40 46S	175 09E
Otranto Italy	27	G4	40 08N	18 30E
Ōtsu Japan	45	C2	35 00N	135 50E
Ottawa Canada	71	C3	45 24N	75 38W
Ouagadougou Burkina	55	B3	12 20N	1 40W
Oudtshoorn RSA	60	C1	33 35S	22 12E
Oujda Morocco	54	B5	34 41N	1 45W
Oulu Finland	16	F4	65 02N	25 27E
Outer Hebrides is. UK	13	A2/A3	58 00N	7 00W
Oviedo Spain	24	C5	43 21N	7 18W
Owen Sound tn. Canada	70	B2	44 34N	80 56W
Oxford UK	15	C2	51 46N	1 15W
Oyama Japan	45	C2	36 18N	139 48E
Oyo Nigeria	55	C2	7 50N	3 55E
Ozero Balkhash l. Kazakhstan	36	H2	46 00N	75 00E
Ozero Baykal l. Russia	37	L3	54 00N	109 00E

P

Place	Page	Grid	Lat	Long
Pacific Ocean	96/97			
Padang Indonesia	46	B2	1 00S	100 21E

Place	Page	Grid	Lat	Long
Paderborn Germany	20	C4	51 43N	8 44E
Padua Italy	26	C6	45 24N	11 53E
Paducah USA	69	J4	37 03N	88 36W
Painesville USA	70	B2	41 43N	81 15W
Paisley UK	13	B1	55 50N	4 26W
PAKISTAN	39	E2/F3		
Pakxé Laos	49	D3	15 00N	105 55E
PALAU	47	E3	7 30N	134 30E
Palembang Indonesia	46	B2	2 59S	104 45E
Palencia Spain	24	C5	41 01N	4 32W
Palermo Italy	27	D3	38 08N	13 23E
Palma de Mallorca Spain	25	G3	39 35N	2 39E
Palmer USA	66	D4	61 35N	149 10W
Palmerston North New Zealand	92	C2	40 22S	175 37E
Palm Springs tn. USA	73	E2	33 49N	116 33W
Palu Indonesia	47	C2	0 54S	119 52E
Pamiers France	22	D2	43 07N	1 36E
Pamplona Spain	25	E5	42 49N	1 39W
PANAMA	76	C1/D1		
Panama Canal Panama	76	D1	9 00N	80 00W
Panama City Panama	76	D1	8 57N	19 30W
Pancevo SM	28	C6	44 52N	20 40E
Panevezys Lithuania	17	E2	55 44N	24 24E
Pangnirtung Canada	67	M4	66 05N	65 45W
PAPUA NEW GUINEA	88/89			
Paraburdoo Australia	90	A3	23 15S	117 45E
PARAGUAY	84	C4/D4		
Parakou Benin	55	C2	9 23N	2 40E
Paramaribo Suriname	83	D3	5 52N	55 14W
Paraná Argentina	84	C3	31 45S	60 30W
Paranaguá Brazil	84	E4	25 32S	48 36W
Pardubice Czech Republic	21	F4	50 03N	15 45E
Parepare Indonesia	46	C2	4 00S	119 40E
Parintins Brazil	83	D2	2 38S	56 45W
Paris France	22	E5	48 52N	2 20E
Parkano Finland	17	E3	62 03N	23 00E
Parker USA	73	F3	34 09N	114 17W
Parkersburg USA	70	B1	39 17N	81 33W
Parma Italy	26	C6	44 48N	10 19E
Parma USA	70	B2	41 24N	81 44W
Parnaíba Brazil	83	E2	2 58S	41 46W
Pärnu Estonia	17	E2	58 28N	24 30E
Páros Greece	29	E2	37 04N	25 06E
Pasadena USA	69	G2	29 42N	95 14W
Pascagoula USA	69	J3	30 21N	88 32W
Passau Germany	20	E3	48 35N	13 28E
Patna India	40	E5	25 37N	85 12E
Patras Greece	29	C2	38 14N	21 44E
Pattaya Thailand	49	C2	12 56N	100 57E
Pau France	22	C2	43 18N	0 22W
Pavlodar Kazakhstan	36	H3	52 21N	76 59E
Peace River tn. Canada	66	G3	56 15N	117 18W
Pecos USA	68	F3	30 00N	102 00W
Pécs Hungary	21	H2	46 04N	18 15E
Pedreiras Brazil	83	E2	4 32S	44 40W
Pegu Myanmar	48	B3	17 18N	96 31E
Pekanbaru Indonesia	46	B3	0 33N	101 30E
Pembroke Canada	71	C3	45 49N	77 08W
Pembroke UK	15	A2	51 41N	4 55W
Pendleton USA	68	C6	45 40N	118 46W
Penrith UK	14	B4	54 40N	2 44W
Pensacola USA	69	J3	30 26N	87 12W
Penticton Canada	66	G2	49 29N	119 38W
Penza Russia	36	E3	53 11N	45 00E
Penzance UK	15	A2	50 07N	5 33W
Peoria USA	69	J5	40 43N	89 38W
Périgeux France	22	D3	45 12N	0 44E
Perm' Russia	36	F3	58 01N	56 10E
Péronne France	19	B2	49 56N	2 57E
Perpignan France	22	E2	42 42N	2 54E
Perth Australia	90	A2	31 58S	115 49E
Perth UK	13	C2	56 42N	3 28W
PERU	82	B1/B2		
Perugia Italy	26	D5	43 07N	12 23E
Pescara Italy	26	E5	42 27N	14 13E
Peshawar Pakistan	39	E3	34 01N	71 40E
Peterborough UK	15	C3	52 35N	0 15W
Peterhead UK	13	D2	57 30N	1 46W
Petrolina Brazil	83	E2	9 22S	40 30W
Petropavlovsk Kazakhstan	36	G3	54 53N	69 13E

154 Index

Name	Page	Grid	Lat	Long
Petropavlovsk-Kamchatskiy Russia	37	R3	53 03N	158 43E
Petrozavodsk Russia	36	D4	61 46N	34 19E
Phayao Thailand	48	B3	19 10N	99 57E
Philadelphia USA	71	C1	39 58N	75 10W
PHILIPPINES, THE	46/47	C3/D4		
Phitsanulok Thailand	49	C3	16 49N	100 18E
Phnom Penh Cambodia	49	C2	11 35N	104 55E
Phoenix USA	68	D3	33 30N	112 03W
Phôngsali Laos	48	C4	21 40N	102 06E
Phrae Thailand	48	C3	18 07N	100 12E
Phuket Thailand	49	B1	7 52N	98 22E
Piacenza Italy	26	B6	45 03N	9 41E
Piatra Neamt Romania	28	F7	46 53N	26 23E
Picton Canada	71	C2	44 01N	77 09W
Picton New Zealand	93	C2	41 18S	174 00E
Pierre USA	68	F5	44 23N	100 20W
Pietermaritzburg RSA	61	D2	29 36S	30 24E
Pine Bluff USA	69	H3	34 13N	92 00W
Pingdingshan China	43	E3	33 50N	113 20E
P'ingtung Taiwan	43	F2	22 40N	120 30E
Pinsk Belarus	30	C5	52 08N	26 01E
Piraeus Greece	29	D2	37 57N	23 42E
Pisa Italy	26	C5	43 43N	10 24E
Pisco Peru	82	B1	13 46S	76 12W
Pisek Czech Republic	20	E3	49 18N	14 10E
Piteå Sweden	16	E4	65 19N	21 30E
Pitesti Romania	28	E6	44 51N	24 51E
Pitlochry UK	13	C2	56 43N	3 45W
Pittsburgh USA	70	C2	40 26N	80 00W
Plainview USA	68	F3	34 12N	101 43W
Plattsburgh USA	71	D2	44 42N	73 29W
Pleven Bulgaria	28	E5	43 25N	24 04E
Plock Poland	21	H5	52 32N	19 40E
Ploiesti Romania	28	E6	44 57N	26 01E
Plovdiv Bulgaria	28	E5	42 08N	24 45E
Plymouth UK	15	A2	50 23N	4 10W
Plzen Czech Republic	20	E3	49 45N	13 25E
Po r. Italy	26	C6	45 00N	10 00E
Pocatello USA	68	D5	42 35N	112 26W
Podgorica SM	28	B5	42 28N	19 17E
Podol'sk Russia	30	E6	55 23N	37 32E
Pohang South Korea	43	F3	36 00N	129 26E
Point Hope tn. USA	66	B4	68 20N	166 50W
Point-Noire tn. Congo	60	B4	4 46S	11 53E
Poitiers France	22	D4	46 35N	0 20E
Pokhara Nepal	40	D5	28 14N	83 58E
POLAND	21			
Poltava Ukraine	30	D4	49 35N	34 35E
Ponca City USA	69	G4	36 41N	97 04W
Pondicherry India	41	C2	11 59N	79 50E
Pond Inlet tn. Canada	67	L5	42 40N	77 59W
Ponta Grossa Brazil	84	D4	25 07S	50 09W
Ponte Leccia Corsica	23	H2	42 28N	9 12E
Pontevedra Spain	24	A5	42 25N	8 39W
Pontiac USA	70	B2	42 39N	83 18W
Pontypool UK	15	B2	51 43N	3 02W
Poole UK	15	C2	50 43N	1 59W
Popacatepetl mt. Mexico	75	E2	19 02N	98 38W
Poplar Bluff tn. USA	69	H4	36 16N	90 25W
Porbandar India	40	A4	21 04N	69 40E
Portadown UK	12	C3	54 26N	6 27W
Portage la Prairie Canada	67	J2	49 58N	98 20W
Port Alberni Canada	68	B6	49 11N	124 49W
Portalegre Portugal	24	B3	39 17N	7 25W
Port Arthur USA	69	H2	29 55N	93 56W
Port Askaig UK	13	A1	55 51N	6 07W
Port Augusta Australia	91	C2	32 30S	137 27E
Port-au-Prince Haiti	77	E3	18 33N	72 20W
Port Austin USA	70	B2	44 04N	82 59W
Port Blair Andaman Islands	41	F2	11 40N	92 44E
Port Elizabeth RSA	60	C1	33 58S	25 36E
Port Ellen UK	13	A1	55 39N	6 12W
Port Gentil Gabon	55	C1	0 40S	8 50E
Port Harcourt Nigeria	55	C2	4 43N	7 05E
Port Hardy Canada	66	F3	50 41N	127 30W
Port Hedland Australia	90	A3	20 24S	118 36E
Portland Australia	91	D2	38 21S	141 38E
Portland USA	68	B6	45 32N	122 40W
Portlaoise RoI	12	C2	53 02N	7 17W
Port Macquarie Australia	91	E2	31 28S	152 25E
Port Moresby PNG	89		9 30S	147 07E
Porto Alegre Brazil	84	D3	30 03S	51 10W
Porto Amboim Angola	60	B3	10 47S	13 43E
Port of Spain Trinidad and Tobago	77	G2	10 38N	61 31W
Porto Novo Benin	55	C2	6 30N	2 47E
Porto-Vecchio Corsica	23	H1	41 35N	9 16E
Pôrto Velho Brazil	82	C2	8 45S	63 54W
Port Pirie Australia	91	C2	33 11S	138 01E
Portree UK	13	A2	57 24N	6 12W
Port Said Egypt	56	C5	31 17N	32 18E
Portsmouth UK	15	C2	50 48N	1 05W
Portsmouth USA	69	L4	36 50N	76 20W
Port Talbot UK	15	B2	51 36N	3 47W
PORTUGAL	24	A2/B4		
Posadas Argentina	84	D4	27 27S	55 50W
Potenza Italy	27	E4	40 38N	15 48E
P'ot'i Georgia	31	F3	42 11N	41 41E
Potosí Bolivia	84	C5	19 34S	65 45W
Potsdam Germany	20	E5	52 24N	13 04E
Powell River tn. Canada	66	F2	49 54N	124 34W
Poznan Poland	21	G5	52 25N	16 53E
Prachin Buri Thailand	49	C2	14 02N	101 24E
Prague Czech Republic	21	F4	50 06N	14 26E
Presidente Prudente Brazil	84	D4	22 09S	51 24W
Presov Slovakia	21	J3	49 00N	21 10E
Presque Isle tn. USA	69	N6	46 42N	68 01W
Preston UK	14	B3	53 46N	2 42W
Pretoria RSA	60	C2	25 45S	28 12E
Pribram Czech Republic	20	F3	49 42N	14 01E
Prieska RSA	60	C2	29 40S	22 45E
Prijedor Bosnia-Herzegovina	26	F6	45 00N	16 41E
Prilep FYROM	29	C4	41 20N	21 32E
Prince Albert Canada	66	H3	53 13N	105 45W
Prince George Canada	66	F3	53 55N	122 49W
Prince Rupert Canada	66	E3	54 09N	130 20W
Pristina SM	28	C5	42 39N	21 20E
Probolinggo Indonesia	46	C2	7 45S	113 12E
Providence USA	71	D2	41 50N	71 28W
Provo USA	68	D5	40 15N	111 40W
Prudhoe Bay tn. USA	66	D5	70 05N	148 20W
Przemysl Poland	21	K3	49 48N	22 48E
Pskov Russia	36	C3	57 48N	28 26E
Pucallpa Peru	82	B2	8 21S	74 33W
Pudasjärvi Finland	16	F4	65 25N	26 50E
Puebla Mexico	75	E2	19 03N	98 10W
Pueblo USA	68	F4	38 17N	104 38W
PUERTO RICO	77	F3		
Pulacayo Bolivia	84	C4	20 25S	66 41W
Pullman USA	68	C6	46 46N	117 09W
Pune India	41	B3	18 34N	73 58E
Punta Alta Argentina	85	C3	38 50S	62 00W
Punta Arenas Chile	85	B1	53 10S	70 56W
Puntjak Jaya mt. Indonesia	47	E2	4 05S	137 09E
Puri India	41	E3	19 49N	85 54E
Pusan South Korea	43	F3	35 05N	129 02E
Putao Myanmar	48	B5	27 23N	97 25E
Pyapon Myanmar	49	B3	16 15N	95 40E
Pyatigorsk Russia	36	E2	44 04N	43 06E
Pyè Myanmar	48	B3	18 50N	95 14E
Pyhäjärvi Finland	17	F3	63 41N	26 00E
Pyongyang North Korea	43	F3	39 00N	125 47E
Pyrénées mts. France/Spain	22	D2	42 50N	0 30E

Q

Name	Page	Grid	Lat	Long
QATAR	38	D2		
Qazvin Iran	38	C3	36 16N	50 00E
Qingdao China	43	F3	36 04N	120 22E
Qinhuangdao China	43	E3	39 55N	119 37E
Qinzhou China	48	D4	21 57N	108 31E
Qionghai China	43	E1	19 17N	110 30E
Qiqihar China	43	F4	47 23N	124 00E
Qom Iran	38	D3	34 39N	50 57E
Quanzhou China	43	E2	24 53N	118 36E
Québec Canada	71	D3	46 50N	71 15W
Queenstown Australia	91	D1	42 07S	145 33E
Queenstown New Zealand	93	B1	45 02S	168 40E
Quesnel Canada	66	F3	53 03N	122 31W
Quezon City Philippines	47	D4	14 39N	121 02E
Quimper France	22	A4	48 00N	4 06W
Qui Nhon Vietnam	49	D2	13 47N	109 11E

© Oxford University Press

Quito Ecuador	82	B2	0 14S	78 30W

R

Rabat-Salé Morocco	54	B5	34 02N	6 51W
Radom Poland	21	J4	51 26N	21 10E
Rae Canada	66	G4	62 55N	115 55W
Raetihi New Zealand	92	C3	39 26S	175 17E
Raichur India	41	C3	16 15N	77 20E
Raipur India	41	D4	21 16N	81 42E
Rajkot India	40	B4	21 18N	70 53E
Raleigh USA	69	L4	35 46N	78 39W
Râmnicu Sarat Romania	28	F6	45 24N	27 06E
Râmnicu Vâlcea Romania	28	E6	45 06N	24 21E
Rampur India	40	C5	28 50N	79 05E
Ranchi India	40	E4	23 22N	85 20E
Rangpur Bangladesh	40	E5	25 45N	89 21E
Rapid City USA	68	F5	44 06N	103 14W
Rasht Iran	38	C3	37 18N	49 38E
Rat Buri Thailand	49	B2	13 30N	99 50E
Ratno Ukraine	21	L4	51 40N	24 32E
Rauma Finland	17	E3	61 09N	21 30E
Ravenna Italy	26	D6	44 25N	12 12E
Ravensburg Germany	20	C2	47 47N	9 37E
Ravensthorpe Australia	90	B2	33 34S	120 01E
Rawalpindi Pakistan	39	F3	33 40N	73 08E
Rawlins USA	68	E5	41 46N	107 16W
Reading UK	15	C2	51 28N	0 59W
Recife Brazil	83	F7	8 06S	34 53W
Redcar UK	14	C4	54 37N	1 04W
Red Deer Canada	66	G3	52 15N	113 48W
Redding USA	72	B6	40 35N	122 24W
Redon France	22	B4	47 39N	2 05W
Red Sea Middle East	38	B2/C1	26 00N	36 00E
Regensburg Germany	20	E3	49 01N	12 07E
Reggio di Calabria Italy	27	E3	38 06N	15 39E
Reggio nell'Emilia Italy	26	C6	44 42N	10 37E
Regina Canada	66	H3	50 30N	104 38W
Reigate UK	15	C2	51 14N	0 13W
Reims France	23	F5	49 15N	4 02E
Rendsburg Germany	20	C6	54 19N	9 39E
Rennes France	22	C5	48 06N	1 40W
REPUBLIC OF IRELAND	12			
REPUBLIC OF SOUTH AFRICA				
	60/61	B1/D2		
Resistencia Argentina	84	D4	27 28S	59 00W
Resita Romania	28	C6	45 16N	21 55E
Reutlingen Germany	20	C3	48 30N	9 13E
Revelstoke Canada	66	G3	51 02N	118 12W
Reykjavík Iceland	16	J2	64 09N	21 58W
Rhein r. Europe	20	B4	50 30N	7 30E
Rhodes Greece	29	G2	36 26N	28 13E
Rhondda UK	15	B2	51 40N	3 30W
Rhône r. Switzerland/France	23	F3	45 00N	4 50E
Rhyl UK	14	B3	53 19N	3 29W
Ribeirão Prêto Brazil	84	E4	21 09S	47 48W
Riberalta Bolivia	82	C1	10 59S	66 06W
Richland USA	68	C6	46 17N	119 17W
Richmond New Zealand	93	C2	41 31S	173 39E
Richmond USA	71	C1	37 34N	77 27W
Riga Latvia	17	E2	56 53N	24 08E
Rijeka Croatia	26	E6	45 20N	14 27E
Rimini Italy	26	D6	44 03N	12 34E
Rimouski Canada	69	N6	48 27N	68 32W
Rio Branco tn. Brazil	82	C2	9 59S	67 49W
Rio de Janeiro tn. Brazil	84	E4	22 53S	43 17W
Rio Grande tn. Brazil	84	D3	32 03S	52 08W
Rio Grande tn. Mexico	74	D3	23 50N	103 02W
Rio Grande r. Mexico/USA	68	E3/F2	30 00N	105 00W
Ripley USA	70	B1	38 49N	81 44W
Ripon UK	14	C4	54 08N	1 31W
Riverton New Zealand	93	B1	46 22S	168 01E
Rivière-du-Loup tn. Canada	69	N6	47 49N	69 32W
Rivne Ukraine	30	C5	50 39N	26 10E
Riyadh Saudi Arabia	38	C2	24 39N	46 46E
Roanne France	23	F4	46 02N	4 05E
Roanoke USA	69	L4	37 15N	79 58W
Rochdale UK	14	B3	53 38N	2 09W
Rochefort France	22	C3	45 57N	0 58W
Rochester USA	69	H5	84 01N	92 27W
Rockford USA	69	J5	42 16N	89 06W
Rockhampton Australia	91	E3	23 22S	150 32E

Rock Hill tn. USA	69	K3	34 55N	81 01W
Rock Springs tn. USA	68	E5	41 35N	109 13W
Rocky Mountains Canada/USA	66	F3/H2	55 00N	125 00W
Roermond Netherlands	18	E4	51 12N	6 00E
Roeselare Belgium	19	C3	50 57N	3 08E
ROMANIA	28	D7/G6		
Rome Italy	27	D4	41 53N	12 30E
Ronda Spain	24	C2	36 45N	5 10W
Rondonópolis Brazil	83	D1	16 29S	54 37W
Roosendaal Netherlands	18	D4	51 32N	4 28E
Rosario Argentina	84	C3	33 00S	60 40W
Roscoff France	22	B5	48 43N	3 59W
Roscommon Rol	12	B2	53 38N	8 11W
Roseburg USA	68	B5	43 13N	123 21W
Rosenheim Germany	20	E2	47 51N	12 09E
Rossano Italy	27	F3	39 35N	16 38E
Rosslare Rol	12	C2	52 15N	6 22W
Rostock Germany	20	E6	54 06N	12 09E
Rostov-na-Donu Russia	36	D2	47 15N	39 45E
Rotherham UK	14	C3	53 26N	1 20W
Rothesay UK	13	A2	55 51N	5 03W
Rotorua New Zealand	92	D3	38 08S	176 14E
Rotterdam Netherlands	18	D4	51 54N	4 28E
Rouen France	22	D5	49 26N	1 05E
Rouyn-Noranda Canada	67	L2	48 15N	79 00W
Roxburgh New Zealand	93	B1	45 33S	169 19E
Royal Tunbridge Wells UK	15	D2	51 08N	0 16E
Royan France	22	C3	45 38N	1 02W
Rubtsovsk Russia	36	J3	51 43N	81 11E
Rudnyy Kazakhstan	36	G3	53 00N	63 05E
Rugao China	43	F3	32 27N	120 35E
Rugby UK	15	C3	52 23N	1 15W
Ruse Bulgaria	28	F5	43 50N	25 59E
Russell USA	68	G4	38 54N	98 51W
RUSSIAN FEDERATION	36/38			
Rust'avi Georgia	31	G3	41 34N	45 03E
Rutland USA	71	D2	43 37N	72 59W
Rutog China	42	A3	33 27N	79 43E
RWANDA	58	A3/B3		
Ryazan' Russia	36	D3	54 37N	39 43E
Rybinsk Russia	36	D3	58 03N	38 50E
Rzeszów Poland	21	K4	50 04N	22 00E

S

Saalfeld Germany	20	D4	50 39N	11 22E
Saarbrücken Germany	20	B3	49 15N	6 58E
Sabhā Libya	56	A4	27 02N	14 26E
Sabinas Hidalgo Mexico	75	D6	26 33N	100 10W
Sacramento USA	72	C5	38 32N	121 30W
Saginaw USA	70	B2	43 25N	83 54W
Saguenay Canada	67	L2	48 26N	71 06W
Sahara Desert North Africa	54	B4/D4	22 50N	0 00
Saharanpur India	40	C5	29 58N	77 33E
St. Albans UK	15	C2	51 46N	0 21W
St. Andrews UK	13	C2	56 20N	2 48W
St. Augustine USA	69	K2	29 54N	81 19W
St-Brieuc France	22	B5	48 31N	2 45W
St. Catharines Canada	70	C2	43 10N	79 15W
St. Cloud USA	69	H6	45 34N	94 10W
St-Dizier France	23	F5	48 38N	4 58E
Ste. Marie Canada	71	D3	46 26N	71 00W
St-Étienne France	23	F3	45 26N	4 23E
St. Gallen Switzerland	23	H4	47 25N	9 23E
St. Helens UK	14	B3	53 28N	2 44W
St. Ignace USA	70	B3	45 53N	84 44W
St. Jerôme Canada	71	D3	45 47N	74 01W
Saint John Canada	67	M2	45 16N	66 03W
St. John's Canada	67	N2	47 34N	52 41W
St. Joseph USA	69	H4	39 45N	94 51W
ST. KITTS AND NEVIS	77	G3		
St. Lawrence r. Canada/USA	67	M2	47 00N	68 00W
St-Lô France	22	C5	49 07N	1 05W
St. Louis USA	69	H4	38 40N	90 15W
ST. LUCIA	77	G2		
St-Malo France	22	B5	48 39N	2 00W
St. Moritz Switzerland	23	H4	46 30N	9 51E
St-Nazaire France	22	B4	47 17N	2 12W
St. Paul USA	69	H5	45 00N	93 10W
St. Petersburg Russia	36	D3	59 55N	30 25E
St. Petersburg USA	69	K2	27 45N	82 40W

Place	Page	Grid	Lat	Long
Saint-Pierre & Miquelon *is.* Atlantic Ocean	67	N2	47 00N	56 20W
St. Pölten Austria	21	F3	48 13N	15 37E
St-Quentin France	22	E5	49 51N	3 17E
St. Stephen Canada	69	N6	45 12N	67 18W
St-Tropez France	23	G2	43 16N	6 39E
ST. VINCENT AND THE GRENADINES	77	G2		
Sakai Japan	45	C1	34 35N	135 28E
Sakata Japan	44	C2	38 55N	139 51E
Sakhalin *i.* Russia	37	Q2/Q3	50 00N	143 00E
Sakhon Nakhon Thailand	48	C3	17 12N	104 09E
Salalah Oman	39	D1	17 00N	54 04E
Salamanca Spain	24	C4	40 58N	5 40W
Salem USA	68	B5	44 57N	123 01W
Salerno Italy	27	E4	40 40N	14 46E
Salima Malawi	61	D3	13 45S	34 29E
Salina USA	68	G4	38 53N	97 36W
Salinas Ecuador	82	A2	2 15S	80 58W
Salisbury UK	15	C2	51 05N	1 48W
Sal'sk Russia	31	F4	46 28N	41 33E
Salta Argentina	84	C4	24 46S	65 28W
Saltillo Mexico	74	D4	25 30N	101 00W
Salt Lake City USA	68	D5	40 45N	111 55W
Salto Uruguay	84	D3	31 27S	57 50W
Salvador Brazil	83	F1	12 58S	38 29W
Salween *r.* China/Myanmar	48	B4	20 00N	103 00E
Salzburg Austria	20	E2	47 48N	13 03E
Samara Russia	36	F3	53 10N	50 10E
Samarinda Indonesia	46	C2	0 30S	117 09E
Samarkand Uzbekistan	36	G1	39 40N	66 57E
Sambalpur India	40	D4	21 28N	84 04E
SAMOA	96	F4		
Samsun Turkey	31	E3	41 17N	36 22E
Samut Prakan Thailand	49	C2	13 38N	100 35E
Samut Sakhon Thailand	49	C2	13 31N	100 16E
Sana Yemen	38	C1	15 23N	44 14E
San Andrés Tuxtla Mexico	75	E2	18 28N	95 15W
San Carlos Philippines	47	D4	10 30N	123 29E
San Cristóbal Argentina	84	C3	30 20S	61 14W
San Cristóbal Venezuela	82	B3	7 46N	72 15W
Sandakan Malaysia	46	C3	5 52N	118 04E
San Diego USA	73	E2	32 45N	117 10W
Sandoway Myanmar	48	A3	18 28N	94 20E
Sandusky USA	70	B2	41 27N	82 42W
San Felipe Venezuela	82	C4	10 25N	68 40W
San Fernando Spain	24	B2	36 28N	6 12W
San Francisco USA	72	B4	37 45N	122 27W
San José Costa Rica	77	C1	9 59N	84 04W
San Juan Puerto Rico	77	F3	18 29N	66 08W
San Julián Argentina	85	C2	49 17S	67 45W
Sanliurfa Turkey	31	E2	37 08N	38 45E
San Lucas Mexico	74	C3	22 50N	109 52W
San Luis Potosí Mexico	74	D3	22 10N	101 00W
SAN MARINO	26	D5	44 00N	12 00E
Sanmenxia China	43	E3	34 46N	111 17E
San Miguel El Salvador	76	B2	13 28N	88 10W
San Miguel de Tucumán Argentina	84	C4	26 47S	65 15W
Sanming China	43	E2	26 16N	117 35E
San Pablo Philippines	47	D4	14 03N	121 19E
San Rafael Argentina	84	C3	34 35S	68 24W
San Remo Italy	26	A5	43 48N	7 46E
San Salvador El Salvador	76	B2	13 40N	89 10W
San Sebastián Spain	25	E5	43 19N	1 59W
Santa Ana El Salvador	76	B2	14 00N	89 31W
Santa Clara Cuba	76	D4	22 25N	79 58W
Santa Cruz Bolivia	84	C5	17 50S	63 10W
Santa Fé Argentina	84	C3	31 35S	60 50W
Santa Fe USA	68	E4	35 41N	105 57W
Santa Maria Brazil	84	D4	29 45S	53 40W
Santa Marta Colombia	82	B4	11 18N	74 10W
Santander Spain	24	D5	43 28N	3 48W
Santarém Brazil	83	D2	2 26S	54 41W
Santa Rosa Argentina	85	C3	36 37S	64 17W
Santiago Chile	84	B3	33 30S	70 40W
Santiago Dominican Republic	77	E3	19 27N	70 42W
Santiago de Cuba Cuba	77	D4	20 00N	75 49W
Santo Andre Brazil	84	E4	23 39S	46 29W
Santo Domingo Dominican Republic	77	F3	18 30N	69 57W
Sanya China	43	D1	18 25N	109 27E
São José Brazil	84	E4	27 35S	48 40W
São José do Rio Prêto Brazil	84	E4	20 50S	49 20W
São Luís Brazil	83	E2	2 34S	44 16W
São Paulo Brazil	84	E4	23 33S	46 39W
SÃO TOMÉ AND PRINCIPE	55	C2		
Sappemeer Netherlands	18	F6	53 10N	6 47E
Sapporo Japan	44	D3	43 05N	141 21E
Saraburi Thailand	49	C2	14 32N	100 53E
Sarajevo Bosnia-Herzegovina	26	G5	43 52N	18 26E
Sarasota USA	76	C5	27 20N	82 32W
Saratov Russia	36	E3	51 30N	45 55E
Saravan Iran	39	E2	27 25N	62 17E
Sardinia *i.* Italy	27	B3/B4	40 00N	9 00E
Sarh Chad	57	A2	9 08N	18 22E
Sarnia Canada	70	B2	42 58N	82 23W
Sarrebourg France	23	G5	48 43N	7 03E
Sasebo Japan	45	A1	33 10N	129 42E
Saskatoon Canada	66	H3	52 10N	106 40W
Sassari Italy	27	B4	40 43N	8 34E
Sassnitz Germany	20	E6	54 32N	13 40E
Satna India	40	D4	24 33N	80 50E
Sattahip Thailand	49	C2	12 36N	100 56E
Satu Mare Romania	28	D7	47 48N	22 52E
SAUDI ARABIA	38/39	B2/D2		
Sault Ste. Marie Canada	70	B3	46 31N	84 20W
Sault Ste. Marie USA	70	B3	46 29N	84 22W
Savannah USA	69	K3	32 04N	81 07W
Savona Italy	26	B6	44 18N	8 28E
Sawankhalok Thailand	48	B3	17 19N	99 51E
Shawinigan Canada	67	L2	46 33N	72 45W
Saylac Somalia	57	D3	11 21N	43 30E
Saynshand Mongolia	43	E4	45 00N	111 10E
Say'ün Yemen	38	C1	15 59N	48 44E
Schwaz Austria	20	D2	47 21N	11 44E
Schwerin Germany	20	D5	53 38N	11 25E
Scilly, Isles of UK	20	C1	49 56N	6 20W
Scotland *country* UK	13		56 10N	4 00W
Scottsbluff USA	68	F5	41 52N	103 40W
Scranton USA	71	C2	41 25N	75 40W
Scunthorpe UK	14	C3	53 35N	0 39W
Seattle USA	68	B6	47 35N	122 20W
Sebes Romania	31	B4	45 58N	23 34E
Sedan France	23	F5	49 42N	4 57E
Sekondi Takoradi Ghana	55	B2	4 59N	1 43W
Selkirk Canada	69	G7	50 10N	96 52W
Semarang Indonesia	46	C2	6 58S	110 29E
Semipalatinsk Kazakhstan	36	J3	50 26N	80 16E
Sendai Japan	44	D2	38 16N	140 52E
SENEGAL	55	A3		
Senj Croatia	26	E6	45 00N	14 55E
Sennar Sudan	57	C3	13 31N	33 38E
Seoul South Korea	43	F3	37 32N	127 00E
Sept-Îles *tn.* Canada	67	M3	50 10N	66 00W
Serang Indonesia	46	B2	6 07S	106 09E
SERBIA AND MONTENEGRO	28	B5/C6		
Seremban Malaysia	46	B3	2 43N	102 57E
Sergiyev Posad Russia	30	E6	56 20N	38 10E
Serra do Navio Brazil	83	D3	1 00N	52 05W
Sétif Algeria	54	C5	36 11N	5 24E
Setúbal Portugal	24	A3	38 31N	8 54W
Sevastopol' Ukraine	31	D3	44 36N	33 31E
Severn *r.* UK	15	B3	52 30N	3 15W
Severodvinsk Russia	36	D4	64 35N	39 50E
Seville Spain	24	C2	37 24N	5 59W
Seward USA	66	D4	60 05N	149 34W
SEYCHELLES	95	C4		
Sézanne France	22	E5	48 44N	3 44E
Sfax Tunisia	54	D5	34 45N	10 43E
Shahjahanpur India	40	C5	27 53N	79 55E
Shakhty Russia	31	F4	47 43N	40 16E
Shanghai China	43	F3	31 06N	121 22E
Shannon *r.* RoI	12	B2	52 45N	8 57W
Sharjah UAE	39	D2	25 20N	55 20E
Shar'ya Russia	30	G6	58 22N	45 31E
Shashi China	43	E3	30 16N	112 20E
Sheffield UK	14	C3	53 23N	1 30W
Shelby USA	68	D6	48 30N	111 52W
Shenyang China	43	F4	41 50N	123 26E
Sherbrooke Canada	71	D3	45 24N	71 54W
Sheridan USA	68	E5	44 48N	106 57W

© Oxford University Press

Name	Page	Grid	Lat	Long
's-Hertogenbosch Netherlands	18	E4	51 41N	5 19E
Shetland Islands is. UK	13	D3/D4	60 00N	1 15W
Shijiazhuang China	43	E3	38 04N	114 28E
Shikarpur Pakistan	39	E2	27 58N	68 42E
Shillong India	40	F5	25 34N	91 53E
Shimla India	40	C6	31 07N	77 09E
Shimonoseki Japan	45	B1	33 59N	130 58E
Shingū Japan	45	C1	33 42N	136 00E
Shīrāz Iran	39	D2	29 38N	52 34E
Shkodër Albania	28	B5	42 03N	19 01E
Shreveport USA	69	H3	32 30N	93 46W
Shunde China	43	E2	22 50N	113 16E
Shymkent Kazakhstan	36	G2	42 16N	69 05E
Siauliai Lithuania	17	E2	55 51N	23 20E
Sibiti Congo	60	B4	3 40S	13 24E
Sibiu Romania	28	E6	45 46N	24 09E
Sibu Malaysia	46	C3	2 19N	111 50E
Sicily i. Italy	27	D2/E2	37 00N	14 00E
Siderno Italy	27	F3	38 16N	16 17E
Sidi Bel Abbès Algeria	54	B5	35 15N	0 39W
Siedlce Poland	21	K5	52 10N	22 18E
Siegen Germany	20	C4	50 52N	8 02E
Siem Reap Cambodia	49	C2	13 21N	103 50E
Siena Italy	26	C5	43 19N	11 19E
Sierra Blanca tn. USA	68	E3	31 10N	105 22W
SIERRA LEONE	55	A2		
Sikar India	40	C5	27 33N	75 12E
Sikasso Mali	55	B3	11 18N	5 38W
Silchar India	40	F4	24 49N	92 47E
Silistra Bulgaria	28	F6	44 06N	27 17E
Silves Portugal	24	A2	37 11N	8 26W
Simao China	48	C4	22 46N	100 59E
Simcoe Canada	70	B2	42 50N	80 19W
Simferopol' Ukraine	31	D3	44 57N	34 05E
SINGAPORE	46	B3		
Sing Buri Thailand	49	C2	14 55N	100 22E
Sinuiju North Korea	43	F4	40 04N	124 25E
Sioux Falls tn. USA	69	G5	43 34N	96 42W
Sioux Lookout Canada	67	J3	50 07N	91 54W
Siping China	43	F4	43 15N	124 25E
Siracusa Italy	27	E2	37 04N	15 19E
Sirte Libya	56	A5	31 13N	16 35E
Sisaket Thailand	49	C2	15 05N	104 20E
Sisophon Cambodia	49	C2	13 37N	102 58E
Sisteron France	23	F3	44 16N	5 56E
Sittard Netherlands	19	E4	51 00N	5 52E
Sittwe Myanmar	48	A4	20 09N	92 55E
Sivas Turkey	31	E2	39 44N	37 01E
Siwa Egypt	56	B4	29 11N	25 31E
Skelleftea Sweden	16	E3	64 45N	21 00E
Skibbereen RoI	12	B1	51 33N	9 15W
Skikda Algeria	54	C5	36 53N	6 54E
Skopje FYROM	28	C4	42 00N	21 28E
Skövde Sweden	17	C2	58 24N	13 52E
Skovorodino Russia	37	N3	54 00N	123 53E
Slave Lake tn. Canada	66	G3	55 17N	114 43W
Sligo RoI	12	B3	54 17N	8 28W
Sliven Bulgaria	28	F5	42 40N	26 19E
SLOVAKIA	21	G3/J3		
SLOVENIA	26	E6/E7		
Slupsk Poland	21	G6	54 28N	17 00E
Smederevo SM	28	C6	44 40N	20 56E
Smolensk Russia	30	D5	54 49N	32 04E
Snowdon mt. UK	15	A3	53 04N	4 05W
Snyder USA	68	F3	32 43N	100 54W
Sochi Russia	31	E3	43 35N	39 46E
Soc Trang Vietnam	49	D1	9 34N	106 00E
Sofia Bulgaria	28	D5	42 40N	23 18E
Sohâg Egypt	56	C4	26 33N	31 42E
Soissons France	22	E5	49 23N	3 20E
Sokhumi Georgia	31	F3	43 01N	41 01E
Sokodé Togo	55	C2	8 59N	1 11E
Sokoto Nigeria	55	C3	13 02N	5 15E
Solāpur India	41	C3	17 43N	75 56E
Solikamsk Russia	36	F3	59 40N	56 45E
Sollefteå Sweden	17	D3	63 09N	17 15E
SOLOMON ISLANDS	96	D4/E4		
Soltau Germany	20	C5	52 59N	9 50E
SOMALIA	57	D1/E3		
Sông Câu Vietnam	49	D2	13 25N	109 11E
Songea Tanzania	61	D3	10 42S	35 59E
Songkhla Thailand	49	C1	7 12N	100 35E
Soria Spain	24	D4	41 46N	2 28W
Sorong Indonesia	47	E2	0 50S	131 17E
Sosnowiec Poland	21	H4	50 16N	19 07E
Souillac France	22	D3	44 53N	1 29E
Sousse Tunisia	54	D5	35 50N	10 38E
Southampton Canada	70	B2	44 29N	81 22W
Southampton UK	15	C2	50 55N	1 25W
Southern Alps mts. New Zealand	93	B1/B2	43 07S	171 13E
Southern Ocean	98			
South Island New Zealand	93	A1/C2	42 30S	172 00E
SOUTH KOREA	43	F3		
SPAIN	24/25			
Spárti Greece	29	D2	37 05N	22 25E
Spittal an der Drau Austria	20	E2	46 48N	13 30E
Split Croatia	26	F5	43 31N	16 28E
Spokane USA	68	C6	47 40N	117 25W
Springbok RSA	60	B2	29 44S	17 56E
Springfield New Zealand	93	B2	43 20S	171 56E
Springfield USA	69	H4	37 11N	93 19W
Springfield USA	69	J4	39 49N	89 39W
Springfield USA	71	D2	42 07N	72 35W
Springville USA	71	C2	42 31N	78 41E
Squamish Canada	66	F2	49 41N	123 11W
SRI LANKA	41	D1		
Srinagar Jammu and Kashmir	40	B6	34 08N	74 50E
Stafford UK	15	B3	52 48N	2 07W
Standish USA	70	B2	43 59N	83 58W
Stanley Falkland Islands	85	D1	51 45S	57 56W
Stara Zagora Bulgaria	28	E5	42 25N	25 37E
Stavanger Norway	17	B2	58 58N	5 45E
Staveren Netherlands	18	E5	52 53N	5 21E
Stavropol' Russia	36	E2	45 03N	41 59E
Stein Netherlands	19	E3	50 58N	5 45E
Sterling USA	68	F5	40 37N	103 13W
Steyr Austria	20	F3	48 04N	14 25E
Stip FYROM	28	D4	41 44N	22 12E
Stirling UK	13	C2	56 07N	3 57W
Stockholm Sweden	17	D2	59 20N	18 05E
Stœng Trêng Cambodia	49	D2	13 31N	105 59E
Stoke-on-Trent UK	15	B3	53 00N	2 10W
Stornoway UK	13	A3	58 12N	6 23W
Strabane UK	12	C3	54 49N	7 27W
Stralsund Germany	20	E6	54 18N	13 06E
Stranraer UK	13	B1	54 55N	5 02W
Strasbourg France	23	G5	48 35N	7 45E
Stratford Canada	70	B2	43 22N	81 00W
Stratford-upon-Avon UK	15	C3	52 12N	1 41W
Stryy Ukraine	30	B4	49 16N	23 51E
Sturgeon Falls tn. Canada	70	C3	46 22N	79 57W
Stuttgart Germany	20	C3	48 47N	9 12E
Subotica SM	28	B7	46 04N	19 41E
Suceava Romania	28	F7	47 37N	26 18E
Sucre Bolivia	84	C5	19 05S	65 15W
SUDAN	56/57	B3/C3		
Sudbury Canada	70	B3	46 30N	81 01W
Suez Egypt	56	C4	29 59N	32 33E
Suez Canal Egypt	56	C5	31 30N	32 20E
Sumy Ukraine	30	D5	50 55N	34 49E
Sunchon South Korea	43	F3	34 56N	127 28E
Sundsvall Sweden	17	D3	62 22N	17 20E
Superior USA	69	H6	46 42N	92 05W
Superior, Lake Canada/USA	69	H6/J6	48 00N	88 00W
Suphan Buri Thailand	49	C2	14 28N	100 07E
Surabaya Indonesia	46	C2	7 14S	112 45E
Surakarta Indonesia	46	C2	7 32S	110 50E
Surat India	40	B4	21 10N	72 54E
Surat Thani Thailand	49	B1	9 09N	99 20E
SURINAME	83	D3		
Suzuka Japan	45	C1	34 52N	136 37E
Swansea UK	15	B2	51 38N	3 57W
SWAZILAND	61	D2		
SWEDEN	16/17	C2/E4		
Sweetwater tn. USA	68	F3	32 27N	100 25W
Swift Current tn. Canada	66	H3	50 17N	107 49W
Swindon UK	15	C2	51 34N	1 47W
SWITZERLAND	23	G4/H4		
Sydney Australia	91	E2	33 55S	151 10E
Sydney Canada	67	M2	46 10N	60 10W
Syktyvkar Russia	36	F4	61 42N	50 45E

Place	Page	Grid	Lat	Long
Sylhet Bangladesh	40	F4	24 53N	91 51E
Syracuse USA	71	C2	43 03N	76 10W
SYRIA	38	B3		
Syzran' Russia	36	E3	53 10N	48 29E
Szczecin Poland	21	F5	53 25N	14 32E
Szeged Hungary	21	J2	46 15N	20 09E
T				
Tabas Iran	39	D3	33 37N	56 54E
Tábor Czech Republic	21	F3	49 25N	14 39E
Tabriz Iran	38	C3	38 04N	46 17E
Tacoma USA	68	B6	47 16N	122 30W
Taegu South Korea	43	F3	35 52N	128 36E
Taejon South Korea	43	F3	36 20N	127 26E
Tai'an China	43	E3	36 15N	117 10E
Taichung Taiwan	43	F2	24 09N	124 40E
Taipei Taiwan	43	F2	25 05N	121 32E
TAIWAN	43	F2		
Taiyuan China	43	E3	37 50N	112 30E
Ta'izz Yemen	38	C1	13 35N	44 02E
TAJIKISTAN	36	G1/H1		
Takamatsu Japan	45	B1	34 20N	134 01E
Takapuna New Zealand	92	C3	36 48S	174 46E
Takayama Japan	45	C2	36 09N	137 16E
Talca Chile	85	B3	35 28S	71 40W
Taldykorgan Kazakhstan	36	H2	45 02N	78 23E
Tallahassee USA	69	K3	30 26N	84 16W
Tallinn Estonia	17	E2	59 22N	24 48E
Taloyoak Canada	67	J4	69 30N	93 20W
Tamanrasset Algeria	54	C4	22 50N	5 28E
Tambov Russia	30	F5	52 44N	41 28E
Tampa USA	69	K2	27 58N	82 38W
Tampere Finland	17	E3	61 32N	23 45E
Tanana USA	66	C4	65 11N	152 10W
Tangier Morocco	54	B5	35 48N	5 45W
Tangshan China	43	E3	39 37N	118 05E
TANZANIA	61	D4		
Táranto Italy	27	F4	40 28N	17 15E
Tarbert RoI	12	B2	52 32N	9 23W
Tarbes France	22	D2	43 14N	0 05E
Taree Australia	91	E2	31 54S	152 26E
Târgu Mures Romania	28	E7	46 33N	24 34E
Tarnów Poland	21	J4	50 01N	20 59E
Tarragona Spain	25	F4	41 07N	1 15E
Tartu Estonia	17	F2	58 20N	26 44E
Tashkent Uzbekistan	36	G2	41 16N	69 13E
Taunton UK	15	B2	51 01N	3 06W
Taupo New Zealand	92	D3	38 42S	176 05E
Tauranga New Zealand	92	D3	37 41S	176 10E
Tavira Portugal	24	B2	37 07N	7 39W
T'bilisi Georgia	31	F3	41 43N	44 48E
Tébessa Algeria	54	C5	35 21N	8 06E
Tegucigalpa Honduras	76	B2	14 05N	87 14W
Tehran Iran	38	D3	35 40N	51 26E
Tehuacán Mexico	75	E2	18 30N	97 26W
Tel Aviv-Yafo Israel	38	B3	32 05N	34 46E
Telford UK	15	B3	52 42N	2 28W
Témiscaming Canada	71	C3	46 44N	79 05W
Temuka New Zealand	93	B1	44 15S	171 17E
Tepatitlán Mexico	74	D3	20 50N	102 46W
Teramo Italy	26	D5	42 40N	13 43E
Teresina Brazil	83	E2	5 09S	42 46W
Termez Uzbekistan	36	G1	37 15N	67 15E
Termoli Italy	27	E4	42 00N	15 00E
Ternate Indonesia	47	D3	0 48N	127 23E
Terni Italy	26	D5	42 34N	12 39E
Ternopil' Ukraine	30	C4	49 35N	25 39E
Terrace Canada	66	F3	54 31N	128 32W
Terracina Italy	27	D4	41 17N	13 15E
Teshio Japan	44	D3	44 53N	141 46E
Tete Mozambique	61	D3	16 10S	33 35E
Tétouan Morocco	54	B5	35 34N	5 22W
Tetovo FYROM	28	D5	42 00N	20 59E
Thai Binh Vietnam	48	D4	20 24N	106 19E
THAILAND	48/49	B1/C3		
Thames r. UK	15	C2	51 32N	0 50W
Thane India	41	B3	19 14N	73 02E
Thanh Hoa Vietnam	48	D3	19 49N	105 48E
Thaton Myanmar	49	B3	16 56N	97 20E
The Hague Netherlands	18	D5	52 05N	4 16E
Thermopolis USA	68	E5	43 39N	108 12W
Thessalon Canada	70	B3	46 15N	83 34W
Thessaloníki Greece	29	D4	40 38N	22 58E
Thika Kenya	59	E4	1 03S	37 05E
Thimphu Bhutan	40	E5	27 32N	89 43E
Thionville France	23	G5	49 22N	6 11E
Thompson Canada	67	J3	55 45N	97 54W
Thun Switzerland	23	G4	46 46N	7 38E
Thunder Bay tn. Canada	67	K2	48 27N	89 12W
Tianjin China	43	E3	39 08N	117 12E
Tijuana Mexico	74	A5	32 29N	117 10W
Tikrit Iraq	38	C3	34 36N	43 42E
Tilburg Netherlands	18	E4	51 34N	5 05E
Timaru New Zealand	93	B1	44 24S	171 15E
Timimoun Algeria	54	C4	29 15N	0 14E
Timisoara Romania	28	C6	45 45N	21 15E
Timmins Canada	67	K2	48 30N	81 20W
Tindouf Algeria	54	B4	27 42N	8 10W
Tipperary RoI	12	B2	52 29N	8 10W
Tiranë Albania	29	B4	41 20N	19 49E
Tiraspol' Moldova	31	C4	46 51N	29 37E
Tiruchirappalli India	41	C2	10 50N	78 41E
Titov Veles FYROM	29	C4	41 43N	21 49E
Tivoli Italy	27	D4	41 58N	12 48E
Tizimin Mexico	75	G3	21 10N	88 09W
Tizi Ouzou Algeria	54	C5	36 44N	4 05E
Tlemcen Algeria	54	B5	34 53N	1 21W
Toamasina Madagascar	61	E3	18 10S	49 23E
Tobol'sk Russia	36	G3	58 15N	68 12E
TOGO	55	C2		
Tokuyama Japan	45	B1	34 03N	131 48E
Tokyo Japan	45	C2	35 40N	139 45E
Toledo USA	70	B2	41 40N	83 35W
Toliara Madagascar	61	E2	23 20S	43 41E
Tolmezzo Italy	26	D7	46 24N	13 01E
Tol'yatti Russia	30	G5	53 32N	49 24E
Tombouctou Mali	55	B3	16 49N	2 59W
Tomsk Russia	36	J3	56 30N	85 05E
TONGA	96	F4		
Tønsberg Norway	17	C2	59 16N	10 25E
Toowoomba Australia	91	E3	27 35S	151 54E
Topeka USA	69	G4	39 02N	95 41W
Torbay UK	15	B2	50 27N	3 30W
Tornio Finland	16	E4	65 50N	24 10E
Toronto Canada	70	C2	43 42N	79 46W
Torre del Greco Italy	27	E4	40 46N	14 22E
Torrente Spain	25	E3	39 27N	0 28W
Torreón Mexico	74	D4	25 34N	103 25W
Toruń Poland	21	H5	53 01N	18 35E
Tot'ma Russia	30	F6	59 59N	42 46E
Tottori Japan	45	B2	35 32N	134 12E
Touggourt Algeria	54	C5	33 08N	6 04E
Toulon France	23	F2	43 07N	5 55E
Toulouse France	22	D2	43 33N	1 24E
Tours France	22	D4	47 23N	0 42E
Townsville Australia	91	D4	19 13S	146 48E
Toyama Japan	45	C2	36 42N	137 14E
Toyota Japan	45	C2	35 05N	137 09E
Trabzon Turkey	31	E3	41 00N	39 43E
Trail Canada	68	C6	49 04N	111 39W
Tralee RoI	12	B2	52 16N	9 42W
Trápani Italy	27	D3	38 02N	12 32E
Trat Thailand	49	C2	12 14N	102 31E
Trento Italy	26	C7	46 04N	11 08E
Tres Arroyos Argentina	85	C3	38 26S	60 17W
Treviso Italy	26	D6	45 40N	12 15E
Trichur India	41	C2	10 32N	76 14E
Trier Germany	19	F2	49 45N	6 39E
Trieste Italy	26	D6	45 39N	13 47E
Trincomalee Sri Lanka	41	D1	8 34N	81 13E
TRINIDAD AND TOBAGO	77	G2		
Tripoli Lebanon	38	B3	34 27N	35 50E
Tripoli Libya	56	A5	32 54N	13 11E
Trivandrum India	41	C1	8 30N	76 57E
Trois-Rivières tn. Canada	71	D3	46 21N	72 34W
Tromso Norway	16	D4	69 42N	19 00E
Trondheim Norway	17	C3	63 36N	10 23E
Troyes France	23	F5	48 18N	4 05E
Trujillo Peru	82	B2	8 06S	79 00W
Truro UK	15	A2	50 16N	5 03W
Tshane Botswana	60	C2	24 05S	21 54E
Tsu Japan	45	C1	34 41N	136 30E

Place							
Tsuyama Japan	45	B2	35 04N	134 01E	Valdivia Chile	85	B3	39 46S	73 15W
Tübingen Germany	20	C3	48 32N	9 04E	Val-d'Or Canada	69	L6	48 07N	77 47W
Tubruq Libya	56	B5	32 05N	23 59E	Valdosta USA	69	K3	30 51N	83 51W
Tucson USA	68	D3	32 15N	110 57W	Valencia Spain	25	E3	39 29N	0 24W
Tucumcari USA	68	F4	35 11N	103 44W	Valencia Venezuela	82	C4	10 14N	67 59W
Tucupita Venezuela	77	G1	9 02N	62 04W	Valjevo SM	28	B6	44 16N	19 56E
Tula Russia	36	D3	54 11N	37 38E	Valladolid Mexico	75	G3	20 40N	88 11W
Tulcea Romania	28	G6	45 10N	28 50E	Valladolid Spain	24	C4	41 39N	4 45W
Tulita Canada	66	F4	64 55N	125 29W	Valledupar Colombia	82	B4	10 31N	73 16W
Tullamore RoI	12	C2	53 16N	7 30W	Vallejo USA	72	B5	38 05N	122 14W
Tulsa USA	69	G4	36 07N	95 58W	Valletta Malta	27	E1	35 54N	14 32E
Tunis Tunisia	54	D5	36 50N	10 13E	Valparaíso Chile	84	B3	33 05S	71 40W
TUNISIA	54	C5/D5			Van Turkey	31	F2	38 28N	43 20E
Tupelo USA	69	J3	34 15N	88 43W	Vancouver Canada	66	F2	49 13N	123 06W
Turin Italy	26	A6	45 04N	7 40E	Vancouver Island Canada	66	F2/F3	49 30N	126 00W
Turiy Rog Russia	44	B4	45 06N	131 54E	Vänern l. Sweden	17	C2	59 00N	13 30E
TURKEY	31				Vännäs Sweden	16	D3	63 56N	19 50E
TURKMENISTAN	36	F1/G1			Vannes France	22	B4	47 40N	2 44W
Turku Finland	17	E3	60 27N	22 15E	Vantaa Finland	17	E3	60 20N	24 50E
Turpan China	42	B4	42 55N	89 06E	VANUATU	96	E4		
Tuscaloosa USA	69	J3	33 12N	87 33W	Varanasi India	40	D5	25 20N	83 00E
Tuticorin India	41	C1	8 48N	78 10E	Varazdin Croatia	26	F7	46 18N	16 21E
TUVALU	96	E4			Vardø Norway	16	G5	70 22N	31 06E
Túy Spain	24	A5	42 03N	8 39W	Västerås Sweden	17	D2	59 36N	16 32E
Tuy Hoa Vietnam	49	D2	13 03N	109 17E	Vättern l. Sweden	17	C2	58 20N	14 20E
Tuzla Bosnia-Herzegovina	26	G6	44 33N	18 41E	Veliko Turnovo Bulgaria	28	E5	43 04N	25 39E
Tver' Russia	36	D3	56 49N	35 57E	Vellore India	41	C2	12 56N	79 09E
Twin Falls tn. USA	68	D5	42 34N	114 30W	VENEZUELA	82	B4/C3		
Tyan-Shan' Kyrgyzstan	42	A4/B4	41 00N	76 00E	Venice Italy	26	D6	45 26N	12 20E
Tynda Russia	37	N3	55 10N	124 35E	Ventspils Latvia	17	E2	57 22N	21 31E
Tynset Norway	17	C3	62 17N	10 47E	Veracruz Mexico	75	E2	19 11N	96 10W
Tyumen' Russia	36	G3	57 11N	65 29E	Vercelli Italy	26	B6	45 19N	8 26E
					Verdun-sur-Meuse France	22	F5	49 10N	5 24E
U					Verín Spain	24	B4	41 55N	7 26W
Ube Japan	45	B1	33 57N	131 16E	Verkhoyansk Russia	37	P4	67 35N	133 25E
Uberaba Brazil	84	E5	19 47S	47 57W	Vernon Canada	66	G3	50 17N	119 19W
Uberlândia Brazil	84	E5	18 57S	48 17W	Véroia Greece	29	D4	40 32N	22 11E
Ubon Ratchathani Thailand	49	C3	15 15N	104 50E	Verona Italy	26	C6	45 26N	11 00E
Udaipur India	40	B4	24 36N	73 47E	Versailles France	22	E5	48 48N	2 07E
Uddevalla Sweden	17	C2	58 20N	11 56E	Verviers Belgium	19	E3	50 36N	5 52E
Udine Italy	26	D7	46 04N	13 14E	Veszprém Hungary	21	G2	47 06N	17 54E
Udon Thani Thailand	48	C3	17 25N	102 45E	Vetlanda Sweden	17	D2	57 26N	15 05E
Ufa Russia	36	F3	54 45N	55 58E	Viborg Denmark	17	B2	56 28N	9 25E
UGANDA	58	B6/C6			Vicenza Italy	26	C6	45 33N	11 32E
Ujung Pandang Indonesia	46	C2	5 09S	119 28E	Vichy France	22	E4	46 07N	3 25E
UKRAINE	30/31				Vicksburg USA	69	H3	32 21N	90 51W
Ulaangom Mongolia	42	C4	49 59N	92 00E	Victoria Canada	66	F2	48 26N	123 20W
Ulan Bator Mongolia	43	D4	47 54N	106 52E	Victoria Chile	85	B3	38 20S	72 30W
Ulan-Ude Russia	37	L3	51 55N	107 40E	Victoria, Lake East Africa	58	C4	2 00S	33 00E
Ul'yanovsk Russia	36	E3	54 19N	48 22E	Vidin Bulgaria	28	D5	44 00N	22 50E
Umeå Sweden	16	E3	63 50N	20 15E	Vienna Austria	21	G3	48 13N	16 22E
UNITED ARAB EMIRATES	39	D2			Vientiane Laos	48	C3	17 59N	102 38E
UNITED KINGDOM	10/11				Vierzon France	22	E4	47 14N	2 03E
UNITED STATES OF AMERICA	68/69				VIETNAM	48/49	D1/D4		
Upper Hutt New Zealand	93	C2	41 07S	175 04E	Viêt Tri Vietnam	48	D4	21 17N	105 25E
Uppsala Sweden	17	D2	59 55N	17 38E	Vigo Spain	24	A5	42 15N	8 44W
Ural Mountains Russia	36	F3/F4	57 00N	60 00E	Villach Austria	20	E2	46 37N	13 51E
Ural'sk Kazakhstan	36	F3	51 19N	51 20E	Villa María Argentina	84	C3	32 25S	63 15W
Uranium City Canada	66	H3	59 32N	108 43W	Vilnius Lithuania	17	F1	54 40N	25 19E
URUGUAY	84	D3			Vilyuysk Russia	37	N4	63 46N	121 35E
Ürümqi China	42	B4	43 43N	87 38E	Viña del Mar Chile	84	B3	33 02S	71 35W
Usol'ye-Sibirskoye Russia	37	L3	52 48N	103 40E	Vinh Vietnam	48	D3	18 42N	105 41E
Uspenskiy Kazakhstan	42	A4	48 43N	72 43E	Vinnytsya Ukraine	30	C4	49 11N	28 30E
Ussuriysk Russia	37	P2	43 48N	131 59E	Virginia Beach tn. USA	69	L4	36 51N	75 59W
Ust'-Ilimsk Russia	37	L3	58 03N	102 39E	Vishakhapatnam India	41	D3	17 42N	83 24E
Ust'-Kut Russia	37	L3	56 48N	105 42E	Vitória Brazil	84	E4	20 20S	40 18W
Ust'-Maya Russia	37	P4	60 25N	134 28E	Vitsyebsk Belarus	30	D6	55 10N	30 14E
Utrecht Netherlands	18	E5	52 05N	5 07E	Vizianagaram India	41	D3	18 07N	83 30E
Uttaradit Thailand	48	C3	17 38N	100 05E	Vladikavkaz Russia	31	F3	43 02N	44 43E
Uvira CDR	58	A3	3 24S	29 08E	Vladimir Volynskiy Ukraine	21	L4	50 51N	24 19E
Uwajima Japan	45	B1	33 13N	132 32E	Vladivostok Russia	37	P2	43 09N	131 53E
UZBEKISTAN	36	F2/G2			Vlissingen Netherlands	18	C4	51 27N	3 35E
Uzhgorod Ukraine	30	B4	48 37N	22 17E	Vlorë Albania	29	B4	40 28N	19 30E
					Volga r. Russia	36	E2	50 00N	45 00E
V					Volgograd Russia	36	E2	48 45N	44 30E
Vaasa Finland	17	E3	63 06N	21 36E	Vologda Russia	36	D3	59 10N	39 55E
Vác Hungary	21	H2	47 46N	19 08E	Vólos Greece	29	D3	39 22N	22 57E
Vadodara India	40	B4	22 19N	73 14E	Vorkuta Russia	36	G4	67 27N	64 00E
Vaduz Liechtenstein	23	H4	47 08N	9 32E	Voronezh Russia	36	D3	51 40N	39 13E
Valdepeñas Spain	24	D3	38 46N	3 24W	Vranje SM	28	C5	42 33N	21 54E
					Vrsac SM	28	C6	45 07N	21 17E

Vung Tau Vietnam | **49** | D2 | 10 21N | 107 04E

W
Wabush Canada | **67** | M3 | 52 45N | 66 50W
Waco USA | **69** | G3 | 31 33N | 97 10W
Wadi Halfa Sudan | **56** | C4 | 21 55N | 31 20E
Wad Medani Sudan | **57** | C3 | 14 24N | 33 30E
Wagga Wagga Australia | **91** | D2 | 35 07S | 147 24E
Wainwright USA | **66** | C5 | 70 39N | 160 10W
Wajir Kenya | **59** | G5 | 1 46N | 40 05E
Walbrzych Poland | **21** | G4 | 50 48N | 16 19E
Walcz Poland | **21** | G5 | 53 17N | 16 29E
Wales country UK | **14/15** | A3/B2 | 52 40N | 3 30W
Walla Walla USA | **68** | C6 | 46 05N | 118 18W
Walsall UK | **15** | C3 | 52 35N | 1 58W
Walvis Bay tn. Namibia | **60** | B2 | 22 59S | 14 31E
Wanganui New Zealand | **92** | C3 | 39 56S | 175 03E
Wanxian China | **43** | D3 | 30 54N | 108 20E
Warrington UK | **14** | B3 | 53 24N | 2 37W
Warsaw Poland | **21** | J5 | 52 15N | 21 00E
Warwick UK | **15** | C3 | 52 17N | 1 34W
Washington D.C. USA | **71** | C1 | 38 55N | 77 00W
Wash, The b. UK | **15** | D3 | 52 55N | 0 10E
Waskaganish Canada | **69** | L7 | 51 30N | 79 45W
Waterford RoI | **12** | C2 | 52 15N | 7 06W
Waterloo Belgium | **19** | D3 | 50 43N | 4 24E
Waterloo USA | **69** | H5 | 42 30N | 92 20W
Watford UK | **15** | C2 | 51 39N | 0 24W
Watseka USA | **70** | A2 | 40 46N | 87 45W
Watson Lake tn. Canada | **66** | F4 | 60 07N | 128 49W
Wau Sudan | **57** | B2 | 7 40N | 28 04E
Weiden Germany | **20** | E3 | 49 40N | 12 10E
Weifang China | **43** | E3 | 36 44N | 119 10E
Weipa Australia | **91** | D4 | 12 35S | 141 56E
Welland Canada | **70** | C2 | 45 59N | 79 14W
Wellington New Zealand | **93** | C2 | 41 17S | 174 46E
Wels Austria | **20** | F3 | 48 10N | 14 02E
Wenshan China | **48** | C4 | 23 23N | 104 17E
Wenzhou China | **43** | F2 | 28 02N | 120 40E
WESTERN SAHARA | **54** | A4 | |
Westerstede Germany | **18** | G6 | 53 16N | 7 56E
West Indies is. Caribbean Sea | **77** | E4/F4 | 22 00N | 69 00W
West Palm Beach tn. USA | **69** | K2 | 26 42N | 80 05W
Westport New Zealand | **93** | B2 | 41 45S | 171 36E
Westport RoI | **12** | B2 | 53 48N | 9 32W
Wetaskiwin Canada | **68** | D7 | 52 57N | 113 20W
Wexford RoI | **12** | C2 | 52 20N | 6 27W
Weyburn Canada | **66** | H2 | 49 39N | 103 51W
Weymouth UK | **15** | B2 | 50 37N | 2 25W
Whangarei New Zealand | **92** | C2 | 35 43S | 174 19E
Whitehorse Canada | **66** | E4 | 60 41N | 135 08W
Whitianga New Zealand | **92** | C3 | 36 49S | 175 42E
Whyalla Australia | **91** | C2 | 33 04S | 137 34E
Wichita USA | **68** | G4 | 37 43N | 97 20W
Wichita Falls tn. USA | **68** | G3 | 33 55N | 98 30W
Wicklow RoI | **12** | C2 | 52 59N | 6 033W
Wiener Neustadt Austria | **21** | G2 | 47 49N | 16 15E
Wiesbaden Germany | **20** | C4 | 50 05N | 8 15E
Wilhelmshaven Germany | **20** | C5 | 53 32N | 8 07E
Williams Lake tn. Canada | **66** | F3 | 52 08N | 122 09W
Williston USA | **68** | F6 | 48 09N | 103 39W
Willmar USA | **69** | G6 | 45 06N | 95 03W
Wiluna Australia | **90** | B3 | 26 37S | 120 12E
Winchester UK | **15** | C2 | 51 04N | 1 19W
Windhoek Namibia | **60** | B2 | 22 34S | 17 06E
Windsor Canada | **70** | B2 | 42 18N | 83 00W
Winnipeg Canada | **67** | J2 | 49 53N | 97 10W
Winnipeg, Lake Canada | **66/67** | J3 | 52 30N | 97 30W
Winnipegosis, Lake Canada | **66** | J3 | 52 10N | 100 00W
Winslow USA | **68** | D4 | 35 01N | 110 43W
Winston-Salem USA | **69** | K4 | 36 05N | 80 18W
Winterthur Switzerland | **23** | H4 | 47 30N | 8 45E
Wloclawek Poland | **21** | H5 | 52 39N | 19 01E
Wolfsburg Germany | **20** | D5 | 52 27N | 10 49E
Wollongong Australia | **91** | E2 | 34 25S | 150 52E
Wolverhampton UK | **15** | B3 | 52 36N | 2 08W
Wompah Australia | **91** | D3 | 29 04S | 142 05E
Worcester UK | **15** | B3 | 52 11N | 2 13W
Worland USA | **68** | E5 | 44 01N | 107 58W
Wrexham UK | **15** | B3 | 53 03N | 3 00W
Wroclaw Poland | **21** | G4 | 51 05N | 17 00E

Wuhai China | **43** | D3 | 39 40N | 106 40E
Wuhan China | **43** | E3 | 30 35N | 114 19E
Wuhu China | **43** | E3 | 31 23N | 118 25E
Wuppertal Germany | **20** | B4 | 51 15N | 7 10E
Würzburg Germany | **20** | C3 | 49 48N | 9 57E
Wuxi China | **43** | F3 | 31 35N | 120 19E
Wuzhou China | **43** | E2 | 23 30N | 111 21E
Wyndham Australia | **90** | B4 | 15 30S | 128 09E

X
Xánthi Greece | **29** | E4 | 41 07N | 24 56E
Xiamen China | **43** | E2 | 24 28N | 118 05E
Xi'an China | **43** | D3 | 34 16N | 108 54E
Xining China | **42** | D3 | 36 35N | 101 55E
Xinjin China | **43** | F3 | 39 25N | 121 58E
Xuwen China | **43** | E2 | 20 25N | 110 08E
Xuzhou China | **43** | E3 | 34 17N | 117 18E

Y
Yakutsk Russia | **37** | N4 | 62 10N | 129 50E
Yamagata Japan | **44** | D2 | 38 16N | 140 16E
Yamaguchi Japan | **45** | B1 | 34 10N | 131 28E
Yamoussoukro Côte d'Ivoire | **55** | B2 | 6 50N | 5 20W
Yangon Myanmar | **49** | B3 | 16 47N | 96 10E
Yanji China | **43** | F4 | 42 52N | 129 32E
Yaoundé Cameroon | **55** | D2 | 3 51N | 11 31E
Yaroslavl' Russia | **36** | D3 | 57 34N | 39 52E
Yazd Iran | **39** | D3 | 31 54N | 54 22E
Yekaterinburg Russia | **36** | G3 | 56 52N | 60 35E
Yellowknife Canada | **66** | G4 | 62 30N | 114 29W
YEMEN REPUBLIC | **38/39** | C1/D1 | |
Yeniseysk Russia | **37** | K3 | 58 27N | 92 13E
Yerevan Armenia | **31** | F3 | 40 10N | 44 31E
Yeu Myanmar | **48** | B4 | 22 47N | 95 26E
Yibin China | **43** | D2 | 28 42N | 104 30E
Yining China | **42** | B4 | 43 50N | 81 28E
Yogyakarta Indonesia | **46** | C2 | 7 48S | 110 24E
Yoichi Japan | **44** | D3 | 43 14N | 140 47E
Yokkaichi Japan | **45** | C1 | 34 58N | 136 38E
Yokohama Japan | **45** | C2 | 35 27N | 139 38E
Yongping China | **48** | B5 | 25 30N | 99 32E
York UK | **14** | C3 | 53 58N | 1 05W
York Factory tn. Canada | **67** | J3 | 57 08N | 92 25W
Yorkton Canada | **68** | F7 | 51 12N | 102 29W
Youghal RoI | **12** | C1 | 51 51N | 7 50W
Yumen China | **42** | C3 | 39 54N | 97 43E
Yuxi China | **48** | C4 | 24 20N | 102 33E
Yuzhno-Sakhalinsk Russia | **37** | Q2 | 46 58N | 142 45E
Yvetot France | **22** | D5 | 49 37N | 0 45E

Z
Zadar Croatia | **26** | E6 | 44 07N | 15 14E
Zafra Spain | **24** | B3 | 38 25N | 6 25W
Zagan Poland | **21** | F4 | 51 37N | 15 20E
Zagreb Croatia | **26** | E6 | 45 48N | 15 58E
ZAMBIA | **60/61** | C3/D3 | |
Zanzibar Tanzania | **61** | D4 | 6 10S | 39 12E
Zaragoza Spain | **25** | E4 | 41 39N | 0 54W
Zaysan Kazakhstan | **42** | B4 | 47 30N | 84 57E
Zeebrugge Belgium | **18** | C4 | 51 20N | 3 13E
Zell am See tn. Austria | **20** | E2 | 47 19N | 12 47E
Zenica Bosnia-Herzegovina | **26** | F6 | 44 11N | 17 53E
Zermatt Switzerland | **23** | G4 | 46 01N | 7 45E
Zhangzhou China | **43** | E2 | 24 31N | 117 40E
Zhengzhou China | **43** | E3 | 34 45N | 113 38E
Zhob Pakistan | **40** | A6 | 31 30N | 69 30E
Zhytomyr Ukraine | **30** | C5 | 50 18N | 28 40E
Zibo China | **43** | E3 | 36 51N | 118 01E
Zielona Góra Poland | **21** | F4 | 51 57N | 15 30E
Zilina Slovakia | **21** | H3 | 49 14N | 18 44E
ZIMBABWE | **60/61** | C3/D3 | |
Zlín Czech Republic | **21** | G3 | 49 14N | 17 40E
Zomba Malawi | **61** | D3 | 15 22S | 35 22E
Zonguldak Turkey | **31** | D3 | 41 26N | 31 47E
Zug Switzerland | **23** | H4 | 47 10N | 8 31E
Zunyi China | **43** | D2 | 27 35N | 106 48E
Zürich Switzerland | **23** | H4 | 47 23N | 8 33E
Zvolen Slovakia | **21** | H3 | 48 34N | 19 08E
Zwettl Austria | **20** | F3 | 48 37N | 15 11E
Zwickau Germany | **20** | E4 | 50 43N | 12 30E
Zwolle Netherlands | **18** | F5 | 52 31N | 6 06E